# JUSTICE AND THE ENVIRONMENT

# JUSTICE AND THE ENVIRONMENT

Conceptions of Environmental Sustainability
and Theories of Distributive Justice

ANDREW DOBSON

OXFORD UNIVERSITY PRESS
1998

Oxford University Press, Great Clarendon Street, Oxford OX2 6DP

Oxford New York

Athens Auckland Bangkok Bogotá Buenos Aires Calcutta
Cape Town Chennai Dar es Salaam Delhi Florence Hong Kong Istanbul
Karachi Kuala Lumpur Madrid Melbourne Mexico City Mumbai
Nairobi Paris São Paulo Singapore Taipei Tokyo Toronto Warsaw
and associated companies in
Berlin Ibadan

Oxford is a registered trade mark of Oxford University Press

Published in the United States
by Oxford University Press Inc., New York

© Andrew Dobson 1998
The moral rights of the author have been asserted

First published 1998

British Library Cataloguing in Publication Data
Data available
Library of Congress Cataloging in Publication Data
Dobson, Andrew.
Justice and the environment : conceptions of environmental sustainability
and theories of distributive justice / Andrew Dobson.
Includes bibliographical references.
1. Environmental justice. 2. Environmental policy. I. Title.
GE170.D63 1998 363.7'03—dc21 98-8745
ISBN 0–19–829482–4
ISBN 0–19–829495–6 (Pbk.)

1 3 5 7 9 10 8 6 4 2

Typeset by Best-set Typesetter Ltd., Hong Kong
Printed in Great Britain
on acid-free paper by
Biddles Ltd, Guildford and King's Lynn

*For Patrick and Carla*
*a future generation with a loud voice*

# ACKNOWLEDGEMENTS

I HAVE incurred a large number of debts while writing this book. Grants from the Leverhulme Trust and the Economic and Social Research Council (ESRC grant number L320253203) allowed me time from other academic duties to research and write it. The ESRC grant was awarded under the Council's Global Environmental Change (GEC) programme, and I owe the programme's director, Jim Skea, and its assistant director, Alister Scott, a special note of thanks for their encouragement and support. During 1996 a distinguished group of academics met three times at Keele University for a series of ESRC-funded seminars to discuss the issues on which I focus in this book, and I benefited more than I can say from those encounters. In particular, Brian Barry, Wilfred Beckerman, Ted Benton, Paula Casal, Alan Holland, Bryan Norton, Jonathon Porritt, and Marcel Wissenburg all helped to deepen my confusion and thereby pave the way to a degree of enlightenment. Chapter 2, which emerged from those conversations, is a version of 'Environmental Sustainabilities: An Analysis and a Typology', *Environmental Politics*, 5/3 (1996), and permission from Frank Cass and Co. to use this material is gratefully acknowledged.

Most of the rest of the book was written during a nine-month stay in Spain. I spent much of that time in the convivial surroundings of the Instituto de Filosofía in Madrid, and I owe a debt of gratitude to the Institute's ex-director, Javier Muguerza, and its present one, Manuel Reyes Mate, for enabling me to use the Institute's facilities. All the Institute's staff were unfailingly helpful during my stay there, and the transient population of the 'sala de becarios' provided just the right amount of daily distraction. I was also taken under the wing of the Centro de Teoría Política at the Universidad Autónoma, Madrid, and I am grateful to Fernando Vallespín, Rafael del Aguila, and Angel Rivero for their intellectual stimulation and 'El Tiro' hospitality. Finally, throughout my stay in Spain, Jorge Riechmann, of the Fundación Primero de Mayo, gave me much more of his time and attention than I deserved, and I benefited enormously from his unfailing energy and intellectual tenacity.

Anonymous referees from several potential publishers made a number of important suggestions, and it is a pleasure to record the contributions made by students at Keele University and Luleå University, Sweden, to the development of my thinking. Luleå has become something of a second home to me while writing this book, and my debt of gratitude to all those who work in the Political Science Department there is deep.

Since 1996, Keele University's Centre for Research on Environmental Sustainability (CRES) and the environmental charity Forum for the Future have been developing a Best Practice for Sustainability Database. The work that has gone into designing the database's architecture has been importantly formative for some of the material in this book, and Paul Ekins, Sara Parkin, and John Proops have all played a larger role in the learning process than they might imagine. Once again, thanks are due to the ESRC's GEC programme organizers for making funds available for the seminars during which the database's sustainability criteria have been discussed and developed. Similarly, I learned much at a marvellous conference on Environmental Justice at Melbourne University, Australia, in October 1997, and I would like to record my thanks to Nicholas Low, John Dryzek, Robyn Eckersley, and Phil McManus for making the trip possible, enjoyable, and intellectually challenging.

As the book neared what I thought were its final stages, close readings by my Keele colleagues John Barry, Margaret Canovan, and John Horton, and by Tim Hayward, Caroline Wintersgill, and Marcel Wissenburg, made me realize how far from 'finishing' I actually was, and each of them saved me from embarrassing mistakes and showed me where positive improvements could be made. It is a real pleasure to work in Keele's friendly and talented Politics Department, and this is the place to record my special thanks to Russell Bentley for so ably and constructively taking my place in it while I was on study leave. Perhaps it is the office staff who make or break an academic department, and I am very grateful to Pauline Weston, Teresa Steele, and Jill Allaway for providing me with assistance at all the right times—and especially for keeping me at arm's length, yet in touch, during my time in Spain. Finally, thanks are due to my editor at Oxford University Press, Dominic Byatt, for his encouragement and his patience.

Needless to say, and despite the best efforts of all those mentioned above, any errors of fact or judgement that remain in this book are entirely my responsibility.

A.D.

*Keele University*
*February 1998*

# CONTENTS

## PART I

## PART II

## PART III

# PART I

# Introduction

THERE are limits to sustainability. About five billion years from now a series of unusually large explosions inside the sun will turn it into a Red Giant, expanding and swallowing everything in its path, including the Earth. It is a fair bet that some time before then, life on this planet will have become untenable, and any possibility of—let alone interest in—environmental sustainability and social justice will have long since disappeared. It is an equally fair bet, though, that until then, the conditions for life and how most fairly to divide up its benefits and burdens will be somewhere near the top of the list of political, social, and economic preoccupations. My intention here is to assess the theoretical relationship between environmental sustainability and social justice. The principal reason for doing so is that we cannot assume that these objectives are compatible, and their potential incompatibility raises issues of political legitimacy for them both. If they were always and everywhere compatible, then 'crises of legitimization' would never occur, but I hope to show in what follows that the empirical evidence for compatibility is patchy at best, and that there are good theoretical reasons for regarding extravagant compatibility claims with some scepticism. (I should say that here I assume, rather than argue for, the desirability of these two objectives, however it is that we turn out to understand them.)

Put differently, it is just possible that a society would be prepared to sanction the buying of environmental sustainability at the cost of declining social justice, as it is also possible that it would be prepared to sanction increasing social justice at the cost of a deteriorating environment. My guess, though, is that neither environmental sustainability nor social justice has such overriding legitimacy that either objective could be pursued at the cost of wholly rejecting the claims of the other. No one would accept as legitimate a society which was environmentally sustainable but wholly unjust, just as no one would accept as legitimate a society which was wholly just, yet destined for ecological collapse within twenty years or so. As far as legitimacy is concerned, then, both objectives will continually vie for attention, and if policy makers and the rest of us are to make sound judgements when faced with choices between them, or when attempting to pursue courses of action which will maximize them both, they, and we, need some guidance on the legitimizing options available. This book is designed to provide that guidance.

Perhaps this is also the place to stress what this book is not designed to do. It is not my intention to provide a guide to policy-making in the strict sense. For example, readers will not find here any predictions of the effects on the distribution of wealth of policy X rather than policy Y for environmental sustainability. Perhaps this is the kind of thing that people will expect from a book carrying the title that this one does, and such an examination is, or would be, obviously of integral importance as far as effective policy-making is concerned. I am, though, less interested here in policy and policy outcomes, and more interested in the legitimizing strategies that might lie behind such policies and their outcomes.

Two questions already clamour for attention. The first is that implicit in what I have said so far is the assumption that the objectives of environmental sustainability and social justice will most often—if not always—conflict. It will be objected, of course, that this assumption is false and that environmental sustainability and social justice stand in a relationship of mutual reinforcement rather than mutual antagonism, such that more of one means more of the other. This view has it that social justice is functional for environmental sustainability, and that environmental sustainability is—at the very least—a necessary condition for social justice. If both parts of this view were correct (and particularly the first) then the legitimizing conflicts between environmental sustainability and social justice on which this book is premised would not exist, and the most we could expect from the examination carried out here would be a discussion confirming the different levels of a fundamentally self-reinforcing relationship between the two social objectives.

I shall have more to say about this argument in Chapter 1 where I consider the nature of 'sustainable development', and of 'environmental justice', but two points are worth mentioning here. The first is that to a large extent the question of whether distributive justice is functional for environmental sustainability can only be answered empirically. Before we can draw any firm conclusions, we need a raft of studies designed to explore this relationship under a number of different conditions, ranging from pastoral farmers in Sudan, through the urban poor in Brasilia and New York, to stockbrokers in south-east England—and all points in between and beyond. The most notable thing about such studies is that they do not exist, or at least not in the numbers we require. So to this extent, and in advance of the range of corroborative evidence required, it would be a mistake to assume that social justice is fundamentally functional for environmental sustainability.

The second point—and this takes me to the second of the questions that clamoured for attention above—is that both environmental sustainability and social justice are contested concepts. The meaning of these terms is not stable and fixed, and so any statement to the effect that 'social justice is functional for environmental sustainability' should immediately be complicated by the question, 'what do you mean by social justice and environmental sustainability?' It might well be the case that one regime of social justice is functional for one understanding of environmental sustainability, but to jump from this relatively narrow compatibility to the conclusion that the compatibility will extend across all possible forms of social justice and all possible conceptions of environmental sustainability would be a mistake.

This present book takes its cue, precisely, from the multiplicity of meanings of social justice and environmental sustainability. I assume, in other words, that the legitimizing relationship between the two objectives will be complex, not so much (or only) because of differing empirical conditions around the world, but because different people and political formations will understand different things by the terms. My aim is to give as comprehensive an account as possible of the compatibilities and incompatibilities between conceptions of environmental sustainability and dimensions of social justice without disappearing under the mountain of material that an exhaustive, purely discursive, approach to the relationship would produce.

In most books of this type, this would probably be the moment to say something about the terms under examination. I shall resist the temptation to do so here, since I devote a whole chapter to each of them in turn—Chapters 2 and 3—and I shall briefly explain the reason for doing so below. Two orientating remarks about meaning are in order here, though. The first is that I distinguish between environmental sustainability and sustainable development, and the book is more about the former than the latter. It will become clear in Chapter 2 that I consider sustainable development to be one theory of environmental sustainability (a theory, precisely, which holds that one particular type of social justice contributes to one particular conception of environmental sustainability), and so the tackling of environmental sustainability gives the book a broader focus than would have been the case had I chosen to deal only with what I regard as the narrower notion of sustainable development.

As far as the second term under examination here is concerned, it will be clear from the book's subtitle that I am primarily interested in social, or distributive, justice (and I shall use these two terms interchangeably). Social justice is most often and most broadly defined as having to do with the distribution of benefits and burdens in the political community. I am, therefore, interested here in the ways in which different principles for distribution, different notions of benefits and burdens, and different understandings of the 'political community' are, or are not, compatible with different understandings of environmental sustainability.

On the other hand, social justice can be regarded as a particular form of the issue that characterizes the idea of justice itself: the giving of their due to whomever are regarded as legitimate and appropriate recipients of justice. Social justice understands what is to be given (or taken away) in a rather particular way—material goods, for instance, but not prison sentences. As the present book progressed, I found myself thinking more and more about justice and the environment in the broader sense of the former—the giving of a certain due—rather than in the narrower sense usually associated with social justice. This is by no means to say that the distributive element disappears from view (for in a sense all justice is distributive), but rather to signal that the 'what?' of distribution broadens in a way unfamiliar in most treatments of justice.

More specifically, thinking about environmental sustainability in terms of social justice invites us to pay considerable attention to perhaps the most primordial (and most often invisible) distributive question: among whom or what is distribution to take place? This is indeed, as I say, a distributive question (what is being distributed is membership of the community of justice) and so can quite properly be thought about in the relatively narrow context of distributive justice. However, this distributive question is primordial for determining the range of application not only of theories of social justice, but also of theories usually regarded as broader than those associated with distributive justice, such as ethical theories. To whom or what do we owe ethical treatment? is a broader question than, to whom or what do we owe justice?, yet they both presuppose an answer to a distributive question—the distribution of membership of the ethical and justice communities, respectively.

Questions regarding the distribution of membership, then, cut across, and run together, a number of fields which are usually kept analytically distinct. Because this distributional issue is so foundational, because it cuts across and ties together what are normally regarded as distinct fields of enquiry, and because it is raised in a particularly acute way in the context of environmental sustainability, I have taken the liberty of relaxing the rigidity of the distinction between 'justice' and 'social justice' in the latter part of this book, and I hope I shall be pardoned for doing so. In this particular context, 'doing social justice' by someone or something amounts to 'doing justice' by them—admitting them to the community of justice in the first place.

I promised, above, a few words on why I have chosen to devote whole and separate chapters to the notions of environmental sustainability and social justice. The need for such sustained treatment derives from my desire to give as full an account as possible of the theoretical and legitimizing relationship between environmental sustainability and social justice. This presupposes a clear view of the variety of options available to theorists of both environmental sustainability and social justice. Armed with this, we will then be in a position to compare and contrast across both domains, with the expectation that different conceptions of environmental sustainability will relate in varying ways to different notions of social justice. There are a number of ways in which a clear view of the multiplicity of both domains might be arrived at. The most obvious would be to give discursive accounts of the territory occupied by both domains. The crucial test of this methodology (as of any other, given what we are trying to achieve) would be the extent of the guarantee incorporated in it that as full a picture as possible of the range of conceptions of environmental sustainability and social justice had been given. Experience suggests that discursive accounts have qualities other than that of comprehensiveness, though, and two examples—one from each of the domains under consideration—will illustrate the point.

In the context of accounts of environmental sustainability, Sharachandra Lélé's (1991) review of the idea of sustainable development has justly attracted critical acclaim. Most surveys of sustainable development and environmental sustainability of this 'review' type are narrative accounts of the development of the term(s), and in this respect Lélé's is a model of its type. This narrative strength, however, is bought at the cost of a degree of analytical weakness. Necessarily, Lélé presents us with a number of different understandings of sustainable development as they have been formulated over time, but—also necessarily, given the overlapping nature of these emergences—they are not presented in an analytically distinct fashion. The 'faultline' differences between these different understandings of sustainable development therefore remain unclear. This drawback is compounded by the lack of any sustained analysis of the component parts of conceptions of sustainable development; we have no clear sense by the end of the survey of the full range of questions that such conceptions set out to answer. In brief, then, the comprehensiveness of narrative accounts of this sort is vitiated—analytically, at least—by two difficulties. First, the *breadth* of conceptions, and the analytical distance between them, is compromised; and second, analytical *depth* is put in doubt by a failure to address the question of the component parts of conceptions of sustainable development (or environmental sustainability, as the case may be).

Accounts of the range of conceptions of social justice often suffer from similar drawbacks—and particularly the second one outlined above. David Miller's *Social Justice* (1976) has deservedly stood the test of time as an outstanding introduction to the concept, but from the point of view of analytical depth it leaves something to be desired. Most of Miller's analytical work in his book is done by the concepts of rights, desert, and need—that is, by the different principles that might underpin regimes of distribution. Such principles are of course central to conceptions of social justice; since one could hardly have a theory regarding the (re)distribution of goods and bads in society without it incorporating a principle (or principles) according to which such (re)distribution would be made.

But theories of justice are not exhausted by such principles. We need to know other things of these theories, such as: among whom are goods and bads to be divided up (the community of justice)?; what is to be divided up?; what is the basic structure of the theory (for instance, is it procedural or consequentialist)? So a full analytical account of the multiplicity of conceptions of social justice would need to make explicit these questions, as well as the one around which Miller organized his book. It is notable, indeed, how often accounts of social justice theory and contributions to it deal primarily with one or another of these analytical categories. Brian Barry's recent work (1995*a*), for example, is principally about an aspect of the basic structure of social justice theory—whether an adequate theory will be impartial or substantive in respect of notions of the good. Michael Walzer's seminal contribution to the subject (1983), on the other hand, is notable at least in part for its careful consideration of the question of the community of justice, while many people remember Bruce Ackerman's (1980) work for his invention of an all-purpose substance ('manna')—the 'what' of distribution.

Most of the wide-ranging descriptions of both environmental sustainability and social justice are therefore not wide-ranging enough for our purposes. We need a methodology that will provide us with the overarching framework for the analysis of the relationship between environmental sustainability and social justice that we wish to carry out. The best way to construct this framework, in my opinion, is analytically, and Chapters 2 and 3 of this book are devoted to deploying an analytical method in the context of sustainability and justice, respectively. I shall describe the analytical method in more detail then, and particularly at the beginning of Chapter 2, but I think it right to flag its general contours here. The intellectual territory in which sustainability and justice move (the *breadth* of the notions) is revealed by establishing the questions to which any conception of environmental sustainability or theory of social justice would have to have an answer, regardless of what the answers actually are. The range of conceptions of sustainability or theories of justice (the *depth* of the notions), in turn, is arrived at by grouping the answers to these questions in family-related groups. This will give a determinate number of analytically distinct conceptions of environmental sustainability and theories of social justice. At that point, these distinct conceptions and theories can be compared and contrasted, and the full account of the relationship between environmental sustainability and social justice that we wanted will emerge. This account is developed in Chapters 4, 5, 6, and 7, and in the Conclusion I offer some thoughts on which type of theory of social justice is best able to cope with the broad range of conceptions of environmental sustainability developed in Chapter 2.

If this book is about the relatively narrow notions of environmental sustainability and social justice, I also regard it as a moment in the broader encounter between environmental questions and political theory more generally. Across the discipline of political science, the phenomenon of environmentalism has been regarded with varying degrees of enthusiasm. Students of political parties and social movements addressed it with perhaps the greatest alacrity, and the result has been an ever more sophisticated capacity for testing theories of party formation, opportunity structures, and political mobilization against the experience of environmentally orientated political formations. The phenomenon has not fared too badly, either, in the context of the study of political ideologies. Pretty soon it was realized that contemporary ecologism (or 'environmentalism', to taste) constituted (and constitutes) an alternative to longer-standing ideological traditions, and surveys of the ideological spectrum can now hardly be regarded as complete without reference to the contested nature of ecologism and its relationship with other ideologies.

By contrast, environmental questions have (with a few honourable exceptions) received little attention from political theorists—those who devote their time to describing and assessing normative proposals for the arrangement of social and political life. The same in reverse is also true: writers on environmental politics have only fitfully addressed themselves to the normative issues raised by environmental programmes, and have hardly begun to take advantage of the intellectual resources developed in political theory for dealing with them. This book, by contrast, is written as a self-conscious attempt to—at least in part—interest political theorists in environmental questions, and encourage those writing from within the environmental matrix to engage more systematically with political theory. I do not in the least intend to suggest that these exchanges of interest should be for their own sake—quite the reverse. I am sure that any feet that might stray into the other camp are more likely to stay there for instrumental and self-interested reasons, rather than because of any sudden awakening to the intrinsic importance of environmental questions or political theory, respectively. So my aim would be to encourage political theorists, and particularly, here, theorists of justice, to the view that their reflections on social justice will not be complete until they take the issues raised by environmental sustainability into account. Likewise, the problems of political legitimacy for the objective of environmental sustainability to which I referred at the beginning of this introduction mean that political theory's legacy of potential assistance on this matter can only be ignored by environmentalists (practicants as well as spectators) at the cost of obtuseness, or worse. Political theory is affected by environmentalism, and environmentalism cannot do without political theory, so even if environmental sustainability and social justice turn out to conflict (perhaps often), this is not to say that the larger sets of enquiries of which they form a part will necessarily do so. More positively, they should be mutually enriching, and the widest intention of this book is to begin to show how.

# 1

# Environmental Politics and Distributive Justice

ONE of the principal curiosities of modern environmentalism is how little it has had to say on the issue of distributive justice. The curiosity derives from the fact that environmentalism and justice share a common organizing concern—the existence of scarcity—but do completely different things with it. Modern environmentalism was founded on the notion of actual or increasing (but always disputed) scarcity. One whole chapter of the seminal report *The Limits to Growth* (Meadows et al. 1972) is entitled 'The Limits to Exponential Growth', in which the report's authors argue that a finite earth necessarily contains a finite amount of non-renewable resources as well as a finite capacity to absorb the waste generated by productive activity. With population increasing and resource availability declining, the unit of resource available to each individual evidently declines too. This is a picture of increasing scarcity in all but name, so it makes at least prima facie sense to say that modern environmentalism—to the extent that it takes its cue from analyses like those outlined in *The Limits to Growth*—has scarcity as one of its central organizing concepts.

Scarcity is also central to the question of distributive justice. John Rawls, basing his own account of what he calls 'the circumstances of justice' on David Hume, writes of 'the condition of moderate scarcity understood to cover a wide range of situations'—and of these situations he refers in particular to those in which '[n]atural and other resources are not so abundant that schemes of cooperation become superfluous' (Rawls 1973: 127). Similarly, but more counterfactually, one of the reasons (but only one) Marx had for refusing to divulge the distributive details of communist society was that once the productive potential held in check by capitalist relations of production was fulfilled under communism, such fabulous amounts of wealth of all kinds would be produced that there would be more than enough of everything for everyone, and the notion of distributive justice would be redundant.

So if scarcity is so central both to political environmentalism and to the very idea of distributive justice, one might have expected political environmentalists to have distributive questions at the heart of their thinking. But typically they have not. Proving this beyond any reasonable doubt would take me too far into the thicket of texts and documents that make up the history of the contemporary politics of ecology. Suffice to say that Sandy Irvine and Alec Ponton hit the nail on the head when they write that 'Fair shares in extinction might be equitable, but as a political statement of faith, it is not the Green way' (Irvine and Ponton 1988: 142). It is the question of 'extinction' that has normally occupied political environmentalists, and not the question of 'sharing'. They have, in other words, had their eye on a different ball—aggregate production rather than its disaggregated distribution. In the context of resource issues, practically the totality of environmentalists' efforts has gone into suggesting ways of reducing the consumption of non-renewable resources, increasing the use of renewable resources, and reducing the amount of waste generated by industrial and other processes. In this sense, green politics is the politics of reducing aggregates rather than distributing disaggregates.

Given the overall objective of environmental protection, however, it is not surprising that environmentalists have been interested in distributive justice for its (potential) effects on environmental protection, even if not for the sake of fair distribution itself. It is arguably this type of connection between environmental protection and distributive justice that underpins much of the meaning of, and support for, the popular notion of sustainable development. (It ought to be pointed out, too, that this instrumentalism works both ways. It is not only that environmentalists look to 'use' justice for their own conservationist ends, but also that people and movements whose primary concern is greater justice have 'piggybacked' their claims on the perceived legitimacy of the project of sustainable development. This latter has, in other words, become a vehicle for a wider movement for greater social justice.)

The WCED Report that encapsulates the notion of sustainable development argues that greater equality will lead to a more securely sustainable environment: 'poverty itself pollutes the environment, creating environmental stress in a different way. Those who are poor and hungry will often destroy their immediate environment in order to survive' (WCED 1987: 28), and this leads the Commission to recommend considerable global and national redistributions of wealth, in the belief that such redistributions will be functional for environmental sustainability. The report also points out that poverty skews the availability of environmental goods away from the poor: 'The number of people living in slums and shanty towns is rising, not falling. A growing number lack access to clean water and sanitation and hence are prone to the diseases that arise from this lack' (WCED 1987: 29). Two dimensions of the relationship between poverty and the environment emerge from this: first, poverty is identified (in the report) as a cause of environmental degradation; and second, relative wealth is regarded as determining access to what we might call environmental goods (or, indeed, the imposition of environmental bads). These two dimensions, in turn, have given rise to the two principal political 'movements' organized around the linking of distributive and environmental issues: first, the sustainable development movement itself; and second, the 'environmental justice' movement, most prominent in the United States, but now with something of an equivalent in Britain in the guise of the Real World Coalition (Real World Coalition 1996).

## Sustainable Development

The Brundtland Report affirms that 'inequality is the planet's main "environmental" problem' (WCED 1987: 6), thereby confirming the Commission's belief that policies for greater material equality are the most important ingredient in any recipe of measures aimed at environmental sustainability. But the report is equivocal as to

whether greater equality or simply the relief of poverty is a necessary condition for such sustainability. These are, of course, not the
same thing—it is perfectly possible to imagine a condition of reduced poverty but increased inequality—and the WCED Report is
not sufficiently clear about the difference. The Commission states,
for example, that 'the "population problem" must be dealt with in
part by efforts to eliminate mass poverty, in order to assure more
equitable access to resources' (WCED 1987: 11). But the elimination
of mass poverty in itself does not necessarily imply greater equality.
It only implies that more people will have access to resources. This
may seem like a merely semantic matter, but failure to make these
distinctions could have the more serious consequence of reducing
the legitimizing appeal of sustainable development by sending the
'wrong' political signals. There is little doubt that in today's climate,
a campaign in favour of poverty relief will have a wider appeal than
a campaign aimed at greater material equality (and even the idea of
poverty relief is unacceptable—for either moral or pragmatic reasons—in many quarters). For legitimizing purposes, then, the sustainable development project would be assisted by a clear statement
indicating that poverty relief, rather than material equality, is the
objective.

The flaw in this suggestion, though, is that the evidence on which
to base it is not available. By this I mean that the systematic studies
which show that poverty relief, rather than greater material equality, is functional for environmental sustainability have not been
made (nor, indeed, have studies which might show the opposite).
I shall have cause to return to this point in Chapter 5; suffice, for
the moment, to register surprise at the fact that, despite sustainable developers' belief that distributive questions are key to
sustainability, research to establish the precise nature of the functional relationship between such questions and environmental
sustainability has not been carried out. In this sense, affirmations
such as the following read more like a programme for research than
a statement on which to base policy: 'Poor people are forced to
overuse environmental resources to survive from day to day, and
their impoverishment of the environment further impoverishes
them, making their survival ever more difficult and uncertain'
(WCED 1987: 27). Prima facie, it is unlikely to be true that poor

people are always forced to overuse environmental resources, since 'overuse' implies an already existing scarcity. Poor people do not always and everywhere live in conditions characterized by environmental resource scarcity, so the conclusion reached by the Commission is not as universally relevant to environmental sustainability as its report suggests. Second, poor people are often, of necessity, absolutely aware of resource problems, and have developed successful and sustainable strategies to cope with them. This suggests that careful analysis of exactly where and why poverty induces unsustainable overuse of resources is required. And third, it is not only poor people who may overuse environmental resources, but rich ones too. In fact, in terms of aggregate consumption, it is well known that the birth of a child in London (particularly well-heeled parts of it) brings with it a much greater strain on the resource base than the birth of a child in Lahore (particularly the poor parts of it). This goes to show that poverty relief (or greater global equality, whichever turns out to be the case) will only ever (at most) be a necessary and never a sufficient condition for environmental sustainability.

Whatever the exact nature of (re)distribution, however, sustainable development's main focus in spatial terms is on the international arena. That is to say that sustainable development is principally concerned with environmental deterioration in 'developing' countries, and the idea is that international redistributions are necessary to halt this degradation: 'It is futile to attempt to deal with environmental problems without a broader perspective that encompasses the factors underlying world poverty and international inequality' (WCED 1987: 3). Of course this does not necessarily rule out the simultaneous enacting of policies *within* countries to reduce poverty (or increase equality), but, as a programme, sustainable development's distributional inclinations are much more international than national. The importance of this point will become clear in Chapter 5 where theories of justice unwilling to countenance the possibility of international justice begin to look incompatible with the project of environmental sustainability.

The one clear exception to this general rule is where the Commission points to inequality of land tenure within countries as contributing to environmentally unsustainable practices. Attention has been focused on this for some time, in particular in connection with the continuing destruction of parts of the Brazilian rainforest. The causes of deforestation are of course multiple, but there is little doubt that landlessness is a crucial contributory factor. Farmers without land are forced into the forest where they cut trees, till the inadequate soil, plant and harvest crops for a year or two, then, when the land becomes unfit for further planting, they move on to the next tract of forest and the process repeats itself. There seems little doubt that in instances like this, national policies aimed at spreading land tenure more widely would make a significant contribution to rainforest protection.

All of these reflections have to do with the way in which poverty and/or inequality may contribute to environmental sustainability and, conversely, the way in which poverty relief and/or measures aimed at increasing equality might be functional for sustainability. As far as issues of justice and sustainability are concerned, this is indeed the principal tenor of the Brundtland Report, but there are occasional references to a different kind of relationship. For example, the report states that 'A growing number of the urban poor suffer from a high incidence of diseases; most are environmentally based and could be prevented or dramatically reduced through relatively small investments' (WCED 1987: 239). The implication here is that poor people typically have poor environments, and it is this insight that has given rise to what has come to be called the 'environmental justice movement'.

## The 'Environmental Justice Movement'

In a very real way, of course, environmental questions in the 'developing' world are so bound up with issues of poverty and distributive justice as to be virtually indistinguishable from them. In this sense, the starting point for considerations of environmental justice as I characterized it above—the observation that 'poor people live in poor environments'—is a starting point not only for environmental justice, but for environmentalism itself, as far as much of the developing world is concerned. In the 'developed' world, though, we find

ourselves drawn to make the distinction between environmentalism and environmental justice because of the place that concern for
the environment 'for its own sake', for example, has in green politics, and the associated (but not necessarily connected) thought that
issues of national and international distributive justice may have
only a tangential bearing on such concern. In the discussion of the
environmental justice movement that follows, I am going to focus
on its manifestation in the United States and, to a lesser extent, in
Britain, and I make the remarks above only to indicate that the
environmental justice movement, *per se*, is much broader based than
such a narrow frame of reference might suggest. I do think, though,
that the structural features that characterize the movement in the
USA are similar to those found in similar circumstances in other
parts of the world, so even if I make no specific reference to
India (say), my remarks on the USA are, *mutatis mutandis*, applicable
elsewhere. This would also be the view of a considerable authority
on the matter, Laura Pulido, who uses the term 'subaltern environmentalism' to capture the connection between developed world
environmental justice activists and developing world environmentalism (Pulido 1996: p. xv).

If one were asked to date the beginning of the environmental
justice movement in the United States, then 2 August 1978 might be
the place to start. This was the day when the CBS and ABC networks first carried news of the effects of toxic waste on the health of
the people of a place called Love Canal (Szasz 1994: 42). It turned
out that decades earlier Hooker Chemical had dumped thousands
of drums of waste into an abandoned navigation canal which was
subsequently (in 1952) filled in. In 1953, Hooker sold the land to the
Niagara Falls Board of Education, a school was built, houses were
erected in the neighbourhood, and people moved in. Twenty or so
years later heavy rains washed the chemicals to the surface and
alarming health problems—including birth defects—began to
emerge.

The link between the relative poverty of many of the inhabitants
of Love Canal and the poisoned environment in which they lived
was immediately made: 'working-class or lower-middle-class
homes . . . barely making ends meet' (Szasz 1994: 43). In the months
and years that followed, more and more similar cases came to light

and the environmental justice movement was born, based on the simple and not very surprising observation that 'Toxic victims are, typically, poor or working people of modest means. Their environmental problems are inseparable from their economic condition. People are more likely to live near polluted industrial sites if they live in financially strapped communities' (Szasz 1994: 151).

Part of the interest of the environmental justice movement and its principles is that it constitutes a useful corrective to the universalism of mainstream environmentalism. It has always been a criticism of environmentalism from those on the left that environmentalists are wrong to claim that everyone suffers equally from environmental degradation. On the contrary, it is argued, the perception, and especially the suffering, of environmental risk is skewed in the direction of those least able to afford to protect themselves against it. Just as natural disasters, such as earthquakes, always cause more death and injury among poor—and therefore poorly protected—populations, so environmental calamities of anthropogenic origin hit the poor hardest. Dowie puts it like this:

During the early years of the movement, in an understandable attempt to build the broadest possible constituency, environmentalists often described the issue as one that affected everyone equally. We all live in the same biosphere, said the gospel, breathing the same thin layer of air, eating food grown in the same soil. Our water is drawn from the same aquifers, and acid rain falls on the estates of the rich as forcefully as on the ghettos of the poor. On closer examination, however, massive inequities in environmental degradations and injustice in the policies used to correct them became evident. While created equal, all Americans were not, as things turned out, being poisoned equally. (Dowie 1995: 141)

Bob Edwards makes a similar point:

The unifying insight of environmental justice recognises that neither the costs of pollution nor the benefits of environmental protection are evenly distributed throughout our society. Uneven distributions of 'socially acceptable' environmental hazards and their long-term corrosion of health and life quality stem from the inequalities of socio-economic and political power . . . Those who live or work in close proximity to the source, storage destination, or waste stream of environmental contaminants bear most of the burden and risks associated with their production. By contrast, the economic benefits of production are concentrated among wealthier groups whose communities are insulated by distance from their daily exposure. Questions of who pays and who benefits from contemporary policies of economic growth, industrial development, and environmental protection are at the heart of the environmental justice agenda. (Edwards 1995: 36)

Similarly, Pulido argues that,

it is . . . the poor and marginalized of the world who often bear the brunt of pollution and resource degradation—whether a toxic dump, a lack of arable land, or global climate change—simply because they are more vulnerable and lack alternatives. The privileged can reduce their vulnerability by insulating themselves from environmental problems through assorted mechanisms including consumption (such as the purchase of bottled water or sunscreens) or exportation (such as the deforestation of other countries). (Pulido 1996: pp. xv–xvi)

Taken together, these quotations make clear the environmental justice belief that the 'environment' is no more—and certainly no less—than a particular form of the goods and bads that society must divide among its members. The movement points out that the principle upon which distribution of these goods and bads takes place is that of 'ability to pay'—that is, those who can afford protection will buy it, in the form, for example, of living on land known to be uncontaminated. Note that 'environmental justice' does not here mean 'justice to the environment', but refers rather to a just distribution of environmental goods and bads among human populations.

The observation that poor people suffer disproportionately as far as the effects of environmental degradation are concerned is sometimes taken a stage further with the finding that 'the racial composition of a community [is] the strongest predictor of hazardous waste site location' (Edwards 1995: 40) in the USA. This has given rise to the notion of 'environmental racism' (see Bullard 1994 and Pulido 1996, for example), and the generalized opposition in the environmental justice movement to this kind of discrimination in environmental policy-making is captured in the second of the 'Principles of Environmental Justice', adopted at the First National

People of Color Environmental Leadership Summit in Washington, DC, in October 1991: 'Environmental justice demands that public policy be based on mutual respect and justice for all peoples, free from any form of discrimination or bias' (in Hofrichter 1994: 237; emphasis in the original; all seventeen principles are collected in Hofrichter 1994: 237–9).

The environmental justice movement in the USA is striking for its grass-roots characteristics. The fact of environmental injustice, as understood by the movement, has not been brought to the public's attention by environmental professionals, or by people already attracted to environmentalism who then became aware of its distributive dimensions, but by ordinary men and women (mostly women) who live(d) in areas of degradation and suffered its effects on a daily basis. Perhaps the best known of these people is Lois Gibbs, one of the original Love Canal protesters. 'When my mother asked me what I wanted to do when I grew up', Gibbs writes, 'I said I wanted to have six children and be a homemaker.' She continues:

I moved into Love Canal, and I bought the American Dream: a house, two children, a husband, and HBO. And then something happened to me, and that was Love Canal. I got involved because my son Michael had epilepsy, and my daughter Melissa developed a rare blood disease and almost died because of something someone else did. I never thought of myself as an activist or organizer. I was a housewife, a mother, but all of a sudden it was my family, my children, my neighbors . . . Every day across the country people distressed about the health and well-being of their families demand justice . . . poor families desperately trying to break the pattern of poverty and give their children a fighting chance: they have typically suffered the greatest inequities . . . These are the people who make up the grass-roots movement for environmental justice. This movement, in hundreds of local and regional organizations, is typically led by women, working-class people, and people of color. Many, particularly the women, have never been involved in any political issue before and have been galvanized primarily by their concern for their children's safety. (Gibbs 1994: p. ix)

Much has been made of the difference in social composition between the grass-roots environmental justice movement and the mainstream environmental movement in the USA. As Bob Edwards writes, mainstream environmentalism's 'core constituency and leadership are centered precisely in the segments of American society least likely to experience environmental injustice' (Edwards 1995: 50). These differences reflect not only different lived experiences, but also—despite views to the contrary—different political objectives. Laura Pulido has rightly pointed out that,

Given the conditions in which marginalized communities find themselves, their point of entry into environmental concerns is usually framed by inequality and often related to access, production and distribution issues in intimate ways. Due to their position, the subaltern are not able to distance themselves from the political and economic consequences of either the problem or the proposed solutions. Because they encounter environmental problems through inequality, their resolutions may be contingent upon an alteration of local power relations, cultural practices, systems of meanings, and economic stuctures. (Pulido 1996: 29–30)

This leads Pulido to suggest that environmental justice activists are 'as interested in changing the prevailing power relations as they are in reducing pollution or preserving biodiversity' (Pulido 1996: p. xiii). I shall have more to say about this shortly, and particularly in the context of what we might regard as the British equivalent of the USA's environmental justice movement.

Also noteworthy is the politicizing effect of campaigning for environmental justice. This is flagged by Gibbs's assertion, above, that 'Many, particularly the women, have never been involved in any political issue before' (see also Krauss 1994 and Epstein 1994). Bob Edwards writes that campaigners typically get angered by 'bureaucratic indifference, political double-speak and scientific equivocation' (Edwards 1995: 44), and Szasz underlines the self-reinforcing effect of action with the following: 'When individuals participate in the movement, they experience what it means to organize, to be an activist; they are exposed to radical perspectives' (Szasz 1994: 150; and see pp. 153–61 for a collection of personal testimonies).

Both of the characteristics of the environmental justice movement mentioned in the previous two paragraphs—its grass-roots composition and its politicizing effect—suggest the possibility of the movement broadening its horizons beyond local toxics issues. From the grass-roots point of view, there is the chance that activists will make connections between not only poverty and environmental discrimination but other forms of injustice as well. As Szasz puts it, 'environmental populism is not only the vehicle for achieving a better environment, but also the most promising candidate for leading the next phase of the larger movement for social change' (Szasz 1994: 6). In this way, broader social justice concerns 'piggyback' on environmental issues in a way that has the potential for reinforcing them both.

Similarly, but this time in the environmental context, Szasz has observed a broadening and deepening movement from pollution control to pollution prevention (Szasz 1994: 5–6), and this observation is repeated in Edwards's affirmation that 'The movement for environmental justice wants to reframe the policy debate over hazardous waste and shift the public agenda away from its current preoccupation with regulating waste disposal toward reducing waste production at source' (Edwards 1995: 49). Dowie claims to have identified an even more impressive widening of horizons: 'Gradually, as toxics were found to contribute to habitat destruction, species extinction, and loss of wetlands, the anti-toxics agenda entered the terrain of the conservationists and the potential for a broad environmental coalition became real' (Dowie 1995: 135). This broader environmental concern is indeed captured by the first and third of the 'Principles of Environmental Justice' to which I referred to earlier, and which read as follows:

1. *Environmental justice* affirms the sacredness of Mother Earth, ecological unity and the interdependence of all species, and the right to be free from ecological destruction.
3. *Environmental justice* mandates the right to ethical, balanced and responsible uses of land and renewable resources in the interest of a sustainable planet for humans and other living things. (in Hofrichter 1994: 237; emphasis in the original)

If all this were seamlessly the case, then Love Canal would certainly have to be seen as the beginning of something really significant. Imagine it: what was in origin a campaign for compensation for the ill-effects of waste dumped in a small town in the United States becomes, in one direction, the force for the tying together of a whole range of other human justice issues across the country and beyond, and, in the other direction, the spark that lights the fire of recognition that the effects of anthropogenic activity extend way beyond the human community into the realms of biodiversity itself. If these connections could then be captured by and expressed in a coherent social movement, then conservationist and leftist (or 'green' and 'red') formations in society, which so often seem to pull in different directions, would be brought into productive harmony.

Three considerations count against jumping too hastily to such a conclusion, however. The first is that the environmental justice movement seems, stubbornly, to be much more about human justice than about the natural environment—or, rather, it is only about the natural environment inasmuch as it (the natural environment) can be seen in terms of human justice. 'The central concern of the new movement is human health', writes Dowie (Dowie 1995: 127), and while there is obviously a link between a healthy environment and human health, concern for the latter will not cover all the objectives of nature conservationists. So when Andrew Szasz quotes from the Citizen's Clearinghouse for Hazardous Waste (founded by Lois Gibbs) that 'Environmental justice is broader than just preserving the environment' (Szasz 1994: 152), we need also to remember that it is *narrower* than preserving the environment, in that not all the environment will be 'preserved' through the medium of environmental justice. In this context, Pulido has noted Pezzoli's important observation that 'communities engaged in what appear to be environmentally related struggles at times may not be committed to an environmental agenda' (Pulido 1996: 16). This needs to be taken seriously by those who argue for a seamless connection between environmental and justice concerns.

In this context it is odd to read supporters of the environmental justice movement criticizing 'traditional' environmental activists for being 'obsessively orientated toward wilderness, public land, and natural-resource conservation' (Dowie 1995: 126). This sounds to me like accusing socialists of being 'obsessively orientated towards equality', or feminists of being too keen on demanding equal substantive rights for women. Such criticism forgets where the centres of gravity of these movements and ideologies lie. In our case, 'traditional' environmentalism just is about wilderness, resource-conservation, and so on, and while there are clearly points at which the human justice and environmentalist programmes will come into contact (precisely those points, indeed, highlighted by the environmental justice movement), it is too much to expect that these programmes will be (or should be) synonymous. This does not invalidate the Dowie-type critique, of course, but it does point up the potential difficulties involved in trying to bring the environmental and justice movements together.

Dowie himself points out that, 'Until recently . . . it [the environmental justice movement] didn't refer to itself as *environmental*—in fact, in some circles, it still doesn't without carefully adding the word *justice*' (Dowie 1995: 144; emphasis in the original). The reason for this is obvious: the movement is principally, and quite properly, a movement for human justice in which the environment is no more (and no less) than the missing word in the social justice question 'the distribution of——?' But what about the explicit reference in the first Principle of Environmental Justice referred to above, to a political-ecological sounding concern for the 'interdependence of all species', and even the 'sacredness of Mother Earth'? Is this not evidence for more far-reaching concern for the natural environment than that derived from considerations of human health? Dowie though, at least, suggests that the reasons for the presence of this principle in the list are primarily tactical, 'as if to reassure traditional environmentalists who believe newcomers to the movement are obsessed with toxics and don't care enough about the preservation of wild nature' (Dowie 1995: 151).

From the environmentalists' point of view, then, the worry will be that the environmental justice movement does not, and does not intend or pretend to, cover the full range of their concerns. For the same reason, the thought that the environmental justice movement might be the vehicle in which 'reds' travel, wholesale, in a 'green' direction, because their causes are all of a piece, looks misplaced. To argue, as Szasz does, that the movement 'brought whole new segments of the population to environmentalism' (Szasz 1994: 165) presupposes a particular understanding of 'environmentalism'—an understanding developed through the prism of the environmental justice movement itself. That is to say that the residents of Love

Canal will have become intimately acquainted with the toxics question, and they may even have broadened their original perspective
from pollution control to pollution prevention, but there are a
number of large steps from there to the wider concerns of what I
would regard as the preoccupations of political ecology: local and
global sustainability, potential resource- and sink-driven limits to
production and consumption, biodiversity, values-in-nature, a focus
on the non-urban environment and its conservation, and so on.
These remarks should not be read as criticisms of the environmental
justice movement; I merely want to point out that while the paths
of these two movements will cross at important points, they by
no means always travel the same road, and they may not even
always head in the same normative direction as far as distributive
issues are concerned. Lived experience, rather than the neat suture
of ideas, is likely to be the determining factor in the extent of
coincidence between the environmentalist and environmental justice movements. Dowie is surely right to say that:

If there is ever a rapprochement between labor and environmentalists it is
unlikely to be between unions and the mainstream environmental movement, and more likely to be between grassroots environmentalists and
the rank and file—organized and unorganized. Many laborers and their
families are drawn to grassroots anti-toxics activism whereas few are
attracted to conservationism. (Dowie 1995: 159)

This is as much as to say that attempts to manufacture a movement
broad enough to contain middle-class environmentalists and leftists
on the one hand, and working-class environmentalists and leftists on
the other, are likely to run into mobilization difficulties.

It is significant that the grass-roots environmental justice movement in the United States has no direct equivalent in Britain, and
that two of the concerted attempts that have been made to bring
'red' and 'green' together have so far failed to rally much public
support. The first of these attempts to which I want to refer has been
made by the 'Red-Green Study Group', founded in 1992. The members of this group echo many of the distributive sentiments found
both in the sustainable development literature and in the declarations of the USA's environmental justice movement. In the first
place they reject the view that ecological protection (for whatever

reason) should take precedence over other desirable social and political objectives: 'Some in the green movement are so convinced of the imminence of ecological catastrophe that they are prepared to give it priority over all other issues—possibly at the expense of social justice, liberty and democracy' (Red-Green Study Group 1995: 13). Second, they support the sustainable development view that there is a causal link between inequality/poverty and environmental degradation: 'social inequalities and oppression are among the causes of environmental degradation', and, 'in some parts of the underdeveloped world poverty is a cause of people overexploiting fragile environments' (Red-Green Study Group 1995: 13). Third, there is explicit recognition from the group of the view that animates the USA's environmental justice movement—the view that poor people will generally live in poor environments: 'Without equality between people, within and between societies, environmental "bads" will continue to be off-loaded onto those with less power' (Red-Green Study Group 1995: 22). This last point is, as I say, central to the notion of environmental justice as understood in the US context, but the crucial difference is that it is made by people whom Bob Edwards (as we saw above) will probably regard as 'least likely to experience environmental injustice' (Edwards 1995: 50). This is not, of course, to call into question either the accuracy or the sincerity of the group's views on the relationship between environmental protection and distributive justice, but the US experience suggests that grass-roots lived experience of a deteriorating environment is a crucial and necessary ingredient for social mobilization.

If this is right, then the second British initiative to which I want to refer is also likely to confront difficulties—this is the initiative that goes by the name of the Real World Coalition. The Coalition describes itself as group of 'non-governmental organisations committed to raising the importance of environmental sustainability, social justice—including the relief and eradication of poverty, in this country and internationally—and democratic renewal in UK political debate' (Real World Coalition 1996: p. vii). Among the thirty-three groups which are signatories to the book from which I quote here, we find Christian Aid, Church Action on Poverty, Friends of the Earth, Oxfam, Save the Children Fund, Black

Environment Network, and the World Wide Fund for Nature. From this brief list it will be clear that the Coalition's membership credentials are impeccable as far as uniting the causes of environmentalism and social justice is concerned—and so are its declarations on the matter. Once again, echoes of the sentiments of the USA's environmental justice movement are evident: 'environmental improvement and poverty eradication go together, since the poor almost always live in the worst environments' (Real World Coalition 1996: 4), and, in an encapsulated form which could almost serve as the starting point for considerations of environmental justice: 'The poorest people almost always live in the worst environments' (Real World Coalition 1996: 24). All this leads the Coalition to conclude that 'This has generated new connections between environmental organisations and those concerned primarily with social justice: the two aims go hand in hand' (Real World Coalition 1996: 4).

I would only enter two caveats to this conclusion. The first is that the aims of environmentalists and social justice activists only go hand in hand up to a certain point, for the reasons I outlined above in connection with the US case. Tucked away at the end of the Coalition's document, indeed, is the implicit recognition that fair distribution in and of itself cannot be the exhaustive medium through which all the questions that concern environmentalists will be solved:

The problem . . . lies in one of the most long-standing assumptions of contemporary politics. This is that 'social and environmental' issues are essentially questions of distribution. The economy produces wealth: this can then be redistributed to alleviate poverty, improve the environment, and so on. But where *the processes of production themselves* are the causes of these problems, this approach is doomed to failure. Concentrating effort on increasing production in order to have more resources available to redistribute only adds to the problems with which such distribution is meant to deal. (Real World Coalition 1996: 118; emphasis in the original)

The second is to point out, once again, that the enunciation of these principles will not in itself be enough to mobilize an environmental justice movement on the scale of the United States. The Real World Coalition is overwhelmingly (but not wholly) made up of organizations run by people who are, to quote Edwards once again in this context, 'least likely to experience environmental injustice' (Edwards 1995: 50). It would of course be absurd to suggest that this somehow disqualifies them from having an opinion on these issues, but the United States experience does suggest that some tough strategic questions as regards social mobilization will need to be asked in Britain as far as issues of environmental justice are concerned. There may well be, as the Real World Coalition believes, 'a substantial groundswell of public opinion in the UK in favour of a "new politics" embracing sustainability, social justice, democracy and community regeneration' (Real World Coalition 1996: p. viii)— although if there is, it received precious little attention, as (unfortunately) did Real World itself, during the 1997 British general election campaign. But given that the social composition of a mass environmental justice movement seems almost by definition to be grass roots, there may only be a limited point in initiatives like the Red-Green Study Group and the Real World Coalition aiming their messages at their habitual middle-class constituencies. The fundamental truth is that social change on the scale hoped for by Real World and similar groups requires grass-roots participation, and this, in turn, presupposes grass-roots lived experience put reflectively at the service of a social movement. For now, there is no sign either of such participation or of such a movement in Britain, although there is no doubt that the *language*, if not a movement, of environmental justice, has a tentative foothold in British political life.

## Conclusion

Whatever the merits and demerits of the sustainable development and environmental justice movements, it would be a mistake to think that their discourses on the relationship between environmental sustainability and social justice were exhaustive. For one thing we shall soon see that there are multiple conceptions of environmental sustainability, and we should not casually assume that egalitarian social and economic policy will be functional for all of them.

For another, social justice is indeed about principles of distribution, but it is about many other things besides, such as among whom or what benefits and burdens are to be distributed, whether justice can or should serve other ends or whether it is an end in itself, and whether we should judge the justice of a situation by its outcome or by how it was arrived at. None of these questions is captured in our discussion of sustainable development and environmental justice thus far, and this strongly suggests that we have a longer road to travel. The remainder of this book is devoted to establishing the nature and whereabouts of the signposts, and to sketching possible destinations.

# PART II

# 2

## Three Conceptions of
## Environmental Sustainability

SHARACHANDRA LÉLÉ's observation that 'Sustainable development is a "metafix" that will unite everybody from the profit-
minded industrialist and risk-minimizing subsistence farmer to the
equity-seeking social worker, the pollution-concerned or wildlife-
loving First Worlder, the growth-maximizing policy maker, the
goal-orientated bureaucrat, and therefore, the vote-counting politi-
cian' (Lélé 1991: 613) neatly summarizes the task facing anyone
proposing to give systematic form to the myriad interpretations
available to us of environmental sustainability and its cousin,
sustainable development.

Attempts to give this debate some shape have been made before,
of course, but not in quite the way I shall do here. Most résumés of
environmental sustainability and sustainable development have
taken one (or sometimes both) of two forms, which I shall call
the 'definitional' and 'discursive' forms. The definitional form is
self-explanatory: commentators attempt to sum up what either
environmental sustainability or sustainable development is by
encapsulating its meaning in a definition. The problem with this
approach is obvious, and it has led to the general demise of the
definitional form: each definition is necessarily contested and
contestable, and with something like 300 definitions available (and
the number increases inexorably) seekers after enlightenment are
often left as confused at the end of their search as at the beginning.
Here, then, I explicitly eschew the definitional approach.

The discursive strategy is, on the face of it, more promising. It
generally works by describing the evolution of terms such as

'sustainability', 'ecodevelopment', and 'sustainable development', and such an approach has the merit of giving a more rounded and complete account than a single definition could ever do. Classic discursive accounts can be found in Lélé (1991), Mitlin (1992), and Pezzey (1992), while Moffatt (1992, 1996) and McManus (1996) provide useful shorter examples of the genre. A principal disadvantage of the discursive approach is that as soon as the account is given it is out of date, and this is because the feature on which it trades—chronological development—never ends. Anyone using a discursive account, then, to orientate their understanding of environmental sustainability will be left with the nagging question of what happened to the concept after the account they are using was completed.

The usefulness of the discursive strategy is further limited by the apparent difficulty of working any analysis of the terms under discussion into it. I say 'apparent' because there is nothing intrinsic to the discursive method that militates against an analytic component, but most discursive accounts conspicuously lack any analysis of the sort that might lead to a *typology* of theories of environmental sustainability, and this is just what I want to produce (McManus's (1996) account is an exception to this rule). Typologies are useful in a rather shallow 'ready reckoning' sort of way, of course, but the principal gain from them is often as much in the process that leads to the typology as in the final outcome. As a minimum, the development of a typology demands that the components of the concept under study be made explicit, thereby bringing it more sharply into focus than a discursive study tends to do.

It is also possible for typologies to be constructed in such a way that they overcome the problem of discursive accounts becoming out of date as soon as they are written. Properly addressed, the typological problem is one of giving a full account of the constitutive dimensions within which discussion of the concept must move, rather than of a permanently up-to-date account of the development of the concept. The latter, as I have pointed out, is an impossible objective, but the former is not—*provided* that sufficient time has elapsed for the dimensions of the concept to have been established. This caveat is important, since there would be no point in developing a typology for a concept which had had little discursive development: there would be no guarantee that the point had been reached beyond which no further dimension of the concept would be revealed. I think we can safely ignore this caveat in the case of environmental sustainability or sustainable development, however, since both terms have been in use for ten years or more, and since enormous amounts have been written and spoken about them both in that period. We should be safe to assume, therefore, that a diligent survey of the material hitherto produced will reveal all the possible dimensions available.

The final advantage of an analytic and typological approach is that one expects to get plural answers from one's investigation. This expectation has advantages in the context of a concept (or concepts) like environmental sustainability or sustainable development whose irredeemably contested nature guarantees plural understandings. The definitional approach discussed above is at fault from this point of view as well—it seeks to make the plural singular (and if this fault is redeemed by admitting a plurality of definitions, we simply find ourselves overwhelmed, rather than enlightened, by the plurality). In other words, an analytical and typological strategy takes advantage of the best features of the definitional and discursive approaches, while avoiding their pitfalls. It takes seriously the discursive demand to pay attention to the concept's track record but refuses to be bound by it, and it takes seriously the definitional demand for clarity but refuses to add to the proliferation of definitions implicit in the contested territories inhabited by environmental sustainability and sustainable development. What we end up with is an ideal-type—rather than a classificatory—typology.

One intention, then, is to provide a form of orientation for finding one's way around the territory of environmental sustainability and sustainable development, and this ought to be useful in itself. But I shall also use this typology, in conjunction with the material worked up in the next chapter, for more creative purposes. I am centrally concerned in this book with the relationship between environmental sustainability and social justice, and as I explained in the Introduction, it would be fatal in this context to take, as given, assertions about the relationship made by parties intent on pushing a particular line. We want, rather, as full a range of possibilities as is feasible to discuss, and I believe that the analytical-typological approach used here is the best way to produce the range of meanings required.

## Method

The analysis of the concept of environmental sustainability which leads to its typology could be carried out in a number of ways, but the general rule implicit in what I said in the previous paragraph is that the analysis must lead to comprehensive coverage of the concept. (From now on I propose to use the term 'environmental sustainability' rather than 'sustainable development' because towards the end of the chapter I conclude that sustainable development is one form, or theory, of environmental sustainability. This is why I believe that the typology developed here is more all-embracing than Michael Jacobs's (1999) which, while admirable, deals explicitly with sustainable development. It would be inappropriate to say any more than this at this stage, since to do so would be to anticipate both the nature of the analytic method and its typological outcome.)

One strategy that would meet the demand of comprehensiveness is suggested by the following quotation from Luke:

As a social goal . . . sustainability is fraught with unresolved questions. Sustainable for how long: a generation, one century, a millennium, ten millennia? Sustainable at what level of human appropriation: individual households, local villages, major cities, entire nations, global economies? Sustainable for whom: all humans alive now, all humans that will ever live, all living beings living at this time, all living beings that will ever live? Sustainable under what conditions: for contemporary transnational capitalism, for low-impact Neolithic hunters and gatherers, for some space-faring global empire? Sustainable development of what: personal income, social complexity, gross national product, material frugality, individual consumption, ecological biodiversity? (Luke 1995: 21–2)

The crucial insight here is that there are questions to which any theory of sustainable development (or, in the case of my target in this chapter, environmental sustainability) would have to have an answer, irrespective of what the answers actually were. This is the insight that provides the form which the analysis of environmental sustainability will take in what remains of this chapter. In sum, I have surveyed a large amount of literature relating to environmental sustainability and sustainable development and have been guided by the following rubric throughout: what are the implicit or explicit questions being asked in these texts? This amounts to a list of questions to which any theory of environmental sustainability would have to have an answer and this list, in turn, amounts to the analytical framework we were looking for.

The analytical framework is not yet, of course, a typology, since the framework is singular and the typology must be plural. The typology is developed through a consideration of the various answers that are given to the questions that compose the framework, leading to a grouping of the answers, and thereby, through a combination of questions and 'family-related' answers, to a limited number of *conceptions* of environmental sustainability. The outcome will look something like Table 1. Two further methodological questions must be addressed before proceeding to the analysis itself. First, what kind of guarantee is there that the literature survey on which this examination is based was a complete one? What guarantee is there, in other words, that we have a full range of questions and answers? At the outset of the survey practically every text I examined produced new questions and new answers to add to the list but, as one would expect, the return on the investment in reading declined as time went on. Soon (but not soon enough!) there came a point where the return approximated to zero, and it was at this point that the survey began to feel complete. It is always

TABLE 1. *Schematic representation of conceptions of environmental sustainability*

|  | Conception A | Conception B | Conception C |
|---|---|---|---|
| Question 1 | Answer A | Answer B | Answer C |
| Question 2 | Answer A | Answer B | Answer C |
| Question 3 | Answer A | Answer B | Answer C |

possible, of course, that the next book/article/report/government document on the list would have produced a new question on which to base the eventual typology, but this seemed increasingly unlikely. Another approach would have been to collect a representative sample of texts and analyse them, but this would have been—inadmissibly—to have anticipated the results, since 'representative' here can only mean 'representative of the range of conceptions of environmental sustainability', which is what I set out to discover in the first place.

The second methodological issue refers to the range of questions and answers—more particularly, should we focus on all possible questions and answers, or on all actual ones? To focus on the former is not at all impossible, since once one has a general grasp of what sustainability is about, an a priori list of questions and answers (and particularly the latter) can be drawn up. Take the question of futurity, for example: how far into the future should whatever we are sustaining be sustained? As Luke suggested above, the answers could range from 'a generation' to 'ten millennia' (with other possibilities either side, of course). Should we include the extremes in our typology as a matter of course, or only if they are actually found expressed in the documentation? In deciding this question, I have been guided above all by the view that the typology of conceptions of sustainability should be useful as well as analytically complete. This means that all the questions and answers that form the basis of the typology can actually be found in the literature on environmental sustainability.

## Results

A summary of the results obtained is presented in Table 2 (and as I shall be referring to the table throughout the rest of the book there may be some profit in xeroxing it and keeping it to hand). In this table, the questions to which all theories of environmental sustainability must have an answer are given down the left-hand side, and there are five of them. Each of these questions has (in the literature) three more or less determinate and self-contained sets of

TABLE 2. *Conceptions of environmental sustainability*

| | A | B | C |
|---|---|---|---|
| What to sustain? | (1) Critical natural capital | (2) Irreversible nature | (3) Natural value |
| Why? | (4) Human welfare | (5) Human welfare and duties to nature | (6) Duties to nature |
| How? | (7) Renewing/substituting/protecting | (8) Substituting/protecting | (9) Protecting |
| Objects of concern Primary Secondary | (10) 1, 2, 3, 4 5, 6 | (11) (1, 5) (2, 6) 3, 4 | (12) (5, 1) (6, 2) 3, 4 |
| Substitutability between human-made and natural capital | (13) Not always possible between human-made capital and critical natural capital | (14) Not always possible between human-made capital and irreversible nature | (15) Eschews the substitutability debate |

*Notes*: Key to 'objects of concern' numbers: 1 = present generation human needs; 2 = future generation human needs; 3 = present generation human wants; 4 = future generation human wants; 5 = present generation non-human needs; 6 = future generation non-human needs.

Numbers in parentheses are 'box' numbers, used in the text for ease of reference.

answers, and it is these groups of answers that give rise to three conceptions of environmental sustainability, lettered A to C. (Those who follow these debates closely may have noticed that in an earlier presentation of these findings—Dobson 1996—I recorded four, rather than three, conceptions of sustainability. To explain in detail how this change came about would take me too far from my present brief, and it is not necessary here to do so.)

The principal organizing question behind theories of environmental sustainability is, perhaps unsurprisingly, what is to be sustained? Alan Holland has written that, 'On any account of sustainability . . . something or other is supposed to be kept going, or at any rate not allowed to decline, over time' (Holland 1994: 169). The question is, what is the 'something or other'? Interestingly, the debate surrounding this question has been largely dominated by economists, partly, at least, because economists are accustomed to thinking in terms of a common *numéraire* which can be pressed into service across space and time. This, of course, is precisely what is required when one is considering the 'what is to be sustained?' component within a theory of environmental sustainability. A *numéraire* commonly used in this context is 'capital', and much of the interest has revolved around (*a*) the creative ways in which this concept can be understood, and (*b*) whether it is a concept appropriate for heading up all conceptions of environmental sustainability—however creatively employed.

At one time I was happy to endorse attempts at characterizing conceptions of sustainability according to the type of capital they sought to sustain. In each case this would be *natural* capital, but the distinctions between conceptions of sustainability would be marked by the presence of a further adjective: *critical* natural capital, or *irreversible* natural capital, for example. I have been persuaded, though, that however clear we make the distinctions between different types of natural capital, the bringing of 'nature' under the sign of 'capital', 'is to look at it ['nature'] in a certain light, as an economic asset of some description' (Barry 1999). As Marx wrote, 'Capital consists of raw materials, instruments of labour, and means of subsistence of all kinds, which are employed in producing new raw materials, new instruments of labour and new means of subsistence' (*Wage Labour and Capital*, in Bottomore and Rubel 1961: 155). While 'nature' *is* largely regarded as 'raw material' and thus as an 'economic asset' in Conception A of environmental sustainability, the same is only very guardedly true of Conception B and not at all true of Conception C. I think it best, therefore, to reserve the term 'capital' for Conception A and to drop the term thereafter. What we thereby lose in terms of a common thread across our three conceptions, we gain in terms of descriptive accuracy.

## Conception A

An essential condition for any theory of sustainability to be a theory of *environmental* sustainability is that it argue for the sustaining into the future of some aspect of the natural environment. This might seem obvious, but bearing it in mind will help us to weed out points of view which claim (or are claimed) to be about environmental sustainability but which are not. So when Nobel Prize-winning economist Robert Solow, for example, writes that 'The duty imposed by sustainability is to bequeath to posterity not any particular thing . . . but rather to endow them with whatever it takes to achieve a standard of living at least as good as our own . . . We are not to consume humanity's capital, *in the broadest sense*' (1992: 15; my emphasis), he is advancing a theory of sustainability, but not of environmental sustainability. Solow's remark—if we take it at face value—is underpinned by a belief in the perfect substitutability of human-made for natural capital. That is to say that every loss of natural capital can be functionally compensated for by increases in capital of human origin. Crudely put, plastic trees which can be designed to perform the same ecological functions as real ones are as good as real ones, and the loss of real ones represents no decline in the 'overall capital base' (Bartelmus 1994: 65).

However, as soon as one not only distinguishes between human-made and natural capital, but also argues that parts or aspects of the latter are not replaceable by the former, and if we add to this the belief that at least some of these parts or aspects need to be maintained into the future, then we are into the realms of environmental sustainability proper. It can be argued that no one believes in the total substitutability of human-made for natural capital, and to this extent all theories of sustainability turn out to be theories of environmental sustainability. Even the villain of the piece for many environmentalists—neoclassical economic theory—turns out only to believe that 'man-made capital is a *near-perfect* substitute for natural resources' (in Daly 1992: 250; my emphasis). So long as substitution is only 'near-perfect' there will be some resources, even if only at the margins, that are not replaceable by human-made capital, and if (for whatever reason) it is held that those resources should be maintained into the future, then we are in the presence of a theory of environmental sustainability. Wilfred Beckerman, the scourge of what has come to be known as 'strong sustainability', is at pains to point out that 'the assumption . . . of infinite substitutability between manmade and natural capital is not made by me or any economist that I know of' (Beckerman 1995: 174). Similarly, Robert Solow, whom I quoted above in the context of perfect substitutability, actually only goes so far as to say that 'Substitution can take place on reasonable terms' (1992: 9), and while he calls this an 'optimistic' view, it is some distance from claiming perfect substitutability. It is therefore a mistake to include theories of sustainability that contain a belief in perfect substitutability in typologies of environmental sustainability.

One further way of glossing this debate on substitutability is to say that those who argue for the maintenance of each category of capital focus on the *complementarity* of different forms of capital rather than on their *substitutability*. 'Capital cannot ultimately substitute for resources because capital itself is composed of resources . . . labour and capital complement the material resources that are transformed into a product', write Daly and Cobb (1989: 409), and then, more graphically, 'To put it crudely, what good is the capital represented by a refinery if there is no petroleum?' (1989: 198). This, of course, is the point at which the sustainability debate meets the limits to growth debate, for:

If natural and manmade capital were substitutes (weak sustainability) then neither could be a limiting factor. If, however, they are complements (strong sustainability), then the one in short supply is limiting. Historically, in the 'empty world' economy, manmade capital was limiting and natural capital superabundant. We have now, due to demographic and economic growth, entered the era of the 'full world' economy, in which the roles are reversed. More and more it is the remaining natural capital that now plays the role of limiting factor. The fish catch is not limited by fishing boats, but by remaining populations of fish in the sea. (Daly 1995: 50)

This quotation introduces a further feature of the debate—the distinction between 'weak' and 'strong' sustainability. In truth, any usefulness that this distinction might have had has been eroded by the proliferation of alternatives: we now read of 'weak', 'strong', 'very weak', and 'very strong' (Pearce 1993: 18–19) and even 'absurdly strong' (Daly 1995: 49) sustainability. To add to the confusion, each of these alternatives takes on different meanings in the hands of different commentators (in addition to Pearce and Daly, above, we might note Beckerman 1994: 194–5 and Jacobs 1995: 61), and it would now be very difficult to give a concise and complete description of them. Fortunately, though, I do not have to try to do so, since it is part of my intention in this chapter to provide a typology which encompasses yet overcomes the proliferation of definitions I mentioned at the beginning of it. No doubt my typology can be read in terms of 'weak', 'strong', etc. sustainabilities, but I do not propose to dwell on that question here.

Assuming, then, that this conception of environmental sustainability (A) is concerned with sustaining a particular aspect or feature of natural capital, what is the best way of describing this aspect or feature? The answers to that question which emerge from the literature are undoubtedly best captured by the term 'critical natural capital', and that is the term we find in Box 1 of Table 2. 'Critical' here is to be understood primarily in terms of 'critical to the production and reproduction of human life', and this points us in the direction of natural capital whose presence and integrity is preconditional for survival.

The term 'critical natural capital' is radically indeterminate, of course, and it might refer us (in the detail) to any number of features of the non-human natural world. There is a tendency in the 'developed' world to think of it in terms of the large-scale 'ecological processes' (Norton 1992: 97), 'biogeochemical cycles' (Pearce 1993: 16), or 'global life support systems' (Bowers 1990: 8) which sustain human life. Pearce speaks elsewhere of an ecological 'glue' (Pearce 1995: 52), and there are echoes of all of this in the increasingly popular notion of 'ecosystem health' (see the whole of *Environmental Values*, 4/4 (1995); and in particular Rapport 1995). Rapport writes that 'it might be said that ecosystem health is the "bottom line" guiding sustainable development—for if the health of the environment is compromised, everything else is undermined' (Rapport 1995: 292). This emphasizes the basic point underlying the 'ecological process' interpretation of natural capital: that ecological processes underpin the rest of human activity, and if they are impaired, a condition for the very possibility of human activity is impaired too.

But much more mundane, yet no less important, interpretations of critical natural capital are possible. Natural capital might be regarded as critical at a local as well as a global level, for instance. The subsistence farmer will regard the topsoil in which she or he grows her or his crops as critical natural capital, as well as the water with which she or he irrigates it, and, perhaps, the worms that aerate it. The general nature of the term 'critical natural capital', then, gives it descriptive strength. It can be applied across a wide range of contexts, and it captures what is fundamental to this conception of environmental sustainability: the sustaining of natural capital that is preconditional for human life. From now on I shall refer to this conception of environmental sustainability either as Conception A, or as the 'critical natural capital' conception.

In the second row of Column A (Box 4) I emphasize the way in which arguments for the sustaining of natural capital understood in terms of ecological processes turn on the instrumental value they have for human beings. This may read oddly to some, and especially to those who argue that 'ecosystem health' (which I mentioned above) is inherently more ecocentric than conceptions of sustainability usually are. Hammond and Holland, for example, argue that: 'the concept of sustainability with its frequent stress on the welfare of future generations of humans seems clearly more anthropocentric than the concept of ecosystem health. An ecocentric conservation policy, therefore, might be thought more likely to gain sustenance from the pursuit of ecosystem health than from the pursuit of sustainability' (Hammond and Holland 1995: 284).

Two points might be made about this. First, the analytical method employed takes seriously the suggestion that we must always ask of a theory of sustainability, *what* is being sustained? As we shall see in the context of Conceptions B and C there is no obvious reason why the answer should always relate to something instrumental to human well-being. In other words, the typology being developed here suggests that environmental sustainability need not be so inherently anthropocentric as Hammond and Holland suggest (although 'sustainable development' is another matter, as I shall show towards the end of the chapter). Second, ecosystem health itself might, of course, be protected *either* because this is a good in itself, *or* because of its instrumental value to human well-being. Whether one adopts the former ecocentric view or the latter anthropocentric view depends largely on how one reads the intentions of ecosystem health proponents. In any case, the anthropocentric view is the one that drives this conception of sustainability.

The third row relates to the issue of *how* critical natural capital is to be sustained. And by 'how' I do not refer to which political/ economic/social tools we should use to bring about the sustaining of critical natural capital, but rather—more broadly—to the technical possibilities inherent in different types of critical natural capital. 'Critical natural capital' might, for instance, be either renewable or non-renewable. Trees in the Himalayan foothills that provide the wood to make a fire on which to cook food can be regarded as renewable critical natural capital for those who depend on it, and the obvious way to sustain this capital is to renew it. If critical natural capital is non-renewable, on the other hand, then an alternative approach to sustaining it is to substitute for it. For present purposes, we can regard oil as an example of non-renewable critical natural capital (for large and increasing sections of the world's population, at least). Once it is gone it is gone (to all intents and purposes) forever. The function of oil (the provision of energy), though, can be met in a number of other ways—ranging from nuclear power to biomass and all points in between—and to this degree substitution may be the appropriate way of sustaining (this type of) critical natural capital. But critical natural capital may also be non-substitutable as well as non-renewable (tropical rainforests, at the heart of the 'ecological processes' or 'biogeochemical cycles' to which I referred above, might be examples of this type of critical natural capital), and in this case such natural capital can only be sustained by maintaining its present integrity through time. In Table 2 I have called this option 'protection' and this option is collected together with renewal and substitution in the figure in Box 7.

The fundamentally anthropocentric reasons for sustaining critical natural capital to which I referred above are reflected in the 'lexical ordering' of the fourth row of Column A (Box 10), where it is made clear that in terms of 'objects of concern' human interests come first, but that this very concern for human interests will devolve secondary concern onto (some) non-human objects, since the former will depend upon the latter. The futurity that is central to all conceptions of sustainability is represented by the way in which future generation human needs take precedence over present generation human wants. This is integral to the idea of at least one notion of what critical natural capital might be—ecological processes—since these operate over long time-scales. It would be odd for those who argue for the sustaining of ecological processes to put the wants of the present generation of human beings (which might threaten those processes) ahead of the needs of future generations of human beings (which depend upon them). It should be stressed that once the interests of future generations are taken into account in this way, concern for many features and aspects of the non-human natural world can be generated. Indeed, Bryan Norton has argued that: 'introducing the idea that other species have intrinsic value, that humans should be "fair" to all other species, provides no operationally recognizable constraints on human behaviour that are not already implicit in the generalized, cross-temporal obligations to protect a healthy, complex, and autonomously functioning system for the benefit of future generations of humans' (Norton 1991: 226; I shall pursue the implications of this at some length in the Conclusion).

Finally, in the fifth row (Box 13), we find Conception A's answer to the substitutability question. The belief here is that substitution between human-made and critical natural capital is not always possible. Where substitution is not possible, and in cases of non-renewable critical natural capital, Conception A points to the necessity of protecting critical natural capital. The implications of all this in the context of justice will be discussed in Chapters 4 and 5.

## Conception B

A second way of focusing on natural capital is flagged in Column B with the introduction of the notion of 'irreversibility'—although in line with my remarks in the introduction to this chapter, I shall drop references to 'capital', and refer to 'irreversible nature'. This is intended to act as a shorthand for natural objects, naturally occurring substances, and organic and inorganic nature, whether individual or collective, and I shall specify these meanings as and when necessary. The idea that animates Conception B, simply, is that what should be sustained are aspects and features of non-human nature whose loss would be irreversible (Box 2), and from now on I shall refer to this conception of environmental sustainability either as Conception B, or as the 'irreversibility' conception.

Before I establish the differences between Conceptions A and B, let me indicate two similarities. First, as I pointed out above in the context of a reference to oil, some critical natural capital also comes under the rubric of irreversible nature. Second, and as a consequence of the first, one of the reasons for protecting (some) irreversible nature is that it is critical to human survival or well-being. In this sense, the reasons for protecting irreversible nature are the same as those for protecting critical natural capital—the protection of the functions it performs for furthering material human welfare.

But the notion of irreversibility as understood here contains an additional dimension: concern for aspects of the natural environment for their own sake. Inherent in the notion of criticality is the question, critical for whom?, and by far the most common answer to this question in the literature is, critical for human beings. Many irreversible natural losses, on the other hand, might not be critical for human beings at all. Arguments in favour of downplaying the importance of preserving biodiversity, for instance, are often couched in terms of lists of species that have disappeared from taxonomists' catalogues without making a dent in standards of human welfare. Those who argue for avoiding the irreversible loss of natural objects and features, therefore, might do so in terms of criticality, but they might also do so in terms of arguments relating to the intrinsic value of whatever it is that is irretrievably lost. This is the sentiment captured in the second row of Conception B (Box 5), and represented by the following thought from Robert Solow (who is more often associated, as will have become apparent, with Column A than with Column B): 'Many though not all, environmental assets have a claim to intrinsic value. That is the case of the Grand Canyon or Yosemite National Park . . . the calculus of trade-offs does not apply' (Solow 1992: 21). Here, obligations to nature are added to the maintenance of human welfare as a reason for protecting (this type of) 'natural capital'.

As a criterion for sustainability, of course, avoiding all irreversible losses is an impossible objective. In the first place, the benefits from some losses need to be weighed against the gains that might result from the loss. The point here is, rather, that the notion of irreversibility needs to be taken into account when calculations of this sort are made. Taking account of potential irreversible losses of nature in this way, as if they matter, would surely make a considerable difference to public policy. Second, we need to distinguish between the irreversible loss of 'types' or 'tokens' of nature. The loss of a species of zebra would be the irreversible loss of a 'type', while the death of a particular member of the same species of zebra would be the loss of a 'token'. As far as this particular zebra is concerned, its loss is irreversible (even cloning cannot get around that) but while its death may be regrettable, sustainability discourses cluster more around concern for the irreversible loss of types than of tokens. Robert Goodin makes the same point with a different example: 'the protection of endangered species is so much more important to greens than the protection of particular specimens . . . what is crucial is that there be some blue whales, not that there be any particular number of them' (Goodin 1992: 61). This indicates that the main concern is for the maintenance of biodiversity, and I shall use this as a *locus classicus* example for this present conception of sustainablility.

As far as the 'how?' question and answer is concerned (Box 8), one of the options available to us in Conception A is by definition ruled out here—the option of renewing natural losses. Irreversible losses cannot be renewed: oil cannot be renewed (yet) and extinct species cannot be brought back to life (yet). (Although renewal as a means of *avoiding* irreversible losses is of course possible in some cases.) This leaves us with either substitution or protection. Once again, oil can be substituted for by other sources of energy, but the language of substitution runs aground in the context of, for example, endangered species. The notion of equivalence, on which substitutability trades, is inappropriate for things which are valued for their uniqueness rather than for the function which they perform. This leaves the likelihood that the idea of mandatory protection will take on greater significance in this conception of environmental sustainability than in the previous one.

As a consequence of the answers here to the 'why?' and the 'how?' questions, the fourth row of Conception B (Box 11) is the first point in the typology where we encounter the present needs of humans and non-humans being satisfied before the wants of humans (present or future). The bracketing of present generation human needs with present generation non-human needs—(1, 5)—is intended to convey the spirit, if not the letter, of proponents of this version of environmental sustainability, as is the prioritizing of present generation non-human needs over future generation human needs suggested by the notation (1, 5), (2, 6). It is not so much that in all cases present generation non-human needs will take precedence over future generation human needs, but rather that if faced with the prospect of the irreversible loss of a species here and now, that loss should be carefully weighed against any putative benefit to future generations obtained by incurring the loss. In this sense, the content and shape of the numeric notation here is intended to indicate the greater weight to be given to the needs of present and future generation non-humans compared to Column A. It is not intended to represent a strict lexical ordering.

Finally (the fifth row of Column B), while there should be no need to belabour the point that this conception of environmental sustainability is underpinned by a belief in the limited and very specific substitutability of human-made capital for irreversible nature, it ought to be pointed out that some commentators for whom irreversible natural capital (and this is what they would call it) is important do talk of substitutability between different types of *natural* capital. David Pearce, for example, argues that definitions of sustainable development must 'allow for the feasible avoidance of irreversible losses of natural assets, or compensation for their loss by other natural assets' (Pearce et al. 1989: 36). Such a view is only applicable in the context of irreversible losses that are, in fact, compensable—whether by human or natural assets. The organizing point behind this conception of environmental sustainability is precisely that some forms and features of irreversible nature are not substitutable, and therefore not compensable in anything other than an attenuated sense. Supporters of this conception of environmental sustainability might just be able to put a price on the disappearance of a given species, but even with the money in their hands they would probably feel seriously cheated. And I suspect they would be even less enamoured at the idea of the extinct species being compensated for by the offer of another 'natural asset'. This consideration points us firmly in the direction of the third conception of environmental sustainability contained in this typology—Conception C.

## Conception C

Conception B—the one I have just described—is Janus-faced. On the one hand, it looks back towards Conception A and the privileging of human welfare over obligations to nature. On the other, it anticipates the themes of Conception C by calling compensation into question through the introduction of the notion of intrinsic value; let us remember that the protection of irreversible natural capital might be argued for in terms of its criticality (anthropocentric), and/ or in terms of its intrinsic value (bio- or ecocentric). We might characterize Conception C as the point at which economists leave the sustainability debate, to be replaced (in yet another form of substitutability!) by philosophers. In an important essay devoted to unpicking David Pearce et al.'s *Blueprint for a Green Economy*, Alan Holland (1994) claims to have detected an unacknowledged commitment to the intrinsic value of nature in Pearce in phrases such as this: 'Each generation should inherit at least a similar natural environment' (Pearce et al. 1989: 37). Why 'similar', we might ask, unless there is something important about the particular configuration of the environment in question? Holland's point is that particular configurations cannot necessarily be defended in terms of non-declining human welfare since it is in principle possible to achieve non-declining human welfare through substitutability across types of capital—and substitutability lays waste to the idea of particular configurations.

So what *will* yield such a defence, asks Holland? The answer, put baldly, is 'a simple ascription of value to nature' (Holland 1994: 180). Expanding on this, and putting it in the context of an answer to the fundamental question in all theories of environmental sustainability, Holland writes that what counts is 'maintaining enough of the particular historical forms of association and their historically particular components—all the better if they have the mark of nature on them'. He continues, 'what is handed down and maintained does need to retain in the process something of its original form and something of its identity: there need to be continuities of form, which constitute what may be called "units of significance" for us, as well as continuities of matter' (Holland 1994: 178). Robert Goodin has called this a 'green theory of value', which 'traces the peculiar value of naturally occurring properties of things to the history of their creation by processes outside ourselves' (Goodin 1992: 61). For short, I shall refer to this as a theory of 'natural value' and this is the name I propose to give to that which is to be sustained in the Conception C notion of environmental sustainability. So this conception will from now on be referred to as either Conception C, or the 'natural value' conception.

Holland is happy to have this view referred to as 'absurdly strong sustainability' (Holland 1997: 128), so long as it is emptied of 'unnecessary' absurdities first—for example, the absurdity that absurdly strong sustainability be taken to mean 'a requirement to preserve intact the environment as we find it today in all its forms' (Beckerman 1994: 194). This *is* absurd, Holland says, because 'it is of the essence of natural processes that they are dynamic', and therefore no one intent on conserving the non-human natural world could cleave to Beckerman's caricature of what they were doing. All this reads to me like a working through of the second of the Janus-faced interpretations with which this section on Column C began. Holland is arguing for 'the recognition that nature, and all its various component events and processes, is a particular historical phenomenon and should be valued as such' (Holland 1994: 179). The physical stock interpretation of natural capital is not exhausted by the importance of that stock to the maintenance of human welfare, but rather 'actually captures something at the heart of environmental concern' (Holland 1994: 179). The concern it captures is that 'the natural world is disappearing' (Holland 1997: 128), and that the defence of the non-human natural world 'requires that we are sometimes called upon to defend [it], even when human interests seem not to be served by such an action' (Holland 1997: 130).

The description 'obligations to nature' contained in the second row of Column C (Box 6) is not intended to convey the impression that this is the *only* reason supporters of this conception of environmental sustainability will argue for the sustaining of 'units of significance'. They might also be able to argue the point in terms of the benefits to human welfare (material and/or aesthetic) derived from doing so. But typically the worry is, as Holland expresses it, whether it is 'in fact true that the actions required to secure justice for future people coincide with those which are required to secure the environmental interest in nature' (Holland 1994: 174). Some people, of course, think that this *is* true, as we saw Bryan Norton arguing above, but this need not detain us now. Here I only want to point out Holland's implication that what he calls an 'environmental' interest in nature is not secured (solely) through concern for either the present or future generations of human beings. This is why I have chosen to characterize the principal motivation underlying this conception of environmental sustainability as 'obligations to nature'.

I pointed out that in Conception A the object of sustainability was critical natural capital, and that such capital can be sustained by renewing/substituting/protecting as appropriate. In Conception B, the 'renewing' option disappears, since the object of sustainability—

'irreversible nature'—is, by definition, non-renewable. Here, renewal is appropriate only in so far as renewal is a feature of the dynamism of ecological systems referred to by Holland above in his qualified acceptance of his notion of environmental sustainability as 'absurdly strong'. As a shorthand, we might say that *anthropogenic* renewal is (one of) the villain(s) of the piece in Conception C: in other words, old-growth forest systems might in principle be renewable over long periods of time, but their 'natural value' will be lost as soon as they are cut down.

This leaves us with the broad options of substituting and/or protecting, and substitution is obviously inappropriate here, for the same reasons it is inappropriate for some forms of irreversible nature (as in Conception B). It might help to recall Holland's reference to the importance of 'particular historical forms of association . . . all the better if they have the mark of nature on them' (Holland 1994: 178), and to note Goodin's point that:

History, by its very nature, is irreproducible. Very talented hydraulic engineers might manage to rush water over another valley in just the right way to create another canyon looking ever so much like the Grand Canyon that was carved by the Colorado. But even if it is identical in every outward respect, that canyon will have the wrong history for us to value it as we do the Grand Canyon, as something created by forces outside of our control. (Goodin 1992: 61)

This leaves us with protection, and we might go so far as to say that Conception C is characterized by focusing solely on protection (Box 9) as the means of bringing about its sustainability objective: the maintaining through time of natural value.

The ordering of figures in Box 12 in the fourth row—(5, 1), (6, 2)—should not be taken to imply either the literal precedence of present non-human needs over present human needs, or the precedence of future non-human needs over future human needs. My intention once again is simply to convey the spirit underlying this conception of environmental sustainability, which is to value the non-human natural world in its own right. None of this does away with the need to make hard policy choices, of course, and the principles of such choices will be discussed in Chapter 7 and the Conclusion, but proponents of Conception C will ask that the non-human natural world has its own seat at the table (as it were) when they are being made.

Finally, the content of the fifth row of Conception C should be self-explanatory: the vocabulary of substitutability simply does not apply here. Just as one interpretation of the injunction to preserve 'irreversible' nature in Conception B involves the belief that such natural capital is unsubstitutable, so 'units of significance' are by definition unsubstitutable.

## *Summing up Table 2*

Perhaps the best way to sum up the typology as we have it so far is to compare it with one drawn up by David Pearce—reproduced here as Table 3. First, Pearce's approach is different. He has drawn heavily on the technocentric–ecocentric distinction which has become common currency and while there is nothing wrong with this distinction in itself, Pearce, in using it, has committed himself to squeezing conceptions of sustainability into a prefabricated mould. I, on the other hand, have tried to allow conceptions of environmental sustainability to 'emerge'. Pearce's tactic leads him up blind alleys—particularly in the first column ('cornucopian technocentrism'). In truth, as I explained earlier, this column only represents a conception of sustainability if we stretch the remit of the word beyond the range of notions of *environmental* sustainability. What is being sustained here (although Pearce does not put it quite like this) is 'economic growth' or, as Solow expresses it, 'productive capacity' (Solow 1992: 7), and this, once again, is not a conception of environmental sustainability at all (although of course it may affect it). This is simply because under this conception of 'environmental' sustainability the non-human world is of no specific consequence due to the underpinning belief in 'infinite sub-stitution possibilities' (Pearce 1993: 18–19). The distinction between the human and non-human worlds collapses, and from this collapse derives the possibility of ignoring any claims the non-human world might have—'Most routine natural resources are desirable for what they do, not for what they are' (Solow 1992: 14). David Pearce and

Michael Jacobs have both pointed out the consequence: 'On the weak sustainability interpretation of sustainable development there is no special place for the environment . . . The environment is simply another form of capital', writes Pearce (1993: 16), while Jacobs suggests that weak sustainability is 'no longer anything much to do with the environment. Once natural capital has been monetised and its benefit stream integrated with that of human-made capital, environmental protection is only contingently connected to the concept of non-declining welfare' (Jacobs 1995: 61).

Characterizing cornucopian technocentrism as a conception of environmental sustainability is therefore misleading, and the problem is compounded (in the detail) when Pearce suggests that this conception involves a belief in 'infinite substitution possibilities'. We have already seen that nobody actually argues for this, so not only is it that cornucopian technocentrism is not a conception of environmental sustainability, but that even if it were, Pearce makes it contain features that are not to be found anywhere except on the wilder shores of neoclassical economic theory. Perhaps the closest real-world approximation to this view is that contained in the United States' 'Wise Use Movement', which argues for 'unrestricted access to all natural resources for (private) economic use, benefit, and profit', on the basis of a 'no-holds-barred utilization of resources for private profit' (Grumbine 1994: 230 and 239; see also Gottlieb 1989). I think we would be hard pushed to recognize any sort of programme for environmental sustainability in this, and my recommendation, therefore, is to erase Pearce's first column from the typology altogether.

'Accommodating technocentrism' (Pearce's second column) has as its organizing focus a 'constant capital rule', and this seems inconsistent with Pearce claiming the 'instrumental value of nature' as an ethical underpinning for this form of sustainability. This is because the undifferentiated constant capital rule renders nature more or less invisible, and leaves little room for incorporating in the scheme any sort of value—even instrumental value—it might have. The critical capital rule which 1 suggest here makes it easier to see where the 'instrumental value in nature' mentioned by Pearce comes from: its value lies in its criticality. Finally (in the accommodating

TABLE 3. *The sustainability spectrum*

| | Technocentric | | Ecocentric | |
|---|---|---|---|---|
| | Cornucopian | Accommodating | Communalist | Deep ecology |
| Green labels | Resource exploitative, growth-orientated position | Resource conservationist and 'managerial' position | Resource preservationist position | Extreme preservationist position |
| Type of economy | Anti-green economy, unfettered free markets | Green economy, green markets guided by economic incentive instruments (EIs) (e.g. pollution charges etc.) | Deep green economy, steady-state economy regulated by macro-environmental standards and supplemented by EIs | Very deep green economy, heavily regulated to minimize 'resource-take' |
| Management strategies | Primary economic policy objective, maximize economic growth (Gross National Product (GNP)) | Modified economic growth (adjusted green accounting to measure GNP) | Zero economic growth; zero population growth | Reduced scale of economy and population |
| | Taken as axiomatic that unfettered free markets in conjunction with technical progress | Decoupling important but infinite substitution rejected. Sustainability rules: constant | Decoupling plus no increase in scale. 'Systems' perspective —'health' of whole | Scale reduction imperative; at the extreme for some there is a literal |

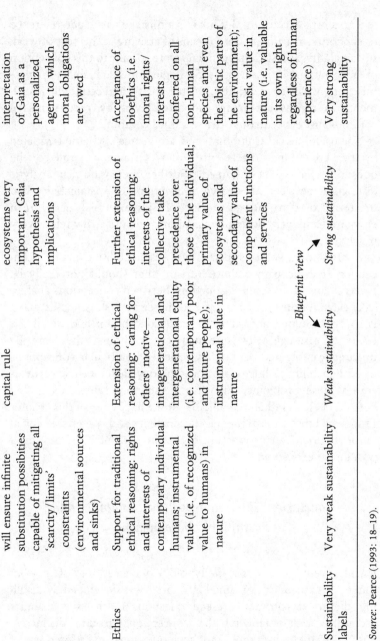

|  | | Blueprint view | |
|---|---|---|---|
| will ensure infinite substitution possibilities capable of mitigating all 'scarcity/limits' constraints (environmental sources and sinks) | capital rule | ecosystems very important; Gaia hypothesis and implications | interpretation of Gaia as a personalized agent to which moral obligations are owed |
| Ethics | Support for traditional ethical reasoning: rights and interests of contemporary individual humans; instrumental value (i.e. of recognized value to humans) in nature | Extension of ethical reasoning; 'caring for others' motive—intragenerational and intergenerational equity (i.e. contemporary poor and future people); instrumental value in nature | Further extension of ethical reasoning: interests of the collective take precedence over those of the individual; primary value of ecosystems and secondary value of component functions and services | Acceptance of bioethics (i.e. moral rights/interests conferred on all non-human species and even the abiotic parts of the environment); intrinsic value in nature (i.e. valuable in its own right regardless of human experience) |
| Sustainability labels | Very weak sustainability | *Weak sustainability* | *Strong sustainability* | Very strong sustainability |

*Source:* Pearce (1993: 18–19).

technocentrism column), I think it is a mistake to include reference to economic instruments as a means of arriving at this sort of weak sustainability, as if such instruments were specific to this conception of environmental sustainability. Strategies for sustainability are promiscuous across conceptions of sustainability, and economic instruments as means are often supported even by proponents of communalist ecocentrism (Pearce's third column).

The usefulness of Columns 3 and 4 in Pearce's scheme is vitiated by their containing no reference to any sustainability rule (or the question: what is to be sustained?). Further, there is no clear analytic distinction between these two conceptions of sustainability and the terms used to indicate distinction (for example, 'deep green economy' and 'very deep green economy' do not really tell us very much).

In brief, then, Pearce's spectrum of sustainability contains a conception (cornucopian technocentrism) that should not really be there; it fails to make the distinctions between conceptions analytically clear; it is insufficiently rigorous in terms of showing just what is to be sustained according to each conception; and, finally, it refers to strategies for sustainability as though they can be uncomplicatedly and definitively related to particular conceptions of sustainability. I hope that the typology developed here overcomes these problems, and that it therefore represents a step beyond Pearce's influential schema. At the beginning of this chapter I suggested that environmental sustainability and sustainable development should on no account be confused, and I am now in a position to explain why.

## Conclusion: Environmental Sustainability and Sustainable Development

It will be remembered that the typology of conceptions of environmental sustainability contained in Table 1 was developed by distilling the most commonly asked questions in the sustainability literature, and organizing the conceptions around distinctive answers to these questions. Two such questions (and related sets of answers) were not included in that table: questions regarding the *causes* of environmental unsustainability and the *solutions* to it. The varying answers to these questions are captured in the form of two 'diagnostic packages' in Table 4. The first package suggests an analysis of unsustainability caused by poverty, a lack of property rights in nature, unpriced ecological services, and protectionism and unsustainable resource use brought about by ineffective economic instruments. The remedial prescription here consists of wealth creation (rather than equity), the conferring of property rights in nature, a marketized environment, free trade, and more effective economic instruments. The second package consists of a series of causes—disempowerment, gender inequality, Western technology, trade, and poverty—with the corresponding remedies of empowerment, women's rights, appropriate technology, protectionism, and equity (rather than wealth creation).

These 'diagnostic packages' represent two 'ideal-type' characterizations of sustainable development theory, and while they serve as indicators of the faultlines between contestants in the battle for definitional supremacy of the notion, we more typically find sustainable development advocates 'borrowing across' the packages in their statements of intent. This habit of borrowing achieves its most sophisticated and widely disseminated form in the Brundtland Report (1987). There is evidence in the report both for wealth

TABLE 4. *Diagnoses and remedies*

| Diagnosis 1 | Remedy 1 | Diagnosis 2 | Remedy 2 |
|---|---|---|---|
| Poverty | Wealth creation | Poverty | Equity |
| Lack of property rights in nature | Confer property rights in nature | Gender inequality | Women's rights |
| Unpriced ecological services | Marketized environment | Disempowerment | Empowerment |
| Protectionism | Trade | Trade | Protectionism |
| Unsustainable resource use | Economic instruments | Western technology | Appropriate technology |

creation ('growth', in Brundtland's terms) and equity, both for the
conferral of property rights and the substantive establishment of
women's rights, both for the pricing of environmental goods and
popular empowerment, and both for economic instruments and
appropriate technology. The only point at which the Brundtland
Report comes down firmly on one side of the diagnosis/remedy
schism represented in Table 4 is on the issue of free trade and
protectionism, with the report broadly in favour of the former and
distinctly reluctant to endorse the latter. The eclecticism in the
report should not surprise us. In fact it is one of the reasons why
the Brundtland analysis of sustainable development has been so
influential—its uninhibited traversal across competing conceptions
of sustainable development is precisely that which has made it all
things to all people.

It should be clear now why earlier in this chapter I said that
sustainable development amounts to one conception or theory of
environmental sustainability, rather than the two things being synonymous. It is a *conception* of sustainability in that it contains views
on what is to be sustained, on why, on what the object(s) of concern
are, and (often implicitly) on the degree of substitutability of
human-made for natural capital. It answers, in other words, all the
questions to which any theory of environmental sustainability must
have an answer. It is a *theory* of environmental sustainability in
that it argues that a particular interpretation of the causes of
unsustainability leads to a determinate view of the remedies for it.
Sustainable development, therefore, amounts to a strategy for environmental sustainability because of the belief that a particular form
of development will provide the conditions within which environmental sustainability can be guaranteed.

This observation, in turn, enables us to make two general and
sustainable (as it were) points about the relationship between the
conceptions of environmental sustainability contained in Table 2
and the theories of sustainable development represented in Table 4.
The first is that the two theories of sustainable development can
most comfortably be associated with Conception A of environmental sustainability, the 'critical natural capital' conception. That is to
say that sustainable development (in either or both of its two ideal-
type guises) is concerned with the sustaining of critical natural

capital, that its principal objective is maintaining or increasing human welfare, that it privileges present and future generation human needs over human wants, and that it has an instrumental attitude to the value of the non-human natural world. Sustainable development (again in either or both of its ideal-type guises) is only compatible with Conception B of environmental sustainability, the 'irreversibility' conception, to the extent that the sustaining of irreversible nature (the objective of Conception B) is important to human welfare—in other words, irreversible nature that can be regarded as critical to the production and reproduction of human life. Irreversible nature which is regarded as worthy of sustaining for its own sake is not generally a part of pictures of sustainable development, and nor is the sustaining of 'natural value', as in Conception C.

All this leads to the second, and broader, point which is that the principal motivation behind any conception or theory of sustainable development is human interest in human welfare. Sustainable development is, therefore, an anthropocentric notion in a way that environmental sustainability need not (but may) be. This distinction ought to be borne in mind in the context of the relationship between environmental sustainability, sustainable development, and social justice. Any theory of social justice must contain a view on who or what the relevant benefits and burdens are to be divided among and between. Clearly, conceptions of environmental sustainability entertain a broader potential community of recipients than do conceptions of sustainable development, and the appropriate regime of social justice may therefore be different in each case. These, however, are speculations that will be redeemed in chapters to come.

# 3

## The Dimensions of Social Justice

WITH the business of the previous chapter complete, half of the framework we needed for our account of the relationship between environmental sustainability and social justice is in place. My task in this chapter is to construct the other half. The analytic method described and deployed in Chapter 2 in the context of environmental sustainability is in practice applicable to any political-theoretical concept. What follows here is the outcome of its application in the context of social justice theory. This involves readings of a number of texts with one overriding intention in mind: to distil from them the principal questions to which any theory of justice would have to have an answer. The results of this enquiry are summarized in Table 5, where the four emergent questions are registered across the top of the table as column headings. The body of the table contains the various answers that have been given to these questions in the social justice literature. I should point out right away that not all the answers to these questions that one can find in social justice theory are represented here—but pretty nearly all of them are. I have left out some because they, while interesting in themselves, do not enable us to make much headway in our study of sustainability/justice compatibility. An example might be 'chance' as an answer to the question 'what is the principle of distribution?' This principle was been ably defended by Barbara Goodwin (1992), but the likelihood of it being compatible with any of the conceptions of environmental sustainability developed in the previous chapter are so slim as to make extended discussion of it here unhelpful.

I had anticipated, as I indicated in the Introduction (p. 10), developing a series of distinct conceptions of social justice from this table

TABLE 5. *The dimensions of social justice*

| What is the community of justice? | | What is the basic structure (the options)? | What is distributed? | What is the principle of distribution? |
|---|---|---|---|---|
| Dispensers[a] | Recipients[b] | | | |
| All human beings | PG HBs[c] | Impartial[d]–procedural[e]–universal[f] | Benefits and burdens | Needs |
| 'Agent-affected'[g] | FG HBs[h] | Impartial–procedural–particular[i] | Environmental goods/bads | Desert |
| | PG sentients | Impartial–consequentialist[j]–universal | Produced environmental goods | Entitlement—including compensation |
| | FG sentients | Impartial–consequentialist–particular | Unproduced environmental goods | Market value |
| | PG non-sentients | Substantive[k]–consequentialist–universal | Preconditional goods | Depends on the mode of production/ good in question |
| | FG non-sentients | Substantive–consequentialist–particular | 'Manna' | To the benefit of the least advantaged |
| | 'Agent-affected' | Substantive–procedural–particular | | Equality |
| | | Substantive–procedural–universal | | Utility |

*Note:* PG = present generation; FG = future generation; HBs = human beings.

[a] Dispensers of distributive justice.
[b] Recipients of distributive justice.
[c] Present generation human beings.
[d] That is, impartial between theories of the good.
[e] That is, procedural in respect of judging the justice of a given situation.
[f] That is, universal in respect of the normative reach of a given theory of justice.
[g] That is, those connected to the agent in some way.
[h] Future generation human beings.
[i] That is, particular in respect of the normative reach of a given theory of justice. Contrasts with 'universal'.
[j] That is, consequentialist in respect of judging the justice of a given situation. Contrasts with 'procedural'.
[k] That is, substantive in respect of having a theory of the good. Contrasts with 'impartial'.

but it turns out that this cannot be done without forgoing the benefits of adopting the analytic method in the first place. This method lays bare the component parts of theories of justice, and this in turn—combined with the results obtained in Chapter 2—makes possible the full exploration of the relationship between environmental sustainability and social justice that we were looking for. Any attempt to force the results obtained in Table 5 into a set of distinctive conceptions of social justice turns out to require a collapsing of components into one another, thereby reducing both their multiplicity and the potential richness of the analysis of the relationship between sustainability and justice. For this reason, *Table 5 contains no conceptions of social justice as such, and no significance should be attached to any patterns that seem to emerge from the answers to the four questions.* (As with the environmental sustainability figure, I suggest that the reader xerox Table 5 and keep it to hand for ease of reference.)

## The Community of Justice

With this general picture in mind, I shall try to put some flesh on the bare bones of Table 5. An overridingly important question in social justice theory involves the nature and extent of the community of justice. Michael Walzer is surely right to say that 'The community is itself a good—conceivably the most important good—that gets distributed' (Walzer 1983: 29), although once the obviousness of this becomes apparent the next surprise is that one finds so little discussion of it. I shall have more to say on Walzer's insight in Chapter 6 (pp. 177–80), but the importance of this element of social justice theory to debates regarding environmental sustainability should hardly need underlining, given the results contained in Table 2 in Chapter 2. It is clear from these results that issues revolving around the question 'sustainable for whom?' are central to conceptions of environmental sustainability. In this sense both sustainability and justice deal in a similar currency, and further examination of the possibilities in justice theory confirm the coincidence.

A fundamentally important distinction to begin with is that

between *distributors* and *recipients* of social justice. One of the few people to point out this distinction is Robert Nozick, who writes:

In considering the distribution of goods, income and so forth, their theories [that is, the theories of those who advance what Nozick calls 'patterned' theories of justice] are theories of recipient justice; they completely ignore any right a person might have to give something to someone. (Nozick 1974: 168)

The theme is picked up by Marcel Wissenburg in the particular context of environmental questions, and in a series of comments to which I shall again have cause to return in Chapter 6 (pp. 190–4) he applies the distinction so as to make clear his view of how non-humans stand in relation to the architecture of social justice theory: 'nature cannot be understood as a distributor . . . we have to restrict ourselves to conceptions of nature . . . as a (collection of) recipients' (Wissenburg 1993: 8). It is Wissenburg's suggestion that leads to my reserving to human beings the role of 'dispensers' of social justice in Table 5, while a broader possible range of recipients (on whom I shall have a little more to say shortly) is registered in the table.

Clearly 'agent-connected' in the table also refers to human beings, and the intention here is to register the difference between universalistic theories of justice ('all human beings') and particularistic theories, for which I have chosen the general descriptive term 'agent-connected'. I take this term from Brian Barry who has referred to such particularistic theories as reserving the role of legitimate dispensers and recipients of distributive justice to 'those connected to the agent in some way' (Barry 1995a: 20), and by Will Kymlicka as involving those bound together in a 'web of relationships' (Kymlicka 1990: 271). Both of these formulations neatly capture the particularistic sense of the community of justice that some theories of distributive justice contain, and which often involve the thought that relations of justice can only be predicated of individuals (or maybe entities) who (or which) are connected in actual relationships of reciprocity. I shall have more to say on a different aspect of the issue of universalism and particularism when I consider the basic structure of theories of justice, below.

Having established the distinction between distributors and recipients, there is little more to say on the former; the interesting
variations are to be found in the category of potential recipients of
distributive justice. I take it that we have no difficulty in this latter
context with including present generations of human beings in the
list of such potential recipients (and when I say 'potential', I mean to
take seriously the possibility that the universalism implicit in the
category may be rejected as unrealistic or undesirable). Most theories of justice, indeed, simply assume that the list of potential recipients is exhausted once contemporary human beings have been
taken into account. A typical expression of this centre of gravity
comes from Tom Campbell, together with a hint of the possibilities
he chooses to eschew:

The illustrative analyses of the concept of justice which have been mentioned so far presuppose that justice, in all its aspects, has to do with states
of affairs which involve persons, or at least sentient beings. Justice does
not arise in our treatment of inanimate things, and possibly not in our
treatment of animals. (Campbell 1988: 11)

The hesitancy here in respect of animals will receive a little attention
below, and considerably more attention in Chapter 6.

The history of social justice theory from the point of view of
thoughts about the community of justice looks rather like the charts
in which the whole of history is telescoped into a 24-hour period. In
these charts, there is a long period at the beginning when nothing
much seems to happen, and then a flurry of activity in the final
minute of the final hour in which *Homo sapiens* emerges from the
plains of Africa and ends up flying to the moon. Social justice theory's equivalent was a long period during which the community of
justice was reserved to (some parts of) the present human generation. Notable and concerted efforts to move beyond this have been
made by, among others, John Rawls (1973), Brian Barry (1991c—an
essay first published in 1977), Joel Feinberg (1981), and Peter Wenz
(1988), and so since the 1970s, at least, I would regard no theory of
justice as complete without some discussion of the possible presence of future generations of human beings in what I am here
calling the community of justice.

Beyond future generations of human beings, however, agree-

ment on who or what to include in the community of justice becomes much (even?) harder to secure. In what follows I shall simply
outline how far it has been suggested that the community of justice
be extended, and some of the issues raised by so extending it, while
leaving detailed comment to Chapters 4, 5, 6, and 7. The next
category registered in the table is 'present generation sentients'.
Clearly this takes us beyond present generation human beings while
including them. The standard way to distinguish these two groups
of sentients (humans and others) is to invoke rationality, so David
Miller (for example) writes that: 'Not every state of affairs can properly be described as just or unjust. It must, first of all, involve
sentient beings, and paradigmatically it involves beings who are
both sentient and rational' (Miller 1976: 18). He goes on to say in the
next breath that 'I shall not discuss whether talk of just treatment of
animals is literal or merely metaphorical' (Miller 1976: 18). This
formulation, of course, leaves the door to talk of justice for animals
ajar, and a number of people (but by no means everybody) have
pushed it open. Perhaps the most determined recent attempt to do
justice to (some) animals has been made by Ted Benton (1993).
Benton writes, for example, that, 'In deciding questions of land use,
I suggest, human communities, or their representative institutions,
have a responsibility to do justice to non-human inhabitants of the
habitats which are liable to be altered by human action' (Benton
1993: 212).

Brian Barry, for one, would think that the vocabulary of this
statement is misplaced, since he writes that 'it does not seem to me
that the concept of justice can be deployed intelligibly outside the
context of relations between human beings. The reason for this is, I
suggest, that justice and injustice can be predicated only of relations
who are regarded as equals in the sense that they weigh equally in
the moral scales' (Barry 1998). In part, the debate between Benton
and Barry and their respective supporters turns on the grammar of
justice: can this grammar be applied to non-human animals and/or
non-sentient nature? I shall consider this question in some detail in
Chapters 6 and 7, but some preliminary remarks are in order here,
if only to indicate how the analytical methodology employed in
arriving at Table 5 enables us to get some early purchase on the
question. In the first place, the distinction between distributors and

recipients of (social) justice needs reiterating: non-human animals cannot distribute justice, but they might receive it (Benton acknowledges this as an irredeemable paternalism in cross-species justice relations; Benton 1993: 212). This sort of distinction shows that the question of whether the grammar of justice is applicable to non-human animals needs careful consideration: it might be that some, but not all, of this grammar is applicable to them.

Second, but without anticipating the detail of what remains for comment on Table 5, a number of features of the architecture (as well as the grammar) of social justice seem appropriate for non-human animals. Issues in the 'basic structure', for example, seem for the most part as relevant to non-human animals as they are to human ones: decisions regarding impartiality/substantiveness, proceduralism/consequentialism, and universalism/particularism will all affect the (putative) distributive claims of non-human animals. Similarly, there is an outside chance that the question of what is being distributed will have repercussions for non-humans, and it is certainly the case that the distributive principle will affect them. All this suggests that non-human animals can be spoken of in terms of the grammar of justice, and that therefore the terms of this grammar in themselves cannot be the reason for excluding them. The stumbling-block, indeed, is more usually located at the entrance to the community of justice itself, and the terms of entrance will occupy us at some length later in this book.

We can return to the theme of this section—the community of justice—by picking up the threads of an issue to which I have just referred, for the distributive principle can itself affect the extent of the community of justice. Benton adopts a needs-based principle, and suggests that the community of justice is thereby widened:

One strength of the socialist [i.e. needs-based] principle of distributive justice is that there is no ontological obstacle to its extension beyond species boundaries. Though, I have argued, the case for attributing rights to non-human animals faces severe intellectual obstacles, their 'neediness' as natural beings is a feature shared with human animals. (Benton 1993: 212)

And Benton continues: 'Need understood in terms of conditions necessary for living well or flourishing is a concept applicable not only to all animal species, but to plant-life as well' (Benton 1993: 212). This formulation takes us to present generation non-sentients in Table 5's 'community of justice', and once they are included as potential recipient members of this community, the way is open for arguments in favour of the inclusion of their sentient and non-sentient future generation counterparts. With this, the list of potential recipients of justice as registered in Table 5 is complete, with the exception of the particularistic notion of being 'agent-connected'. This, though, is easily explained as the recipient reflection of the distributor original: the particularistic community of justice comprises distributors and recipients bound together by an actual and identifiable web of relationships. It is worth noting that the notion of 'agent-connectedness' need not necessarily be confined to human beings: particular humans are bound to particular animals by identifiable webs of relationships (we need only think of the relationship between domestic pets and their owners, for example), and so particularistic conceptions of justice are in principle compatible with cross-species conceptions. I shall say something more about this in the concluding chapter of this book in connection with Peter Wenz's 'concentric circle' theory of justice (1988).

## Basic Structure

Each of the eight sets of options recorded in Table 5 alongside the question 'What is the basic structure?' represents a combination of answers to questions regarding impartiality, proceduralism, and universalism. Each of these three terms is mirrored by an alternative which I have called (in turn) substantiveness, consequentialism, and particularism. (I should emphasize that I am not using the term 'basic structure' here in the Rawlsian sense.)

The issue at stake in the first case (impartiality v. substantiveness) is whether any given theory of justice should be impartial in respect of notions of the good for human beings, or whether it should be read off from, or even be in the service of, the given notion of the good. Brian Barry has neatly illustrated both alternatives, and the first is explicit in what follows: 'A crucial task of justice as impartiality', he writes, 'is to mediate between conflicting notions of the good' (Barry 1995*a*: 12). (Barry distinguishes this sort of impartiality—i.e. impartiality between theories of the good—from impartial theories of the good, which do not 'give any special weight to the interests or concerns of the agents but [treat] all interests and concerns in the same way'; Barry 1995*a*: 20. It is the first sort with which we are concerned here.)

Barry himself believes, of course, that theories of justice should be impartial in this sense, and he contrasts this with utilitarianism and Thomism (following Alasdair MacIntyre's example) in both of which,

the relation between justice and morality is a simple one . . . we start with a conception of the good that is to be achieved as far as possible. We then assess potential rules of justice by their conduciveness to the achievement of that good. Principles of justice have a purely derivative status: they function as guides to the selection of appropriate rules. (Barry 1995*a*: 76)

The difference between impartial and substantive theories of justice could hardly be clearer.

The next line in the structural section of Table 5 registers the distinction often drawn in theories of justice between procedural and consequentialist justice. This distinction has to do with how one judges the justice of a given situation at, say, time *t*. Proceduralists will say that so long as the situation has arisen through just procedures, then the situation is just; there is no independent datum outside of the procedure, so to speak, by which to judge the outcome otherwise. Consequentialists, on the other hand, will assess the outcome of procedures against some external standard, and will judge that outcome just or unjust accordingly. This view is captured in Ronald Dworkin's assertion that 'Justice is a matter of outcomes: a political decision causes injustice, however fair the procedures that produced it, when it denies people some resource, liberty or opportunity that the best theories of justice entitle them to' (Dworkin 1993: 140). Dworkin's view contrasts with Robert Nozick's proceduralist argument that 'Whatever arises from a just situation by just steps is itself just' (Nozick 1974: 151). These quotations neatly capture the consequentialist/proceduralist distinction to which I want to draw attention here.

Two features of the basic architecture of theories of social justice are now in place. The third deals with the issue of universalism and particularism—an issue which is, in truth, complicated by the fact that the terms can be applied to a range of features in social justice theory. They could, for example, be applied to the principle of distribution, in which case the question might be: is the principle of desert universally applicable across all societies, or is it that in some societies, perhaps at different stages of development, an alternative principle—say distribution according to need—is more appropriate? Similarly, as Michael Walzer famously pointed out in his *Spheres of Justice*, it may be wrong to assume that all goods (for distribution) are valued the same way in all societies. Then again, particularism might be diachronic instead of (or as well as) synchronic: Marx, for instance, entertained the view that principles of distributive justice were tied to particular historical modes of production.

In this structural section, however, I intend the universal/particular distinction to refer in the broadest sense to the norms that underpin theories of justice. A forceful exponent of the universalist view is Brian Barry, who opens his *Justice as Impartiality* with this: 'I continue to believe in the possibility of putting forward a universally valid case in favour of liberal egalitarian principles' (Barry 1995a: 3). He goes on to say that this 'appears to be a deeply unfashionable view among contemporary anglophone political philosophers', because, 'From a number of premises, including Burkean conservatism, concern for "stability", worries about "cultural imperialism" and postmodernist "irony", they [anglophone political philosophers] have tended to converge on the conclusion that the so-called "Enlightenment project" of addressing the reason of every human being of sound mind was a gigantic error and that all we can aspire to is articulating the shared beliefs of members of our own society' (Barry 1995a: 3–4).

As Barry implies here, the most principled recent opposition to universalism (in the context of social justice) has come from the so-called 'communitarian' political theorists. Warnke neatly sums up the communitarian view as follows: 'The interpretative turn in political philosophy abandons the attempt to ground universally valid principles of justice in features of human action or rational choice and attempts, instead, to articulate those principles of justice that are suitable for a particular culture and society because of that culture and society's traditions' (Warnke 1992: 158). This makes clear the distinction between universalist and particularist pretensions, and completes this brief descriptive survey of the choices to be made when considering the basic structure of theories of distributive justice.

The three pairs of choices just discussed produce eight technically possible combinations of the three terms, and it is these that are registered in Table 5. As I see it, two of these technical possibilities are logically and practically unlikely—the two at the right-hand end of the basic structure section of the table. In terms of what we have seen so far, the combinations substantive/procedural/particular and substantive/procedural/universal involve the non-guaranteeable (because procedural) eventuality that a procedural approach to justice will produce the substantive outcomes required for a given view of the good for human beings. Put differently, a theory of justice that involves a substantive view of the good for human beings will be uncomfortable with what Rawls calls 'imperfect procedural justice', the distinguishing feature of which is that while 'there is an independent criterion for the correct outcome, there is no feasible procedure which is sure to lead to it' (Rawls 1973: 86). The only context in which proceduralism might be compatible with substantiveness would be that in which the people 'operating' the procedure were of such similar mind that the substantive outcome would be 'written into' their procedural decisions. A Rousseauian community of individuals, overseen by Rousseau's Lawgiver who has 'changed human nature' and 'transformed each individual, who is by himself a complete and solitary whole, into part of a greater whole' (Rousseau 1762/1968: 84), suitably bolstered by an appropriate civil religion (Rousseau 1762/1968: 176–87), might be a case in point. Evidently if this civil religion were to be a green one, then the point would be brought even closer to home. However, 'proceduralism' understood in this way collapses into consequentialism and much of what one might want to say about it could be captured under other, 'live', alternatives in our basic structure typology. Given this, and with half an eye on the use to which this table is to be put in subsequent chapters, I propose to pay attention in those chapters to only the first six combinations in the basic structure section.

Each of these six combinations is to be regarded as something of an ideal type, and it would therefore be wrong to expect to find each combination distinctively represented in identifiable theories of justice. Having said that, though, these analytic distinctions do have their real-world counterparts, and I shall stick my neck out (in the expectation that it will be promptly chopped off) by saying—without detailed supporting comment, and for illustrative purposes only—what they are. The first combination (impartial, procedural, and universal) is most closely represented in Robert Nozick's theory of justice as found in *Anarchy, State and Utopia* (1974). The second (impartial, procedural, and particular) has no obvious real-world analogue, but the third set (impartial, consequentialist, and universal) can be found in Rawls's early work (1973), where 'consequentialism' refers to judging the justice of given situations (distribution is just when it is to the benefit of the least advantaged), as well as in Brian Barry's current work. The fourth set (impartial, consequentialist, and particular) broadly represents Rawls's later position (1993), where 'consequentialist' has the meaning referred to in the previous combination, and where the particularism has to do with Rawls's current view that justice as fairness has to be viewed 'in conjunction with . . . the idea of a well-ordered society . . . effectively regulated by a public political conception of justice' (Rawls 1993: 35). The relative scarcity of such societies and the contingent dependence of justice as fairness upon them is what gives Rawls's later work its particularistic dimension. The fifth combination (substantive, consequentialist, and universal) is archetypically represented by utilitarian theories of justice, and the sixth (substantive, consequentialist, and particular) by Michael Walzer's theory of justice as expressed in his seminal (1983) work.

## What is Distributed?

At its broadest, social justice is about the distribution of 'benefits and burdens' (the first item in the row in Table 5) in society (Miller 1976:

18), and there are a number of ways in which these very broad categories can be disaggregated. Again with half an eye on the uses to which this table is to be put in the context of environmental sustainability, the disaggregation can usefully take the form outlined in the table.

In the first place, there are what David Miller has referred to as 'environmental goods' which he defines as 'any aspect of the environment to which a positive value may be attached' (Miller 1999). As examples he refers to 'the maintenance of the ozone layer, having rivers free of pollution, the continued existence of the Siberian tiger, the availability of open uplands for hikers, and the preservation of ancient monuments . . . [as] . . . all count[ing] potentially as environmental goods in my sense' (Miller 1999).

I want to differ from Miller's presentation in two respects. First, in keeping with the general rubric of social justice as being about the distribution of benefits *and* burdens, I would refer to environmental goods *and* bads (the second item in the row in Table 5)—which means that we are dealing with 'any environmental feature that may be positively *or* negatively valued'—rather than just to the former, as in Miller's formulation. To his list, then, we might add such examples as landfill sites, toxic waste dumps, and so on. This move enables us to capture issues at the heart of the environmental justice movement, to which I made reference in Chapter 1.

Second, I want (as far as possible) to keep produced and unproduced environmental goods (e.g. the Pyramids and the ozone layer, respectively—and in so far as we can call the Pyramids an environmental good at all) apart (the third and fourth items in the row in Table 5). This is in itself a contentious proposal, since there are many who think that the reach and range of human activity is such that no part of the non-human natural world remains unaffected by human artifice (McKibben 1990). In this sense, humans have 'mixed their labour' everywhere, and therefore all goods—including environmental goods—are 'produced'. For the moment I shall say no more than that there seems to me to be a difference of the sort that makes a difference between the ozone layer and the Pyramids, and that this difference can be summed up in the distinction between unproduced and produced environmental goods. Perhaps it would now help to drop the Pyramid example altogether and refer, instead, to the difference between, say, the forests of Central New Guinea and London's Hyde Park to capture the kind of distinction I intend here between unproduced and produced environmental goods.

Environmental goods that are essential for human existence are a specific type of the next kind of good in the table—what I have called preconditional goods (the fifth item in the row in Table 5). These may be even more controversial in the detail than environmental goods, but it is hard to avoid discussion of the idea, and the reference point for such discussions is often John Rawls's notion of primary goods. Such goods are, in Rawls's terms, goods 'that every rational man is presumed to want', and this is because they 'normally have a use whatever a person's rational plan for life' (Rawls 1973: 62). The idea of primary—or what I have here called preconditional—goods is of course radically indeterminate, and Rawls himself gives examples of various types of 'social' and 'natural' primary goods (Rawls 1973: 62). I shall have more to say on what filling out this indeterminacy might imply for the relationship between environmental sustainability and social justice later on (and particularly in Chapter 4), and here I only wanted to establish the existence of the idea of preconditional goods—so obviously bound up with the issue of environmental sustainability—in social justice theory.

One more answer to the question 'What is distributed?' requires mention here: Bruce Ackerman's 'manna' (the final item in the row in Table 5). In Ackerman's exploration of social justice we are asked to imagine that we are on a spaceship, having left 'our previous wealth and position' far behind (Ackerman 1980: 31), and we unexpectedly come across a planet. We scan this planet with our instruments, 'and learn that it contains a single resource, manna, which has some remarkable properties. Most important, manna is infinitely indivisible and malleable, capable of transformation into any physical object a person may desire' (Ackerman 1980: 31). The rest of Ackerman's book is taken up with an investigation of the principles of justice that might emerge from this otherworldly situation. I do not want to say much about 'manna' here, although I shall

return to it in Chapter 5. It is worth noting, however, that
Ackerman's decision to deploy an infinitely fungible substance of
this sort in his theory puts down important markers in both social
justice and environmental sustainability theory. As far as social justice theory is concerned, it will be clear that Ackerman's view contrasts vividly with that of Michael Walzer, for example. Walzer, it
will be remembered, distinguishes between various sorts of goods
precisely because he thinks that different principles will regulate the
just distribution of different goods. Ackerman's expository decision
to make different goods infinitely fungible evidently precludes
him from broaching such a possibility (although in the second part
of his book he does come back to Earth to consider the non-
substitutability case).

Similarly, in the context of environmental sustainability,
Ackerman's 'manna' has uncannily similar characteristics to those
displayed by conceptions of sustainability that turn on a belief in
infinite substitutability between human-made and natural capital—
i.e. conceptions of sustainability which I argued in Chapter 1 cannot
properly be regarded as *environmental* conceptions. It will be remembered that according to this view, natural capital requires no special
protection since its functions can be adequately substituted for by
human-made equivalents. Whether this apparently neat match between an aspect of Ackerman's theory of justice and one particular
notion of sustainability makes Ackerman's theory prima facie unsuitable for conceptions of *environmental* sustainability is a question
I shall broach in Chapter 5.

## *The Principle of Distribution*

The final question to which all theories of social justice must have
an answer is, 'What is the principle of distribution?', and some of the
many answers that have been given to this question in such theories
are recorded along the bottom line in Table 5.

I pointed out in the Introduction that David Miller (1976) organized his book on the subject around a consideration of three of the
answers presented here: need, desert, and entitlement. These an-

swers are indeed central to social justice theorizing and instances of each of them are abundant. Marx, for example, in the context of need, talked famously of a 'higher phase of communist society' in which the distribution of society's benefits and burdens would be based on the principle 'from each according to his ability to each according to his needs' (Marx 1969: 160). In almost the same breath, and prefacing his remark regarding need, he also glosses a version of what distribution according to desert might look like: 'the individual producer receives back from society . . . exactly what he gives to it' (Marx 1969: 159). The calculation of desert is of course as notoriously difficult and contested as the assessment of need, so making either of these principles work in practice is no easy task. But the conceptual space between them is considerable and most contemporary theories of justice are organized around one or the other principle—or, more commonly, some combination of them in conjunction with the third common principle of distribution, entitlement.

Here I take Robert Nozick's entitlement view of just distribution to be paradigmatic. Nozick suggests that 'The general outlines of the entitlement theory illuminate the nature and defects of the other conceptions of distributive justice. The entitlement theory of justice is *historical*; whether a distribution is just depends upon how it came about' (Nozick 1974: 153; emphasis in the original). In contrast, he continues, '*current time-slice principles* of justice hold that justice of a distribution is determined by how things are distributed (who has what) as judged by some structural principle(s) of just distribution' (Nozick 1974: 153; emphasis in the original).

Structural principles of this sort, maintains Nozick, lead to what he calls 'patterned' theories of justice, and he is opposed to patterning because the transfers involved inevitably undermine what he regards as the fundament of just transfer, which is history: 'Justice in holdings is historical; it depends on what actually happened' (Nozick 1974: 152). This, in turn, is tied to a remark already noted in the context of the earlier discussion regarding proceduralism and consequentialism in the basic structure of theories of justice. It will be remembered that Nozick's contribution there was to argue that 'Whatever arises from a just situation is itself just' (Nozick 1974: 151), so as long as the transfers of holdings made in the past are just, then the present set of holdings is by definition also just.

Importantly, Nozick's entitlement theory of justice depends on an elision of production and distribution. As he says: 'To think that the task of a theory of distributive justice is to fill in the blank in "to each according to his——" is to be predisposed to search for a pattern; and the separate treatment of "from each according to his——" treats production and distribution as two separate and independent issues. On an entitlement view these are *not* two separate issues' (Nozick 1974: 159–60; emphasis in the original). Acceptance of this depends on acceptance, in turn, of the just acquisition of property, since this is what justifies him (in his mind at least) in claiming that 'Things come into the world already attached to people having entitlements over them' (Nozick 1974: 160).

The historical and property-based nature of entitlement as a principle of distribution should now be clear, and both of these features of the principle will merit discussion in the contex of environmental sustainability. It might turn out that the suitability of the principle for the context of environmental sustainability will turn on the eliding of production and distribution, referred to in the previous paragraph. This is because this elision amounts to the elision of two categories of goods developed as answers to the previous question in the table, 'What is distributed?' It will be remembered that there we developed a category of unproduced environmental goods, and it would seem that Nozick's theory has no purchase on such goods. Nozick's assertion, referred to above, that 'Things come into the world already attached to people having entitlements over them' (Nozick 1974: 160), depends on such things being owned, through either just acquisition or just transfer. Original just acquisition is based, in a Lockean sense adopted without question by Nozick, on individuals 'mixing their labour' with objects in the world. Unproduced (environmental) goods, though, have by definition had no work done on them, and so Nozick's affirmation that 'Things come into the world already attached to people having entitlements over them' cannot be true of all things.

It would be inappropriate to discuss this potential hiatus between entitlement as an exhaustive principle of distribution and particular conceptions of environmental sustainability any further now, but it is worth pointing out that the problem was dimly visible to Nozick himself. To the discussion glossed above he attached, as something of an afterthought, a reference to a 'limit case' of objects that 'appear from nowhere, out of nothing', before going on to say that 'A complete theory of justice might cover this limit case as well; perhaps here is a use for the normal conceptions of distributive justice' (Nozick 1974: 160). One of my expectations in bringing distributive justice and environmental sustainbability into interrogative contact was that the strains in conceptions of either or both would soon show. This may be the case here, but corroboration of this suspicion is required, and I shall try to produce it in later chapters.

I take Friedrich Hayek's work to be illustrative of the next principle mentioned in the table—market value. Like Nozick, Hayek rejects the idea of a distributive principle as such. He argues, instead, that 'only that "natural price" [for the sale of somebody's labour] could be regarded as just which could be arrived at in a competitive market . . . determined not by any human laws or decrees but . . . on so many circumstances that it could be known beforehand only by God' (Hayek 1993: 132). The resulting distribution of wealth, says Hayek, will often be totally unrelated to merit or need:

The long and the short of it is that men can be allowed to decide what work to do only if the remuneration they can expect to get for it corresponds to the value their services have to those of their fellows who receive them; and that these values which their services have to their fellows will often have no relations to their individual merits or needs. (Hayek 1993: 128)

The connection between market value and chance is made explicit by Hayek:

though people resent that their remuneration should in part depend on pure accident, that is in fact precisely what it must if the market is to adjust itself promptly to the unavoidable and unforeseen changes in circumstances, and the individual is to be allowed to decide what to do. (Hayek 1993: 139)

So far there has been no suggestion that these various principles for fair distribution should be anything other than universally applicable, both in time and across space. This assumption (or, in some cases, this argument) has been challenged across both dimensions by some theorists of social justice, and I have chosen to illustrate this challenge with reference to Marx and to Michael Walzer. The challenge is captured in Table 5 under the rubric: 'depends on the mode of production/good in question'.

Marx's reasons for eschewing the universalizing route have to do with the specialized form of his theory of history, but a description of the theory is unnecessary here. Suffice to say that Marx's materialist view of history leads him to the conclusion that each mode of production 'produces' a different principle according to which distribution will be fairly carried out. Wood glosses this as follows: 'Any mode of distribution is determined by the mode of production of which it is a fundamental part' (Wood 1993: 172). This much was hinted at earlier in this consideration of distributive principles when we saw Marx referring to principles of both desert and need: desert is the principle appropriate to the capitalist mode of production, with labour as an indicator of desert as the transition to communist society takes place. Once the transition is complete, as we saw, need becomes the appropriate distributive principle. For Marx, therefore, no single principle of distribution can be considered universally valid; rather, different principles relate to different modes of production in such a way as to make such principles depend on the stage of development of the economic relations in question, and therefore to make distributive principles both diachronically and synchronically variable.

Michael Walzer arrives at a similar position, but by focusing on the nature of the goods themselves and the cultural context within which they are valued and distributed, rather than on developing social and economic relations. He puts it like this:

I want to argue . . . that the principles of justice are themselves pluralistic in form: that different social goods ought to be distributed for different reasons, in accordance with different procedures, by different agents; and that all these differences derive from different understandings of the social goods themselves—the inevitable product of historical and cultural particularism. (Walzer 1983: 6)

Walzer's views have been the object of considerable and deserved discussion, not least for his fervent refusal to countenance any universalizing of the value of social goods. This discussion is of abiding interest in the context of environmental sustainability, both because the valuation of such goods seems often to be tied to cultural context, and because such goods may have a distributive principle 'attached' to them for Walzerian reasons. The question, though, might well be whether any conception of sustainability can afford anything other than universalism, given what could be regarded as a set of non-negotiable objectives.

Three further answers to the question regarding the principle of distribution remain for brief explanation. The first—that the principle works to the benefit of the least advantaged—will be instantly recognizable as a dictum drawn from John Rawls. In their intermediate form (the final form is importantly different from this from the point of view of future generations, but not for reasons that make a difference here) Rawls's two principles read as follows:

First: each person is to have a right to the most extensive basic liberty compatible with a similar liberty for others. (Rawls 1973: 60)

Second: social and economic inequalities are to be arranged so that they are both (a) to the greatest benefit of the least advantaged and (b) attached to offices and positions open to all under conditions of fair equality of opportunity. (Rawls 1973: 83)

This second principle obviously sanctions inequalities, but it only does so if they are 'to the greatest benefit of the least advantaged'. While 'greatest benefit' can be interpreted in a number of ways, particularly in the way in which it allows present inequalities to be justified in terms of benefits to the least advantaged at some unspecified point in the (often long-distant) future, Rawls's principle does allow some rough-and-ready judgements to be made. For instance, the Rowntree Foundation's *Inquiry into Income and Wealth* in Britain, carried out in 1995, came to the following conclusion:

In the period 1961–79, the incomes of the poorest 20 per cent of the population grew at or above that average rate for society as a whole, while those of the top 20 per cent rose slightly more slowly than the average. From 1979–1992, average incomes in Britain rose by 36 per cent, with those of the richest 20 per cent growing faster than this (the top 10 per cent by over 60 per cent). But the incomes of the poorest 20 per cent of the population failed to rise at all, and those of the bottom 10 per cent actually *fell* by 17 per cent. (Real World Coalition 1996: 67; emphasis in the original)

During the 1979–92 period, then, income inequalities increased, and according to Rawls's principle these inequalities could only be justified if they were to the 'greatest benefit of the least advantaged'. The fact, though, that during this period the incomes of the least advantaged fell suggests that on Rawlsian terms the Thatcher period in Britain was one of growing injustice (assuming, among other things, the potentially tendentious point that 'the least advantaged' are those with the lowest incomes).

Rawls's theory will be discussed at length in a number of contexts in the chapters that follow, and it is fair to say that his 'difference principle', which incorporates the idea of inequalities being to the benefit of the least advantaged, is not necessarily the most interesting part of his theory from the point of view of environmental sustainability. It needs mentioning, though, both for its broad importance, and for its relation to our penultimate principle for distribution—equality.

As a 'prioritarian' principle (it gives priority to the least advantaged), Rawls's principle is non-relational. The justice of a given situation is not judged by comparing some people in relation to others, but in terms of the well-being of a determinate and in principle isolatable group of people. Equality, on the other hand, is a relational principle, in that relational comparisons need to be made before judgements on equality (and inequality) can be arrived at. Equality as a principle of distribution has always been associated with the most radical tendencies in political thought and practice, and the environmental context is no exception to this. It has been suggested, for example, that the total amount of (unproduced) environmental goods available to the human race can be calculated, and that the only fair way to divide up these resources is on the basis of equality. This idea of equal 'ecological space' possesses considerable polemical, if not theoretical, force (part of its theoretical weakness is that it fails to recognize the elementary point that fair treatment might require unequal treatment). The polemical force derives from comparing the idea of ecological space with that of the 'ecological footprint', defined as 'the aggregate land (and water) area required by people in a region to provide continuously all the resources they presently consume and all the wastes they presently discharge' (Selman 1996: 36). People who live in areas of high consumption will generally make a larger ecological footprint than their nominal allotment of environmental space would warrant them to make, and this discrepancy has been used to highlight the unsustainability of certain lives and lifestyles. Closer to our theme of the relationship between justice and sustainability, the discrepancy has also been used to argue for significant inter- and intranational transfers of wealth on the basis that if some people are overconsuming, then others are underconsuming, and these latter should be entitled to sell their surplus environmental space to overconsumers. These remarks are only intended to hint at considerations which will be taken up more fully in Chapters 4, 5, 6, and 7.

The final principle for distribution to which I want to refer here is 'utility'. Believing that 'The principle of utility is capable of being pursued', and that 'it is but tautology to say, that the more consistently it is pursued, the better it must ever be for humankind' (Bentham 1789/1948: 13), Jeremy Bentham adopted an unashamedly instrumental view of the role of justice and its principles. He wrote that 'Justice . . . is nothing more than an imaginary instrument, employed to forward on certain occasions, and by certain means, the purposes of benevolence' (Bentham 1789/1948: 125–6 n. 2). So the justice of a given distribution is determined by the extent to which it contributes, or otherwise, to what John Stuart Mill referred to as 'social utility' (Mill 1863/1972: 54). In our connection, there is a potential structural compatibility between the consequentialistic and aggregative framework for utilitarian calculation and the seemingly objective-driven nature of conceptions of environmental sustainability.


## Conclusion


My explication of Table 5 is now complete, and with it, the framework for the exploration of the relationship between environmental sustainability and social justice that follows. This exploration would have been neater than it turns out to be if it had been possible to demarcate distinct conceptions of social justice in the same way as I was able to do for conceptions of environmental sustainability in Chapter 2. I would then have been able to take each conception of environmental sustainability in turn, and test it for compatibility against each conception of social justice.

It turns out, though, that, as I explained near the beginning of this chapter, the answers to the four organizing questions in Table 5 cannot be usefully herded into family groups. This is principally because the number of answers 'overflows' any reasonable number of conceptions of justice. This is the case, for example, with what I have called the 'basic structure'. Here there are eight options (or six, if we count only the 'live' ones), and each of them is worthy of separate discussion in the context of environmental sustainability. To have forced these options into a smaller number of conceptions of justice would have been to reduce the potential richness of the encounter between environmental sustainability and this aspect, at least, of social justice theory.

The best way to proceed, then, is to take each of the three conceptions of environmental sustainability developed in Chapter 2 in turn, and to pick out the points in Table 5 where this encounter between sustainability and justice is at its most interesting. This will inevitably mean that not all of the features of Table 5 will receive equal attention in each of the subsequent four chapters, but something of a pattern will emerge, and I shall refer to the significance of this in the concluding chapter.

# PART III

# 4

## 'Critical Natural Capital' and Social Justice (Part I)

LET me begin by recalling the principal features of the 'critical natural capital' conception of environmental sustainability that I developed in Chapter 2. Of the four organizing questions, the first, 'what to sustain?', is answered by the notion of critical natural capital—for example 'ecological processes'. This answer is underpinned by a belief in the possibility of considerable substitutability between human-made and natural capital, but not between human-made and some critical natural capital. In this conception of environmental sustainability the question of why capital availability should be sustained through time is answered by the importance to human welfare (material and aesthetic) of such capital over time. The implications of this answer, in turn, are reflected in the objects of concern for Conception A: present and future generation human needs take precedence over present and future generation human wants, and secondary concern is devolved onto the non-human natural world to the extent that a sustained natural environment is functional for human welfare.

There are five fundamental contexts in which this conception of environmental sustainability bears upon distributive justice (and vice versa). In the order in which I propose to deal with them these are: international justice, future generations, the relationship between human welfare and environmental sustainability, the role of property ownership in policies for sustainability, and substitutability between human-made and natural capital. Consideration of these contexts is divided between this chapter (the first two) and the next chapter (the last three): to have dealt with them all here would have produced a chapter more ungainly than it already is.

In each of these contexts I shall be asking slightly different questions, relating to different parts of the analysis of distributive justice
developed and discussed in Chapter 3. For my purposes, the interesting issues in the context of international justice centre on the
extent of the community of justice and on the basic structure of
theories of justice. In other words, assuming that justice (whatever
that might mean) has an international character in this conception
of environmental sustainability, which types of theories of justice
can best deal with this internationalism? Put differently again, advocates of this conception of sustainability need to legitimize their
preferred distributions in an international context. Are there any
types of theories of justice which will not enable them to do this?
Are there any ways of theorizing justice which advocates of the
'critical natural capital' conception should be warned off?

The second theme is the very large one of distributive justice in
relation to future generations. Once again the debate here largely
turns on the community of justice, and how different theories of
justice might deal with sustainability's demand to include future
generations in that community.

As far as the third issue is concerned, it is practically an article
of faith for the sustainable development movement that environmental sustainability is a distributional issue. And not only that,
but that particular types of distribution (more equitable ones) are
linked to greater environmental sustainability. In other words, of
the principles of distribution identified in Chapter 3, advocates
of sustainable development will argue that some combination of
equality and needs-meeting is functional for environmental
sustainability as well as for improved human welfare. I shall discuss
this argument, both in its self-contained form and (bearing in mind
the full range of principles of distribution we have identified) in the
form of a further question: might not other principles of distribution
be functional for sustainability too? My conclusions will have the
potential effect of widening the legitimizing frame of reference
(in distributive terms) beyond that offered by the sustainable
development lobby.

The fourth theme, that of property ownership, arises in connection with that of international justice, in the sense that measures
aimed at improving the chances of environmental sustainability

often involve the proposed transfer of various forms of benefits and burdens between nations. I shall examine the arguments in favour of such transfers and the difficulties with them here, but I shall leave the wider question of the very legitimacy of the ownership of various forms of natural capital until the next chapter. This theme of property links the objective of this conception of environmental sustainability (i.e. the maintaining of critical natural capital availability) with the question that is common to all theories of justice of what is to be distributed (the answer here is property).

Finally, this seems the right place to introduce the issue of compensability since compensation, as well as being fundamental to some conceptions of justice, also presupposes the possibility of substitutability, and substitutability plays a considerable part in this notion of environmental sustainability. Perhaps the most interesting and controversial uses of the idea of compensation are made in the context of future generations, so this section is linked to the second one. In terms of the analyses of environmental sustainability and of social justice carried out in Chapters 2 and 3, then, the issue of compensability links that of substitutability (in environmental sustainability) with that of what is to be distributed (in distributive justice).

## International Justice

'Part of what is keyed by the phrase "global environmental justice"', writes Dale Jamieson, 'is the idea that we may owe duties of justice to entities that have traditionally been regarded as beyond the pale. These may include wild animals, plants, species, populations, ecosystems, forests, canyons and so on.' But most people, he suggests, 'believe that global environmental justice centrally concerns relations among humans rather than relations between humans and non-humans' (Jamieson 1994: 202). In what follows in this section I shall be guided by the latter intuition, but I quote Jamieson's wider-ranging frame of reference to flag what is in store in Chapters 5 and 6.

It will become clear in those chapters that there is a considerable reluctance to talk of the non-human natural world in terms of justice because of the apparent difficulties involved in simultaneously preserving a series of conditions for participation in the justice game, and admitting a realm (non-human nature) to the game which cannot meet those conditions. The anatomy of this reluctance is relevant to us here in the solely human context in that within the so-called realist school of international relations there is the belief that international justice is a meaningless concept because of the lack of a particular precondition for justice. Supporters of this school 'deny that moral considerations, including those of justice, can or should apply beyond the bounds of particular societies' (Simon 1984: 183), because they argue that a fundamental prerequisite for relations of justice—reciprocity—simply does not exist in the international context.

There have been a number of types of response to this. The first, baldly, is to say that while reciprocity may have been hard to identify in the past, the contemporary globalization of political life brings with it a 'network of relationships' (Belsey 1995: 40) which amount to reciprocity in all but name. This looks like a sensible approach to take, and indeed it is so obvious to some that they relegate the view that there can be no such thing as international justice to prehistory: 'One old philosophical wrangle which appears quaint in the context of today is the debate over whether and why there are duties and obligations that transcend national boundaries' (Jamieson 1994: 199).

A second, more theoretical approach, and one which is of considerable relevance to us in view of what follows, is flagged by Kai Nielsen. Nielsen suggests that it is a mistake to stick with the idea that a 'skein of actual co-operative reciprocity [is] essential for the circumstances of justice'. What is required, he goes on, is 'mutual reciprocity not resting on actual schemes of co-operation for mutual advantage but instead on a broadly Kantian conception of moral equality in which justice requires that we all treat each other as equals' (Nielsen 1995: 39–40). The significance of placing one's bets on Kantian transcendentalism rather than on mutual advantage as far as founding and motivating justice are concerned will soon become clear. Remember that a guiding question for us is: are there any ways of theorizing about justice that advocates of international justice should be warned about? Already it looks as though theories which take reciprocity and/or mutual advantage as their guiding star will have, at the very least, some tough empirical questions to answer in the international context before the theory can get going (has globalization really brought about the kind of reciprocity required?). Of course, supporters of Kantian equality might themselves be accused of putting the cart before the horse in that the preconditions for justice (a recognition of moral considerability) are a part of what justice itself is supposed to be (or to bring) about.

What appears to be an important logical point emerges from these last remarks. International justice presupposes two types of universality: first, a community of potential distributors and recipients which in principle includes everyone on earth; and second, a universality of prescriptive reach. In the terms used in the table of distributive justice, the potential dispensers of justice and the potential recipients of justice are coterminous: all present generation human beings. Similarly, the idea of universal prescriptive reach contrasts in the table with the 'particularism' of restricted reach (in the 'basic structure' section).

Both these types of universality are called into question in some contemporary justice theory. What has come to be called 'communitarian' theory opposes both the idea of a planet-wide community of justice, and the notion that prescriptions for justice can have universal reach; while so-called 'care' theory suggests that obligations to others decrease in strength the further one moves from one's immediate circle, thereby undermining any pretensions to a universal community of justice.

Communitarians argue that 'the demands of distributive justice can and will differ across different societies and at different moments in history' (Taylor 1986: 47), and this particularism may be underpinned by the view that ideas of social justice are linked to theories of the good for human beings. Since such theories themselves differ across societies, so will prescriptions for justice. Alasdair MacIntyre puts it like this: 'conceptions of justice and of practical rationality generally and characteristically confront us as closely related aspects of some larger, more or less well-articulated, overall view of human

life and of its place in nature' (MacIntyre 1988: 389), and the varia-
tion he observes across human societies of such overall views leads
him to the conclusion that 'There is . . . only . . . the justice-of-this-
or-that-tradition' (MacIntyre 1988: 346).

In terms of the basic structure dimension of theories of justice
outlined in Table 5, MacIntyre subscribes to a notion of justice
which is *substantive* (it has a theory of the good), *consequentialist* (in
terms of judging the justice of a given situation), and *particular* (in so
far as the prescriptive reach of ideas of justice is concerned). This
cocktail, and especially the last ingredient in it, seems unpromising
from the point of view of international justice, and it looks even
worse if we mix in the particularism of community since this fore-
closes the in-principle possibility of there being a theory of the good
which all human beings could share. And at the end of this particular
track we find Jacques Derrida who argues that every attempt to
speak justice is always already an injustice because it presupposes
appropriation of the other's language:

To address oneself to the other in the language of the other is, it seems, the
condition of all possible justice, but apparently, in all rigor, it is not only
impossible (since I cannot speak the language of the other except to the
extent that I appropriate it and assimilate it according to the law of an
explicit third) but even excluded by justice as law (*droit*), inasmuch as
justice as right seems to imply an element of universality, the appeal to a
third party who suspends the unilaterality or singularity of the idioms.
(Derrida 1992: 17)

Derrida cannot, of course, be regarded as a member of the
communitarian persuasion, but his radical particularism highlights
the difficulties that anyone of that frame of mind will have with the
idea of international justice. At the root of this lies a conflict between ways of theorizing about justice. As David Miller puts it in his
introduction to Michael Walzer's theory of 'spheres of justice', on
one reading, a theory of justice is 'meant to look a bit like a scientific
theory in which a small number of fundamental laws are established, and these are then applied to a range of concrete cases,
bringing them into a common fold and showing how, despite their
superficial differences, they share the same essential properties'
(Miller 1995: 2). The 'laws' to which Miller refers are universal in

character and therefore give the universal prescriptive reach that a theory of international justice will require.

But, continues Miller, 'Walzer's account of justice is developed in conscious opposition to this approach. It is radically pluralistic in nature. There are no universal laws of justice. Instead, we must see justice as the creation of a particular political community at a particular time, and the account we give must be given from within such a community' (Miller 1995: 2). The only way to make sense of international justice, given this starting point, would be to view the whole of humanity as a political community, but Walzer himself bluntly refuses to entertain such an idea: 'The only plausible alternative to the political community is humanity itself, the society of nations, the entire globe. But were we to take the globe as our setting, we would have to imagine what does not yet exist: a community that included all men and women everywhere' (Walzer 1983: 29).

Unlike (to my knowledge) MacIntyre, Walzer has reflected at some length on the implications of his radical pluralism for aspirations to international justice. The centrepiece of Walzer's edifice is his theory of 'complex equality': the idea that inequalities in the holdings of one particular good should not translate into inequalities of other social goods. As Walzer himself puts it: 'My purpose in this book is to describe a society where no social good serves or can serve as a means of domination' (Walzer 1983: p. xiv). In the context of our present discussion of international justice, Walzer says the following:

In a limited way, the theory of complex equality can be extended from particular communities to the society of nations, and the extension has this advantage: it will not ride roughshod over local understandings and decisions. Just for that reason, it will also not yield a uniform system of distributions across the globe, and it will only begin to address the problems raised by mass poverty in many parts of the globe. (Walzer 1983: 30)

This last remark of Walzer's is not designed to win him many friends among those who think that mass poverty is a global evil that should be eradicated. Brian Barry, for one, acidly remarks that: 'It is an immediate implication of Walzer's particularism [or 'conventionalism', p. 75; or 'hyper-conventionalism', p. 76]—and one he happily embraces—that there can be no such thing as international distributive justice. For there is manifestly no international community in Walzer's sense of a set of people with shared understandings of the meaning of social goods' (Barry 1995b: 79).

(I should point out that Walzer has shifted his position slightly in more recent work, but surely not enough to satisfy critics like Barry. A principal current caveat to his *Spheres* maxim that 'distributive justice is relative to social meanings' is that such justice is 'not relative simply', since 'the very idea of "justice" . . . provides a critical perspective and a negative doctrine' (Walzer 1994: 26). This critical perspective does not allow him to move much beyond the radical pluralism of *Spheres*, however. It is still not legitimate, he says, to 'wag our fingers' at distributions of social goods in other societies, but we can criticize them 'insofar as we think of these as options for ourselves' (Walzer 1994: 30). It is Walzer's continuing refusal to countenance the move from a particular 'ourselves' to a universal 'everyone'—he explicitly rejects the presuppositions of a Habermasian 'ideal speech situation' (Walzer 1994: 27), for example—that prevents him from endorsing the idea of an international community that might underpin a conception of international justice.)

Walzer would want to make it clear that his view that there can be no such thing as international *justice* does not imply that he thinks there should be no international *concern*. (He would also, of course, want to make clear that he is talking of the impossibility of the idea of international *distributive* justice, as opposed to international justice *per se*: he might still be able to make sense of the idea of a 'just war', for example.) In reply to Barry's point, though, he writes, 'I am inclined to think that . . . ordinary moral principles regarding humane treatment and mutual aid do more work than any specific account of distributive justice' (Walzer 1995: 293). This amounts to a reworking of the view of 'realist' international relations theorists that the incoherence of the idea of international justice for technical reasons (lack of reciprocity) does not invalidate attempts to render international assistance (e.g. aid) on other grounds (e.g. charity). This begs the question of why, if charity (or 'humane treatment' or 'mutual aid' in Walzer's words) will do the trick, we should bother with justice at all—and why charity can legitimately cross international boundaries while justice cannot. Judging by results, of course, neither charity nor justice is doing the trick, as the number of people in absolute poverty worldwide grows year by year, but the reasons why the poor are likely to choose justice over charity as the source of alleviation of their condition are twofold. First, justice implies a ground-level equality between distributor and recipient which charity does not; and second, obligations born of justice are more binding and less revocable than those born of charity.

In sum, Walzer's rejection of both of the constitutive terms of 'international justice' makes him an unlikely source of succour for those for whom international justice is functional for environmental sustainability—i.e. practically everyone in the sustainable development movement. And we can see from Table 5 that Walzer's is an outstanding example of a broad band of theories of justice (or ways of theorizing about justice) that have at their heart two sorts of radical particularism: first, the particularism of social communities; and second, the particularism of prescriptive reach of theories of justice. These sorts of particularism disable attempts to generate an international theory of justice, and so the conception of environmental sustainability with which we are currently engaged seems incompatible—in this context at least—with particularist theories of justice.

The second type of particularist theory of justice with which I want to deal is that which has come to be called 'justice as care'. (I realize that it is somewhat idiosyncratic to refer to this theory as a theory of justice at all, since it is much more often regarded as an alternative to justice than as an instance of a theory of it. However, an ethic of care—to give it its more normal name—does include views on the proper distribution of goods and bads, and therefore unavoidably deals with the same type of subject matter as standard theories of justice. This seems enough, for my purposes here, to refer to care in terms of justice. It will also become apparent a little later that attempts to oppose 'care' and 'justice' may be misplaced.) The notion of 'care' derives principally from the work of Carol Gilligan whose research suggests that different moral principles from those derived from Kantian autonomy, which often serves to underpin universalist theories of justice, might emerge from 'a life spent in intimate and generative relationships' (Gilligan 1982: 151). She claims to have observed just such an ethic at work, and notes that it is most often advanced by women (although it is wrong to say that she thought such an ethic to be exclusive to women; Gilligan 1982: 2). This ethic, she writes, 'evolves around a central insight, that self and other are interdependent' (Gilligan 1982: 74), and she expresses the implications of this for justice as follows:

The values of justice and autonomy, presupposed in current theories of human growth and incorporated into definitions of morality and of the self, imply a view of the individual as separate and of relationships as either hierarchical or contractual, bound by the alternatives of constraint and cooperation. In contrast, the values of care and connection, salient in women's thinking, imply a view of the self and the other as interdependent and of relationships as networks created and sustained by attention and response. (Gilligan 1996: 242)

Brian Barry has glossed Gilligan's 'different voice' thesis as implying that 'Obligations . . . can arise only out of relations with other people' (Barry 1995a: 250), and this evidently has important repercussions in the context of arguments for and against international justice. In a suggestion that is designed for the context of intergenerational rather than international justice, Gregory Kavka hopes to argue for an intuitive sense of the former by analogy with the latter. He writes: 'Location in space is not a morally relevant feature of a person . . . [so] . . . why should location in time be any different?' (Kavka 1981: 110). The problem for Kavka is that proponents of justice as care will resist his premiss on the grounds that location in space *does* matter. (There might appear to be something of a jump in my argument here in that the relationships of which Gilligan speaks—'networks created and sustained by attention and response'—do not necessarily entail close location in space. But I am sure that the spirit of her work, and certainly of those who follow her, supports my interpretation.)

A similar conclusion can be drawn from the same argument by analogy put by Tyler Cowen and Derek Parfit, with the addition that their appeal contains a hypothetical example that highlights the dangers of applying the principles of justice as care to the international arena:

Suppose [the US] government decided to resume atmospheric nuclear tests. If it predicts that the resulting fallout would cause several deaths, should it discount the deaths of aliens? Should it therefore move these tests from Nevada to the South Pacific, so that those killed would not be Americans? It seems clear that, in such a case, the special relations make no moral difference. We should take the same view about the harms that we may impose on our remote successors. (Cowen and Parfit 1992: 150)

Once again, these 'special relations' do make a difference to supporters of the idea of justice as care since it is precisely such relations that generate obligations in the first place. On the face of it, justice as care is hard to square with impulses to international justice, and its usefulness in the context of environmental sustainability is doubly questionable if arguments for intergenerational justice (central to our 'critical natural capital' conception of environmental sustainability) are made to piggyback on intuitions regarding international justice.

On the other hand, justice as care can be useful for proponents of environmental sustainability because of its potential for widening the scope of the community of justice itself. Near the beginning of this chapter I pointed out that decisions as to membership of this community are crucial, and we have already seen its effects as far as international justice is concerned. Membership is usually decided through possession of a prerequisite 'X' which members must have, and in Gilligan's words (above), 'X' involves 'networks created and sustained by attention and response'. Usually these networks are assumed to be forged between people, but there is no prima facie reason why they should not be understood in terms of the bonds created between humans and non-humans (and even the non-human environment at large)—at the very least, reciprocal 'attention and response' is part and parcel of the relationship between pets and their owners, for example.

The idea that justice as care, so interpreted, might widen the community of justice is deployed by Peter Wenz in his groundbreaking book *Environmental Justice* (although Wenz does not relate his theory directly to the care paradigm). Wenz concludes with a 'concentric circle' notion in which obligations are based on 'closeness', generated in turn in the following ways:

I have benefited from another's kindness or help; I am in a particularly good position to help the other; another person and I have undertaken a project together; the other person and I are working to realize the same goal, foster the same ideal, or preserve the same traditions; I have unilaterally made a commitment to another; my actions have a particularly strong impact upon the other; and I have perpetrated or benefited from a past injustice toward the other, or a past injustice which adversely affects the other. (Wenz 1988: 316)

Wenz refers to 'persons' here, but his concentric circles of obligation are designed to include non-human interpretations of the 'other' to which he also refers. I shall discuss Wenz's 'concentric circles' theory of justice in detail in the Conclusion.

Immediate relations and/or contact as constitutive of relations of justice seem therefore to be potentially compatible with conceptions of sustainability that involve obligations to (parts of) the non-human natural world (Conceptions B and C in particular in our typology), even if problematic for notions of international justice. In addition, the fully fledged impartiality that might be thought to ground international justice itself can lead to unattractively counter-intuitive conclusions involving the possibility of sacrificing our nearest and dearest for distant causes. These conclusions are resisted by proponents of justice as care precisely because our nearest and dearest have precedence over distant causes. From this point of view, enthusiasts for international justice wave their wand of obligation too cavalierly, and are usually not careful enough to set the limits (or degrees) of obligation appropriately.

But does the adoption (even partial) of justice as care eliminate the possibility of grounding international justice? On the face of it the answer would seem to be yes, but what if we try for *both* care *and* impartiality rather than one or the other, on the grounds that they both make a valuable (and non-contradictory) contribution to our thinking about obligations in this context? I should like to explore this possibility via a discussion of two attempts to give care and impartiality their respective due, rather than have one of them wholly supplant the other. These attempts have been made by Onora O'Neill and Brian Barry.

O'Neill's view is that the two poles of the distinction between care and impartiality have been overdrawn. She distinguishes between what she calls 'relativized' and 'idealized' theories of justice—a distinction that incorporates (but is not exhausted by) what I have been calling care and impartiality—and comments as follows:

> *Idealized* accounts of justice stress the need to abstract from the particularities of persons. They paint justice as blind to gender and nationality. Its principles are those that would regulate the action of idealized 'abstract individuals', hence take no account of differences between men and women and transcend national boundaries. *Relativized* accounts of justice not only acknowledge the variety and differences among humankind but ground principles of justice in the discourse and traditions of actual communities. (O'Neill 1995: 50–1)

International justice seems to presuppose idealization and abstraction, and to this degree cannot be underpinned by, or even incorporate, context-sensitivity. But O'Neill disagrees:

> Discussions of international and gender justice both legitimately demand that principles of justice abstract from differences between cases and that judgements of justice respond to differences between them. Abstraction and sensitivity to context are often treated as incompatible: abstraction is taken to endorse idealized models of individual and state; sensitivity to human differences is identified with relativism. Neither identification is convincing: abstract principles do not entail uniform treatment; responsiveness to difference does not hinge on relativism. (O'Neill 1995: 50)

O'Neill believes that the incompatibility between idealized and relativized theories of justice dissolves once we see that it is based on unwarranted 'enhancements' (O'Neill 1995: 58) of both theories:

> the reason for the incompatibility may be that many advocates of abstraction and of sensitivity to context are making other, stronger claims that are indeed incompatible. What these debates term 'abstraction' is often a set of specific, unargued *idealizations* of human agency, rationality and life and of the sovereignty and independence of states. And in each debate what is

described as attention to actual situations and contexts in *judging* in fact often extends to building recognition of differences into fundamental *principles*—and so amounts to *relativism*. These conflations are avoidable. (O'Neill 1995: 57)

The point is to keep abstraction and sensitivity in their place or, in O'Neill's words, to give 'both abstraction and sensitivity to context their due—but only their due' (O'Neill 1995: 52). This involves generating abstract principles which will regulate but not determine decisions of justice: 'The principles of justice can be determined for any possible plurality . . . Judgements of the justice of actual situations are regulated but not entailed by these principles' (O'Neill 1995: 72–3). The idea that impartial principles of justice might regulate but not determine our decisions leaves the door ajar to making 'justice' and 'care' compatible, and Brian Barry—the second thinker to whom I want to refer here—pushes it open.

As a response to criticisms from the care perspective, Barry deploys the distinction (as we saw in Chapter 3) between two sorts of impartiality, outlined in his *Justice as Impartiality* (1995a). What he calls 'first-order impartiality' involves 'not being motivated by private considerations', while 'second-order impartiality' refers to 'principles and rules that are capable of forming the basis of free agreement among people seeking agreement on reasonable terms' (Barry 1995a: 11). If justice as impartiality entailed universal and constant adherence to both sorts of impartiality then care critics would have a point, says Barry, since then the option of taking private considerations into account could never be exercised. But, he continues, 'second-order impartialist theories do not entail universal first-order impartiality' (Barry 1995a: 217). Barry believes it perfectly possible to develop rules of justice that are impartial in respect of theories of the good for human beings, such that justice is not seen to serve the cause of any theory of the good (second-order impartiality), while preserving space for moral discretion in particular cases (first-order partiality). He therefore sees an ethic of justice and an ethic of care as complementary; they do not 'dispute the same terrain', but work in different ones—a view very similar to O'Neill's: 'When the "voices" of justice and care', writes O'Neill, 'are presented as alternatives between which we must choose, each is viewed as a complete approach to moral issues. However, the two in fact focus on different aspects of life' (O'Neill 1995: 60). Sometimes, Barry continues, 'plausible rules of justice do not determine the choice, so it is perfectly legitimate to use a "caring" approach to decide what to do . . . [and sometimes] . . . plausible rules of justice do determine the choice, so that it is a mistake to suppose that it is necessary to make a choice between the deliverances of rival "ethics" that both bear on the case' (Barry 1995*a*: 249). In conclusion, Barry writes that 'The case I wish to argue is that both of Gilligan's "different voices"—the "ethic of justice" and the "ethic of care"—are valid, and should be incorporated within any satisfactory account of morality' (Barry 1995*a*: 250).

If Barry and O'Neill are right, then both the particularism of care and the impartiality of justice can be taken to pathological extremes. In our context, a no-holds-barred adherence to care would make any notion of international justice impossible to sustain since the community of justice is simply too restricted. Likewise, the notion of international justice needs the underlying universalism presupposed by impartiality, but potential dispensers of international justice also need the discretion afforded in particular cases by Barry's first-order partiality. To this extent both care and impartiality seem fit to underpin notions of international justice, but only if neither (and particularly the first) is taken to pathological extremes.

On the other hand, the communitarian view explored earlier seems far less amenable to incorporation in an impartialist view since it is the communitarian's belief that second-order impartiality, as defined by Barry, is impossible. There can be no 'principles and rules that are capable of forming the basis of free agreement among people seeking agreement on reasonable terms', communitarians will say, since such principles and rules are inextricably linked to different communities' self-understanding(s). Here, the impossibility of impartiality is synonymous with the impossibility of the universalism which is apparently essential to notions of international justice, so the 'communitarian' critique of universalism seems to lead to an incompatibility with the idea of international justice in a way that the 'care' critique does not (necessarily). Michael Walzer himself appears to recognize as much as far as communitarian theory is concerned when he writes that 'Ideal contractualism or

undistorted communication, which represents one approach—not
my own—to justice in particular communities, may well be the only
approach for the globe as a whole' (Walzer 1983: 30). In other
words, if we want to work up a notion of international justice,
Walzerian communitarianism, at least, will not get us there. Taking
the issue at its broadest, I would conclude by endorsing Brenda
Almond's view that 'a localized notion of justice is not the one at
issue in cases of international . . . justice. In [this] case, it is the
universal conception that must be invoked as a guide to formulating
appropriate local laws and just international agreements' (Almond
1995: 15).

At this level, theories of justice apparently as diverse as those
advanced by John Rawls (the early Rawls, in any case) and Robert
Nozick possess a similarity that makes them in principle applicable
to the international arena in a way that Walzer's and MacIntyre's
theories are not. The similarity is the belief that the principles they
(Rawls and Nozick) advance are uncontroversially applicable across
time and space so that, as Dale Jamieson observes, 'The case for
transfers from the North to the South seems very strong from the
perspective of most major theories of justice. A Rawlsian might see
the Difference Principle as warranting such transfers; an entitlement
theorist [e.g. Nozick] might base them on the need to rectify past
injustices' (Jamieson 1994: 204), and this last point is supported by
Kai Nielsen who writes that 'Nozickian notions of justice in rectifi-
cation would require redistribution between North and South'
(Nielsen 1995: 30). On the other hand it is practically impossible to
make a case for such transfers from within the frames of reference
developed by Walzer, MacIntyre, and Charles Taylor; since the very
idea of international justice presupposes an 'in-principle' universalism of distributors and recipients, and of the prescriptive reach of
the principles for distribution.

## Future Generations

The future is built into the idea of sustainability in a fundamental
way and the problems thereby created for notions of social justice

are among the best documented—and most intractable—in this whole area of enquiry. The starting point is James Fishkin's observation that 'no defensible theory of justice can neglect the facts that people are born and die and that our actions may have serious effects on the interests of those yet to be born' (Fishkin 1992: 9). If Fishkin is right, then the issue of sustainability ineluctably adds a whole new dimension to social justice theorizing, and, once aware of it, no self-respecting social justice theorist should ignore it in her or his deliberations. Put differently, theories of social justice need (from now on) to be tested not only against how well they work under the already stressful conditions of contemporary everyday life, but also in the quagmire of the future, and we should not be satisfied with a prescription for justice unless it gives us some convincing guidance regarding distributions between present and future.

Of course, Fishkin may be wrong, since, as Robert Heilbroner has awkwardly asked, 'Why should I lift a finger to affect events that will have no more meaning for me seventy-five years after my death than those that happened seventy-five years before I was born? There is', Heilbroner avers, 'no rational answer to that terrible question' (Heilbroner 1981: 191). If there is an answer to Heilbroner's question, part of it must surely consist in persuading him that the community of justice contains future people as well as present ones (I shall say something about the complications hidden in that innocent pair of words—'future people'—a little later). To this extent, the challenge to theories of justice presented by futurity is similar to that encountered in the context of international justice: broadening the community of justice to the required degree. And once again, a prerequisite for relations of justice appears to be missing—that of reciprocity: future generations cannot harm or benefit us. It seems evident that any theory of justice that has reciprocity as its basis for creating obligations will not work for future generations. This has been pointed out by, among others, Brian Barry (1991*c*: 244) and by Peter Laslett and James Fishkin (1992*b*: 9–11), and John Rawls puts the dilemma like this: 'It is a natural fact that generations are spread out in time and actual exchanges between them take place only in one direction . . . This situation is unalterable' (Rawls 1973: 290–1).

Rawls is without doubt expressing the consensus opinion on this issue, although it is worth noting a dissenting view from John O'Neill who argues that 'Future generations can benefit or harm us: the success or failure of our lives depends on them for it is they that are able to bring to fruition our projects' (O'Neill 1993: 34). O'Neill's observation is part of a determined attempt to describe an *actual* transgenerational community, and this strategy stands in opposition to the *hypothetical* constructions that some theorists have used to try to make sense of intergenerational justice, and which I shall discuss below.

The idea of an actual transgenerational community is not new, of course, and its principles were enunciated with great elegance by Edmund Burke: 'As the ends of partnership cannot be obtained in many generations, it becomes a partnership not only between those who are living, but between those who are living, those who are dead, and those who are yet to be born' (Burke 1790/1982: 194–5). Much more recently, Avner de-Shalit has picked up the challenge of describing an actual transgenerational community in (and on) which to found obligations of justice. He begins by assuming that, 'if and when one admits the existence of a community, and if one acknowledges that the community constitutes one's identity, then it is absurd at the same time to deny any obligation to the community and its members' (de-Shalit 1995: 15). As far as the existence of the community itself is concerned, de-Shalit argues that 'One of three main conditions has to be met in order for a group of people to count as a community. These conditions are interactions between people in daily life, cultural interaction, and moral similarity' (de-Shalit 1995: 22). De-Shalit recognizes that the first of these conditions cannot be met between generations, but he suggests that the second two can be, based on the succeeding and overlapping of generations. So there is, for example, a 'cultural interaction between Michael Tippett [the contemporary composer] and the musicians of tomorrow' (de-Shalit 1995: 43), and at the same time, 'moral similarity will extend into the future' (de-Shalit 1995: 50).

These remarks are buttressed by what de-Shalit calls the 'psychological fact' that 'most of us fear the loss of life, and that the end of one's own ideas, norms, and values the moment one passes on is perceived by most of us as a tragic possibility which we should wish to prevent . . . not only the future selves of one's own lifetime are part of oneself, but the future can also be regarded as part of oneself . . . This future is also the future of one's ideas' (de-Shalit 1995: 40). There is a sonorous echo here of John O'Neill's reference to the success or failure of our personal projects in the future, and both O'Neill and de-Shalit trade on the idea of a transgenerational self as the basis for a transgenerational community. In truth, as far as de-Shalit is concerned, this is a different idea from that expressed in the notion of enduring cultural and/or moral similarity across generations. In that notion, entirely 'new' selves are born into circumstances that are recognizably similar to ours, and it is these similar circumstances that constitute the glue that holds the transgenerational community together. From the point of view of the idea of the transgenerational self it is the self (itself) that threads the generations together by continually 'throwing itself' towards the future (as Jean-Paul Sartre might have said).

We could argue for some time about the extent of the success of attempts like this to establish the existence of an actual trans-generational community, but let me point out two difficulties that arise even if we assume total success. The first concerns the sting in the tail of an apparent advantage of adopting de-Shalit's type of intergenerational community. The apparent advantage is that de-Shalit can deal with the problem of how much the present generation might be required to sacrifice for future generations. Laslett and Fishkin put this problem of sacrifice starkly: 'Let us start', they say,

with what looks to be the core of a defensible principle of justice over time, certainly with respect to the environment. This principle states that every member of every generation must have equal access to the resources of the world, quite irrespective of the generation into which he or she was, is, or will be born.

But, they continue, this leads to absurd conclusions, since:

the resources of the human world, social, political, and material, cannot themselves possibly be infinite, even if it is uncertain how large they are in fact and how far technical ingenuity could spread them out. Now a finite quantity divided by an infinite number must have a zero result—no one gets anything at any time. (Laslett and Fishkin 1992*b*: 6)

I shall come back to the general question of calculating present generation sacrifice later, but it is not hard to see how de-Shalit might claim to have a solution to it. De-Shalit's view is that the ties that bind the transgenerational community together—cultural and moral similarity—decline in strength over time, so our obligations to future generations ' "fade away" ' as the ties weaken (de-Shalit 1995: 13). We decide between conflicting obligations, he says, by referring to 'the intensity of relations in the community, the criteria for intensity being personal and emotional ties together with moral similarity. The more intense the relations are, the stronger the obligations the community imposes' (de-Shalit 1995: 52). In other words, Laslett and Fishkin's dilemma is more of a problem for those who might be tempted to argue for intergenerational equality of outcome, than it is for de-Shalit.

There are evidently difficulties of calculation here for de-Shalit, but even leaving these aside, his apparent assumption that intensity will fade at a uniform rate surely cannot be made. There may be no decline at all, for example, in which case we are back with the Laslett/Fishkin scenario of no one getting anything, ever. Or there may be a very rapid decline, in which case our obligations will last for a very short period of time—too short to deal with the long-term problems with which environmentalists are often concerned (the decay of radioactive waste, for example).

These problems are compounded by the fact that there is no world community in the sense in which de-Shalit would want to understand it—a community sharing moral and cultural similarity. This means that there is no transgenerational community either, just a series of transgenerational communities to which each present generation community is bound by (presumably varying) degrees of transgenerational moral and cultural similarity. This implies that present-day obligations towards the future vary in strength from place to place, opening up the uncomfortable possibility of nuclear waste (for example, again) being legitimately shipped from areas of 'high' intergenerational obligation to areas of 'low' intergenerational obligation.

So the attractive-looking solution in de-Shalit's theory to the first problem I wanted to raise comes out in spots when examined a little more closely. The second problem arises even if we assume that intergenerational obligations behave as de-Shalit hopes they will (especially if they do, indeed). If such obligations 'fade away' at a more or less constant rate, then there may be no room in the theory for obligations in respect of the long-term problems to which I referred above. The half-life of Uranium-235, used as a fuel in nuclear reactors, is $7.1 \times 10^9$ years, and we might imagine that our moral and cultural similarity to the relevant future generation that many years down the road will be small, if not non-existent. (Or we might not; but that just goes to show how ill-advised it probably is to try to calculate one variable, namely the extent of the sacrifice of present generations for future ones, by introducing another, namely the decline in moral and cultural similarity.)

In sum, de-Shalit's 'actual community' approach to inter-generational justice has a number of drawbacks. First there is the problem of accepting the make of glue (Moral and Cultural Similarity) that holds the generations together. Then there is the problem of the variety of communities of moral and cultural sim-ilarity around the planet, compounded by the different rates of decay of similarity between them. And finally there is the difficulty involved in generating obligations in respect of long-term 'sleeper'-type environmental problems. Taken together, and thinking in terms of the dimensions of theories of justice outlined in Table 5, these problems suggest that the cause of intergenerational justice is poorly served by particularistic conceptions of the recipient com-munity of justice. If we add to this the conclusions reached at the end of the discussion about international justice, particularistic conceptions of both the distributive and recipient communities of justice seem broadly incompatible with the spatial and temporal demands of our current 'critical natural capital' conception of environmental sustainability.

One way of spreading the community of justice recipients more evenly into the future is to ascribe rights to future people. The idea that lies behind this is summed up by Joel Feinberg: 'Protecting our environment now is . . . a matter of elementary prudence, and insofar as we do it for the next generation already here in the persons of our children, it is a matter of love. But from the perspective of our remote descendants it is basically a matter of justice, of respect for their rights' (Feinberg 1981: 139). Love, in other words, is (or may be) the source of obligation to our nearest and dearest, but since, by definition, future generations are neither near nor dear (beyond the generation of our great-grandchildren, at the limit, at any rate), we need something to replace love as the source of obligation, and Feinberg suggests that rights will do the job.

A common objection to ascribing rights to members of future generations is that they lack a necessary (but not at all a sufficient) condition for the possession of rights: existence. Charles Taliaferro points out that what he calls 'present generationism' gives preference to those who are alive, and he says that 'The rationale for this policy is typically grounded upon a theory of rights . . . [and] . . . in order to have a right one must exist' (Taliaferro 1988: 245). Edwin Delattre suggests in this vein that 'existence itself should be seen as a prerequisite for other rights' (Delattre 1972: 256), and he is supported in this view by Bryan Norton who (with a technical shift from 'existence' to 'identity', the importance of which will only become clear when we discuss the so-called 'non-identity problem' later) argues that 'Any reference to interests, rights, or duties presupposes an identifiable individual who has that interest or right' (Norton 1982: 320). This leads Norton to conclude, indeed, that 'assigning rights to life to possible members of future generations is both theoretically incoherent and practically self-defeating' (Norton 1982: 331).

A typical reponse to the 'non-existence' objection put by Delattre is to make the possession of interests, rather than existence itself, the precondition for rights-holding. (Again, this does not in itself meet Norton's 'identity' worry, but I shall come back to that.) Joel Feinberg, for one, defends the 'interests' perspective, and he does so by considering a spectrum of cases, ranging from rocks to human beings. Most people, he says, will accept that rocks cannot have rights and that human beings can, but why? And also, 'In between the clear cases of rocks and normal human beings . . . is a spectrum of less obvious cases, including some bewildering borderline ones . . . [such as] . . . dead ancestors . . . individual animals . . . whole species of animals . . . plants . . . idiots and madmen . . . foetuses . . . generations yet unborn' (Feinberg 1981: 140).

As far as individual animals are concerned, says Feinberg, we will most likely agree that they cannot have duties, and some will say that they cannot have rights, either, because they cannot claim those rights. But Feinberg argues that this objection falls once the possibility of proxy representation (as for children) is considered. The counter-objection now may be that representatives always represent interests, and animals cannot have interests. Feinberg says that this is simply wrong: 'Many of the higher animals at least have appetites, conative urges, and rudimentary purposes', and they can have an interest in having these fulfilled (Feinberg 1981: 143; and the list of animals might be enlarged by referring to Feinberg's own list of other features that might give a thing interests: 'latent tendencies, direction of growth, and natural fulfillments'; Feinberg 1981: 142).

Feinberg now says that

we can extract from our discussion of animal rights a crucial principle for tentative use in the resolution of other riddles about the applicability of the concept of a right, namely, that the sort of beings who *can* have rights are precisely those who have (or can have) interests. (Feinberg 1981: 143)

Applying the principle to the context with which we are concerned here—future generations of human beings—Feinberg concludes that future generations will have interests, for example in respect of 'living space, fertile soil, fresh air, and the like' (Feinberg 1981: 143), and that they therefore have a right to have them fulfilled.

If the glue that held de-Shalit's intergenerational community together was called Moral and Cultural Similarity, then Feinberg's might be dubbed 'Possession of Interests'. My own view is that this is a more convincing foundation on which to base obligations to future generations than de Shalit's communitarian one, although the problem of the extent of present sacrifice for future gain remains—and I shall return to it.

Feinberg's 'Possession of Interests' brings with it problems of its own, in any case. Some will say that the possession of interests, even if demonstrated, need not entail rights possession, and it need not even imply anything regarding the 'proper treatment' of the possessor. Then it might be said that if the possession of interests does involve such an implication, why bother with rights at all? Finally, even if we can ascribe rights on the basis of interests, and even if there is a point in doing so, there is still the thorny difficulty associated with the difference between formal and substantive rights. From one point of view, the granting of rights—their formal inclusion in a Bill of Rights, for example—is the tiniest of small steps on the way to rectifying the abuses that rights-possession is supposed to deal with, and this is simply because rights-possession does not guarantee the necessary material conditions for rights-enjoyment. But of course, rights-possession can be seen as a regulating idea on which demands for material change may be based, and even someone as wary of the promise of formal rights as Ted Benton has pointed out that 'A substantial core of the arguments used by feminists, anarchists, black rights and gay rights activists, "disablement" campaigners and others rely on the contrast between formal possession of rights and substantive enjoyment of them' (Benton 1993: 4).

Given that most theories of justice—and most practices too—make reference to future generations only as an afterthought, it practically goes without saying that bringing them closer to the centre of attention will be transformative of both theory and—particularly—practice. From this point of view, rights-talk can perform the useful function of providing a benchmark against which to test present practices. The project of ascribing rights to future generations is subject to all the strategic criticisms that might be made against ascribing rights to disadvantaged present generation humans, but the hard core of a standard on which to base demands for transformation will remain. Principally for this reason I think that the ascription of rights will have an important part to play in working up a theory of justice for future generations, and such ascription can also generate obligations of justice for distant generations (unlike de-Shalit's communitarian theory).

The problem of the extent of present sacrifice for future gain has ghosted the whole of this discussion, and it is now time to confront it head on. Let me recall Laslett and Fishkin's presentation of the dilemma, mentioned above. An egalitarian principle of distribution across generations, they say, such that 'every member of every generation must have equal access to the resources of the world, quite irrespective of the generation into which he or she was, is, or will be born', does not make sense since, as we saw earlier, 'a finite quantity divided by an infinite number must have a zero result' (Laslett and Fishkin 1992*b*: 6).

Even if we follow Laslett's and Fishkin's implications and accept that some generations are likely to have a greater share of benefits than others, the question of *how much* greater still arises. Robert Heilbroner makes the sacrificial point graphically (as ever): 'suppose we . . . knew with a high degree of certainty that humankind could not survive a thousand years unless we gave up our wasteful diet of meat, abandoned all pleasure driving, cut back on every use of energy that was not essential to the maintenance of a bare minimum. Would we care enough for posterity to pay the price of its survival?' (Heilbroner 1981: 191).

As far as this question of present sacrifice for future gain is concerned, the most formal way of achieving the de-Shalit 'fade' without recourse to his metric of declining moral and cultural similarity is through discounting the future. Economists are accustomed to discounting because 'future costs are less burdensome than current costs' (Pearce et al. 1989: 7). More picturesquely,

we all possess a degree of impatience. We would rather that the new car arrived tomorrow than wait for a year. We would prefer our wages or salary now than wait until the end of the week or the month . . . Respecting time preference is just as much a feature of 'consumer sovereignty' as respecting people's rights to buy and sell what they choose in the market place. (Pearce et al. 1989: 7–8)

A positive discount rate justifiably pushes the costs of present activities into the future, and the results can be spectacular: 'At a 5% discount rate . . . one life today is equivalent in value to two lives in 14.4 years, four lives in 28.8 years, eight lives in 43.2 years, sixteen lives in 57.6 years and so on.' 'In 489.6 years, for example,' Peter Wenz continues, 'doubling of value has taken place thirty-four times . . . making one life today worth more than sixteen billion lives then' (Wenz 1988: 230). A 5 per cent discount rate therefore justifies the sacrifice of 16 billion deaths in 490 years' time for the sake of saving one life today.

One can have endless fun fiddling about with the discount rate so as to arrive at a figure that seems more in line with intuition, but we always end up trading multiples of future lives for present single ones. More fundamental objections than those related to the correct discount figure have been entered against discounting. In the first place, there is the thought that costs and benefits are not the kinds of things that it makes sense to talk of as being affected by time. Tyler Cowen and Derek Parfit have put it like this:

> Why should costs and benefits receive less weight, simply because they are further in the future? When the future comes, these benefits and costs will be no less real. Imagine finding out that you, having just reached your twenty-first birthday, must soon die of cancer because one evening Cleopatra wanted an extra helping of dessert. How could this be justified? (Cowen and Parfit 1992: 145)

Strictly speaking, the implications of this question would be resisted by a supporter of the present 'critical natural capital' conception of environmental sustainability, because it (the question) places the satisfaction of present generation human wants (Cleopatra's pudding) ahead of the meeting of future generation human needs (the conditions for my remaining alive beyond my twenty-first birthday). A glance at Box 10 in Table 2 will show that in Conception A, the satisfaction of future needs should take precedence over indulging present wants.

More generally, Cowen and Parfit make a point for time by relying on the analogy with space: 'no one suggests that . . . we should adopt a spatial discount rate . . . at some rate of $n$ percent per yard' (Cowen and Parfit 1992: 158). (This may be true in the detail, but as we saw in the 'care' discussion, there are certainly those who think that space makes a difference, and such people will not be at all persuaded by Cowen and Parfit's analogy.) John Rawls makes a similar point to Cowen and Parfit's, and takes it a stage further: 'The mere difference of location in time, of something's being earlier or later, is not in itself a rational ground for having more or less regard for it . . . the different temporal position of persons and generations does not in itself justify treating them differently' (Rawls 1973: 294–5).

Note Rawls's implication here that there may be a case for treating future generations differently, but not on the grounds of their being *future* generations. Cowen and Parfit pick up this theme by pointing out that a discount rate might be justified because we believe future generations will be better off than this one (Cowen and Parfit 1992: 148). In this case the discount is not defended on the grounds of the benefits being in the future, but—simply—because our successors are better off.

Similarly, Cowen and Parfit observe that the reason we may feel driven in the direction of a discount rate is that otherwise, 'We may seem morally required to choose policies that would impose great sacrifice on the present generation' (Cowen and Parfit 1992: 148). Once again, though, they point out that if we do opt for a discount rate, we do so not because the 'importance of future benefits declines', but because 'no generation can be morally required to make more than certain kinds of sacrifice for the sake of future generations' (Cowen and Parfit 1992: 149).

By this point, however, the argument has become irritatingly circular. We are all agreed, apparently, that the Laslett/Fishkin dilemma ('no one gets anything at any time') is a real one, but the idea that we can deal with this by having less regard for future benefits than present ones seems unsound. This leaves us with the possibility of disengaging the idea from its normal operative conclusion; in other words, we accept the necessity of something like a social discount rate, not because we think future benefits are worth less than present ones, but because the kinds of present sacrifices towards which the Laslett/Fishkin dilemma pushes us are unacceptable. At the same time, the felt need to do something like discount the future is underwritten by the future's essential unknowability. Greens are well acquainted with this feature of the future, and a whole discourse around the idea of the 'precautionary principle' has been developed to deal with it. The precautionary principle, however, is based on the (usually unstated) assumption that the future (and the people who inhabit it) is of just as much concern as the present. Discounting (positive discounting, at any rate) is based on a very different assumption. The tension between these two views of the underlying value of the future is evident, and it may be best resolved by using a social discount rate 'as a crude rule of thumb', as Cowen and Parfit put it. But as they also go on to say, 'this rule would often go astray' (Cowen and Parfit 1992: 158), and one of the crossroads at which this might happen is illustrated by the Cowen/Parfit Cleopatra's pudding example I quoted above. In deciding the nature and extent of present sacrifice we need at least to take into account the difference between needs and wants, and supporters of Conception A will say that future generation needs should have precedence over present generation wants. In other words, the social discount rate will only come into operation at the level of need satisfaction across generations.

In the end, this is a problem of numbers. We are faced with decreasing resources and increasing numbers of human beings across the generations, and even allowing for enhanced technology, heightened efficiency, and changes in social organization that might improve the production/consumption ratio across time, the numbers are still against us. At this point I can no longer put off discussion of the 'non-identity' problem which adds a layer of initially confusing detail to this particular numbers game. William Galston paraphrases the issue as follows:

All long-run social policies affect the composition of the population to such an extent that after a relatively small number of generations (six to eight) the chances are infinitesimal that any individual who exists under the regime of a long-run policy would have existed if the policy had not been adopted, and conversely. We cannot then say that any individual would have been better, or worse off, given different policies, since the policy populations have no members in common. (Galston 1980: 252)

Our present policies affect future generations, and they affect them in such a way that 'we are able to affect not just the conditions under which future generations will live, but also to determine their composition and identity' (Grey 1996: 162). Now it is a common thought that harm can only be said to be done if people are made worse off by the action that causes the harm—the 'person-affecting' view (Grey 1996: 165). But as Galston shows us above, our peculiar relation with the future means that no one can be said to be worse off in the future as a result of actions taken today. The paradox, then, is the idea of bad outcomes that make no one worse off.

The paradox depends, though, on two assumptions. The first is that existence is itself desirable: we might produce an extraordinarily bad future for our descendants, but at least they have 'descended'. This seems counter-intuitive, and not in the sense that we hear it said of street children in London or Jakarta that 'they'd be better off dead', but in the sense that we would see existence as a precondition for benefit or harm rather than a benefit in itself. This would lead us to seek to provide the street children with shelter and food rather than to have them rounded up and disposed of.

The second assumption is the person-affecting one that 'an action is wrong only if it makes someone worse off than they would otherwise have been' (Grey 1996: 165). So as Grey says, 'If you accept the policy-dependence of the identity of human populations . . . and if you also believe that we should be concerned about the interests of persons who will exist in the remote future, the principles to substantiate this concern cannot take a person affecting form' (Grey 1996: 168). To the extent that both of these 'ifs' are confirmed by supporters of Conception A (and they will probably all accept the first, if not the second—depending on how far off 'remote' is taken to be), then concern for future generations 'has to be expressed through impersonal formulations' (Grey 1996: 168). But a fully impersonal formulation would take us right the way back to the Laslett/Fishkin dilemma in which an infinite number of people have equal claims on a finite amount of resources. Once again,

This is [a] . . . manifestation of the domain problem. Either we take the class of moral patients to be the class of presently existing individuals, which is far too narrow, or we take them to be the class of merely possible individuals, and that is far too wide. (Grey 1996: 173)

In sum, I agree with Grey that 'we need to recognise impersonal obligations because we need to recognise constraints on actions which can affect persons, even though there are not (now) persons who we can affect' (Grey 1996: 174), and we have to add to this some sort of discount rate which reflects the need not to ask present generations to make unacceptable sacrifices for the sake of future ones. In our present 'critical natural capital' conception of environmental sustainability, moreover, discounting will not come into effect until we get to the level of the meeting of needs across generations; the trading of present wants against future needs is not permitted in this scheme (Table 2, Box 10).

All of this invites reflection on the thorny issue of population and population control: it is generally (although not unanimously) accepted that resources will last longer if fewer people consume them (and if well-off people in developed countries consume less). Opinions regarding the relationship of justice to the population question vary widely. Marcel Wissenburg, for example, writes that 'none of the ecological arguments that are commonly used to defend legal limitations to procreative rights is compatible with a stringent interpretation of liberal democracy . . . there is no just or equitable way of attributing limits to individuals' procreative liberties' (Wissenburg 1998). Brian Barry, on the other hand, canvasses the idea of a policy 'restricting women to one child' and suggests that 'it does not contravene any principle of intragenerational justice, and is a requirement of intergenerational justice' (Barry 1999). The only thing about which these two agree is that population policy is related to questions of justice, so how do they arrive at such different conclusions?

Barry's position is quite simple. He regards sustainability as being about the maintaining of some value X into the 'indefinite future', as far as we are able to do so (Barry 1999). Clearly, if this X is to be measured over individuals, '[T]he demands of justice will . . . be more stringent the larger we predict the future population to be' (Barry 1999). Since we (the present generation) cannot be held responsible for increases in population in future generations (except, presumably, in so far as our actions provide for or discourage the conditions in which population reductions might or might not be possible), Barry argues that:

The conception of sustainability that makes it appropriate as a necessary condition of intergenerational justice may be formulated as follows:

Sustainability requires at any point in time that the value of some X per head of population should be capable of being maintained into the indefinite future, on the assumption that the size of the future population is no greater than the size of the present population. (Barry 1999)

Barry knows that this is a large assumption, but the essential point is that he considers population control to be a condition for justice, whereas Wissenburg regards it as contravening justice.

The big difference between Barry and Wissenburg here is that the former deals with generations as collectivities while the latter is concerned with individuals within generations. From Wissenburg's point of view, '[G]iven the deep and possibly extreme intrusions on people's lives and bodies involved in population policies, there is good reason to draw attention to the moral status of individuals' procreative rights' (Wissenburg 1998). He rejects Barry's arguments about the importance of maintaining the right size of the total population because it leaves the question of 'the *distribution* of procreative activities unanswered' (Wissenburg 1998; emphasis in the original), and if Barry were to reply with his across-the-board-one-woman-one-child policy, Wissenburg will suggest that 'there may be valid reasons other than overall welfare why some people would be more deserving [of having more children] than others' (Wissenburg 1998). Wissenburg will also deny that what he calls the 'quasi-welfarist perspective' embodies 'the only or the most important moral code', on the grounds that 'individual rights . . . should be considered too' (Wissenburg 1998).

As it happens, I think that Barry's one-woman-one-child position has more force than Wissenburg might allow, and its fundamental strength is its egalitarianism. As Wissenburg says, 'all individuals should be treated as equals unless good reasons for unequal treatment exist' (Wissenburg 1998), but he uses this as an argument against antinatalist positions on the assumption that these positions will allow some people to procreate and others not. Barry's position transfers the boot to the other foot by acknowledging the need for equal regard and asking for reasons why people should procreate rather than why they should not.

On the other hand, Wissenburg makes it clear that he is considering 'the moral validity of purely ecological reasons for *coercive* population control' (Wissenburg 1998; emphasis in the original), and if he concludes that there are none (as he does), then neither Barry nor most supporters of environmental sustainability as an objective of public policy will disagree with him. The solution lies in creating the appropriate conditions under which reproductive decisions are taken, rather than in leaving the conditions as they are and arbitrating in the fight over the scarce resource which is the right to procreate. On this point, Wissenburg and Barry are, happily, in agreement. Wissenburg writes of the importance of 'providing information and education, instigating public debate and making preservatives and other alternatives to procreation available to those who, as yet, do not have the freedom to choose . . . [P]olicies of this sort empower individuals; they enlarge rather than limit their procreative liberties' (Wissenburg 1998). Barry argues that

[W]e know that stabilisation of population is perfectly possible as a result of voluntary choices made by individuals because a number of western countries have already arrived at the position at which the (non-immigrant) population is only barely replacing itself, if that. Although they stumbled into it without any particular foresight, the formula is now known and can be applied elsewhere. Women have to be educated and to have a possibility of pursuing rewarding occupations outside the home while at the same time compulsory full-time education and stringent child labour laws make children an economic burden rather than a benefit. (Barry 1999)

My point would be that under these conditions the problem of justice 'withers away', and that putting it in these terms does not expose it to the criticisms of utopian impossibilism that assailed Marx, Engels, and Lenin in a different context. As Barry says, and as countless studies have shown, these conditions have been created in many parts of the world, and if doing justice means doing away with the need for justice then here is one place where, if the conditions are not exactly ripe, their contours are clearly visible.

If we put what we have seen up to now in the terms developed in Chapter 3 and captured in summary form in Table 5, the basic features of a theory of justice which is capable of dealing adequately with the claims of future generations will be the following: the dispensers will be all (present) human beings, although some sort of 'ability to pay' criterion within the present generation is appropriate; the recipients will be future human beings (question 1) whose needs (question 4) should be met consistent with an acceptable level of sacrifice for present generations; and the basic structure will require universality of prescriptive reach of the theory, as well as a degree of consequentialism (question 2) to ensure—at least—that preconditional goods (Row 3) are distributed in such a way as to observe the 'lexical ordering' of meeting present and future generation needs ahead of present generation wants. (I shall hold over comment on the relevance to future generational justice of substantiveness and impartiality regarding theories of the good until the next chapter.)

A goodly proportion of these characteristics is present in the most influential theory of justice of the past thirty years, that of John Rawls, so this is an appropriate moment to consider the usefulness of Rawls's theory in this particular context. To deal with future generations, the early Rawls (1973) stipulates the following about people deciding the principles of justice behind the veil of ignorance: 'The parties do not know to which generation they belong . . . The veil of ignorance is complete in these respects. Thus the persons in the original position are to ask themselves how much they would be willing to save at each stage of advance on the assumption that all other generations are to save at the same rates' (Rawls 1973: 287). This results in the so-called 'just savings principle', and a final formulation of the second principle of justice which now reads like this:

social and economic inequalities are to be arranged so that they are both:

(a) to the greatest benefit of the least advantaged, consistent with the just savings principle, and
(b) attached to offices and positions open to all under conditions of fair equality of opportunity. (Rawls 1973: 302)

The difficulty for Rawls with all this derives from his own assumptions—assumptions which lead to a 'motivational problem'. 'Why', as we saw Robert Heilbroner ask earlier, 'should I lift a finger to affect events that will have no more meaning for me seventy-five years after my death than those that happened seventy-five years before I was born?' (Heilbroner 1981: 191)—and Rawls's contractors will ask themselves the same question. This is because Rawls makes them assume that they are self-interestedly deciding the principles of justice behind the 'veil of ignorance', and they would therefore appear to have no motivation to save for future generations. As Rawls himself says: 'Those in the original position know . . . that they are contemporaries, so unless they care at least for their immediate successors, there is no reason for them to agree to undertake any saving whatever' (Rawls 1973: 292). Rawls then turns the 'unless they care . . .' clause into the motivational basis he needs by saying that, 'it is assumed that a generation cares for its immediate descendants, as fathers say care for their sons' (Rawls 1973: 288), and 'The parties [to the agreement] are regarded as representing family lines, say, with ties of sentiment between generations' (Rawls 1973: 292).

One difficulty with this solution is that it does not give us a cast-iron 'contractarian justification for obligations to people of the distant future' (Wenz 1983: 202, and see also Goodin 1985: 171–2) because the 'chain of obligation' does not work for problems that jump generations. Wenz points out that there would be nothing inconsistent from this point of view in fitting explosive devices to nuclear repositories timed to detonate in 200 years' time, since our immediate progeny would not be affected (Wenz 1983: 202). This is not the kind of result we might expect from an impartialist and universalist theory like Rawls's; we might expect, on the contrary, that it would solve, rather than reproduce, the difficulties we encountered in this respect in de-Shalit's communitarian theory.

The second problem with Rawls's 1973 solution to the motivational problem is that it obliges him to modify one of the assumptions about people in the original position which has most intrigued commentators: the assumption of self-interest. As Brian Barry puts it: 'the postulate of self-interest is relaxed to allow concern for successors', and this, for Barry, undermines the 'intellectual fascination' of Rawls's position—that of taking self-interested agents, and, 'by the alchemy of the "original position", forc[ing] them to choose principles of universal scope' (Barry 1991c: 253).

By 1993 Rawls recognizes that his account of future generations and just savings is 'defective' (Rawls 1993: 20 n.) for just the reasons Barry advances (Rawls 1993: 274 n.). Before proposing an alternative solution, he rehearses the general background:

in order to establish fairness between generations (for example, in the agreement on a principle of just savings), the parties, who are assumed to be contemporaries, do not know the present state of society. They have no information about the stock of natural resources or productive assets, or the level of technology beyond what can be inferred from the assumption that the circumstances of justice obtain. The relative good or ill fortune of their generation is unknown. For when contemporaries are influenced by a general description of the present state of society while agreeing how to treat each other, and the generations that come after them, they have not yet left out of account the results of historical accident and social contingency found within the basic structure. And so we arrive at a thicker rather than a thinner veil of ignorance. (Rawls 1993: 273)

One apparently obvious solution to the conundrum would be to drop the 'contemporaries' stipulation, such that those in the original position would not know which generation they were to be born into; this additional thickening of the veil of ignorance would ensure that no principles of justice would be chosen that might favour any one particular generation. This has been suggested by many people, and Brian Barry puts it like this: 'It might appear that the obvious way out of the difficulty is to drop the postulate that the people in the "original position" are contemporaries, and this is I believe the path Rawls should have taken to be true to his own theory' (Barry 1991c: 252, and see also Goodin 1985: 172 for support for Barry).

In fact, though, Rawls takes another route, and he describes it as follows: 'Rather than imagine a (hypothetical and nonhistorical) direct agreement between all generations, the parties can be required to agree to a savings principle subject to the further condition that they must want all *previous* generations to have followed it' (Rawls 1993: 274). At first sight it might appear that if the magician uses this particular wand the rabbit will remain firmly stuck in the hat, since what is to stop a generation (say '$X$') bingeing on the savings generation $X - 1$ dutifully left for them? The answer, of course, is that generation $X$ might in fact turn out to be generation $X + 1$, and given that people in the original position do not know which generation they will belong to, the only way they can be guaranteed a stock of capital is by agreeing to want all previous generations to have followed the required just savings principle.

This certainly keeps the motivational assumptions of the original 'original position' intact, and so would Brian Barry's alternative. There may be two reasons why Rawls chooses to eschew this latter alternative. First, given that 1993's *Political Liberalism* was largely a response to his communitarian critics with their concern at the hypothetical and non-historical nature of Rawls's theory of justice, Rawls felt that to have thickened the veil of ignorance any more would have simply created more hostages to fortune. Second, to accept Barry's alternative would be to risk falling foul of the Laslett/ Fishkin problem of dividing a finite quantity by an infinite number. Either way, Rawls's recent theory appears capable of coping with the idea of justice between generations, and in its most recent guise it does so even to the extent of taking into account remote generations. It therefore seems able to satisfy the demands on a theory of justice likely to be made by proponents of the 'critical natural capital' conception of sustainability, in this context at least (for further detailed and constructive discussion of Rawls's later 'future generationism', see Wissenburg 1999).

There are those who believe that the 'motivational problem' in Rawls just cannot be solved, and that we need another way of generating obligations of justice to the future, but without falling into the traps apparently set by de-Shalit's communitarian argument and others like it. Robert Goodin, for example, has developed an idea based on the notion of 'vulnerability' (Goodin 1985). Goodin argues that it is wrong to think of our widely recognized responsibilities towards 'our families, friends, clients, compatriots and so forth' as being based foundationally on any voluntary commitment towards them (Goodin 1985: p. xi). He considers it more persuasive to view these responsibilities as deriving from the '*vulnerability* of the beneficiary rather than [from] any voluntary commitment per se on the part of the benefactor' (Goodin 1985: p. xi; emphasis in the original). This is obviously an attractive idea in the context of future generations who clearly are vulnerable to our actions. Goodin turns the standard 'no reciprocity' argument against itself by suggesting that we should derive intergenerational obligations 'from precisely the fact that we enjoy "unilateral power" over the generations that succeed us' (Goodin 1985: 177). So, '[T]he vulnerability of succeeding generations to our actions and choices seems to be the strongest basis for assigning to present ones strong responsibilities for providing for them' (Goodin 1985: 177).

The theoretical basis for Goodin's position lies in the distinction he draws between two models of reasons for obligation. The first is the idea of obligations born of voluntary commitments, of which the obligation to keep a promise is the paradigm case. This model, says Goodin, cannot cater for at least two types of responsibility, itemized by Sidgwick in his *The Methods of Ethics* (1874) and commonly regarded as important: 'duties arising out of comparatively permanent relationships not voluntarily chosen, such as Kindred' and 'duties that seem due to special need' (in Goodin 1985: 33). More specifically, Goodin suggests that the voluntaristic model 'is ill equipped to account for the intuition . . . that we owe something special to our children. In my alternative model', he continues, 'I take that intuitive obligation as the central case, and I proceed to build a theory of our special responsibilities around it' (Goodin 1985: 33).

There is much to be said in favour of Goodin's position from our point of view. The paradigm case to which he refers— responsibilities to infants—is an intuitively powerful place from which to start, and the problem of motivation which plagues (some readings of) Rawls is largely solved. Of course this would not be doing much if that was all it did, since the idea of responsibility to the immediate next generation can be worked up in a number of ways and is largely an accepted idea. It is Goodin's deployment of the idea of vulnerability that potentially carries this motivation beyond the immediate next generation by providing us with a conceptual and affective bridge across the generations. Intergenerational justice is therefore canvassed without the problems associated with the need, as in de-Shalit's case, to identify 'moral and cultural similarity'. Goodin's theory can also deal, in principle, with the 'sleeper' type of environmental problem that de-Shalit struggles to accommodate.

Goodin and Rawls (in his 1993 guise) therefore provide us with
differing solutions to the so-called 'motivational problem' but they
both end up in the same place—owing duties of justice to proximate
and distant future generations. To that extent we may not need to
choose between them (and Goodin, in any case, argues that the
contractual basis for obligation can be read in his terms of vulnerability; Goodin 1985: 42–5). What Goodin and Rawls also share—
apart from the terminus of their arguments—is an in-principle
commitment to universalism, in terms of both the normative and
performative reach of their theories. It must be said, though, that
the architecture of Goodin's theory invites him to let the principle
slip earlier than Rawls might do. Goodin makes it a virtue of his
position that the 'vulnerability model can . . . explain the cultural
relativity of special responsibilities' (Goodin 1985: 35). He then gives
a series of examples which are really about different, culturally
specific, ways of discharging universally recognized responsibilities,
such as care for the elderly. But what if a culture did not recognize
care for the elderly as a responsibility at all? Closer to our present
context, what if a culture felt that it had no special responsibility
towards future generations? So much for normative universality.
The performative element touches, of course, on the thorny issue of
discounting: how do we value future well-being in comparison with
our own? Goodin is intuitively opposed to the implications of discounting, at least in its crude geometric-progression guise, but his
vulnerability thesis does lead him to say that, from an affective point
of view at least, we are permitted 'to give more to our nearer
temporal neighbors and less to our distant descendants' (Goodin
1985: 178). He feels that this can be countered, though, by what he
calls 'material vulnerabilities' which can override the 'fading' produced by the affective calculus. His conclusion is that, 'although the
vulnerability argument may allow for some discounting of the
future, it does not allow for anything like the dramatic discounting
that is practiced at present' (Goodin 1985: 178). Truth be told, this is
something like the conclusion most of us would want to reach, on
the grounds that cleaving to a non-declining commitment leads us
to the Laslett/Fishkin dilemma of no one ever getting anything,
described above.

In sum, and from the point of view of future generations, Rawls and Goodin provide useful resources for those seeking ways of reconciling social justice theory with our present conception of environmental sustainability. A question for us now is what Rawls's theory can make of Conception A's interest in critical natural capital. There are two ways of approaching his 'just savings principle' from this point of view: one through interpreting 'capital' in Rawls in the requisite way, and the other via a specific interpretation of his notion of 'primary goods'.

'Capital' certainly looks open to interpretation in Rawls. Examples of capital are 'not only factories and machines, and so on, but also the knowledge and culture, as well as the techniques and skills, that make possible just institutions and the fair value of liberty' (Rawls 1973: 288). Rawls appears to have in mind here a preconditional role for capital—preconditional for the construction of 'just institutions', for example. Critical natural capital is, of course, preconditional capital *par excellence* in that it is critical precisely because without it human life would not be possible. Russ Manning, for one, has picked up the baton provided by Rawls, and he thinks it perfectly consistent with everything Rawls says about capital to suggest that 'just savings' must include the passing on of such natural capital as 'clean air and water . . . [and] . . . land' (Manning 1981: 162). Given, though, that Rawls understands just savings as involving capital *accumulation* (Rawls 1973: 285) we will need to understand this in ways that make sense in the context of critical natural capital. I suggest that we think of accumulation here in terms of *enhancement*, whereby each generation has an obligation to improve 'ecosystem health' (Rapport 1995) to a reasonable degree. So what would the just savings principle, understood in this way, now look like? Casting our minds back a little we will remember Rawls's 1993 dictum that in 'all generations, the parties can be required to agree to a savings principle subject to the further condition that they must want all *previous* generations to have followed it' (Rawls 1993: 274). If we were now to follow the words 'savings principle' with the phrase 'including the enhancement of ecosystem health', then the role that critical natural capital might play in Rawls's scheme becomes clear. On the strength of all this, it looks possible to answer our original question ('can Rawls's theory cope not only with extending the community of justice into the future, but also with saving the 'right sort' of capital?') in the affirmative.

I think that the success of the other route in Rawls to the same objective (via the notion of 'primary goods') is more equivocal. Rawls defines primary goods in the following way:

> things which it is supposed a rational man wants whatever else he wants. Regardless of what an individual's rational plans are in detail, it is assumed that there are various things which he would prefer more of rather than less. (Rawls 1993: 92)

It would seem reasonable, given this definition, to include critical natural capital in the list of primary goods since (*a*) it has the required preconditional characteristics, and (*b*) Rawls himself distinguishes between social and natural primary goods: 'the assumption is that though men's rational plans do have different final ends, they nevertheless all require for their execution certain primary goods, natural and social' (Rawls 1973: 94). But Rawls does not have quite the same understanding of 'natural' here as that contained in Conception A. Social primary goods, he says, are things like 'rights and liberties, opportunities and powers, income and wealth' (Rawls 1993: 92), while natural primary goods include 'health and vigor, intelligence and imagination' (Rawls 1973: 62). Given the apparent centrality of the natural environment in the preconditional sense that Rawls evidently wants to give to the idea of primary goods, it is odd that he makes no special reference to it. He says, indeed, that 'I shall not argue the case for the [contents of the] list of primary goods here, since their claims seem evident enough' (Rawls 1973: 434), and even by 1993 nothing had persuaded him that environmental goods should have a place in the list of primary goods (Rawls 1993: 181).

So on this reading, the link between 'critical natural capital' and Rawls's 'natural primary goods' is tenuous if not non-existent, and the hold of Rawlsian theory on the relationship between distributive justice and critical natural capital seems to be loosened even further when we read that, for Rawls, natural primary goods are not the kinds of things that are distributable anyway. This is because although it makes sense to talk of the distribution of social primary goods 'on the principle that some can have more if they are acquired in ways which improve the situation of those who have less' (Rawls 1973: 94), natural primary goods are peculiar in that while 'their possession is influenced by the basic structure [of society], they are not so directly under its control' (Rawls 1973: 62).

One way to shift the balance here in favour of critical natural capital is to point out that Rawls has put health in the wrong category of primary goods. It has long been an environmentalist argument that health is related to the distribution of environmental goods and bads, and so Manning suggests that health should be included in Rawls's list of social primary goods (Manning 1981: 158), with the conclusion that:

If health and opportunity are accepted as primary goods to be distributed by social institutions, and if it is accepted that resource consumption has a limiting effect on health and opportunity, then we have the justification for environmental controls within Rawls's theory of justice. To allow unrestricted resource competition would cause an inequitable and unfair distribution of the primary goods of health and opportunity, a violation of the second principle of justice, which requires the distribution of primary goods to be to everyone's advantage and which guarantees an equal opportunity within the society. (Manning 1981: 160)

Extrapolating a little in the language of Conception A, critical natural capital 'piggybacks' on health: clean water (for example) should be distributed in such a way that the distribution is 'to everyone's advantage'. This line of thinking leads to the conclusion that in so far as critical natural capital is distributable, Rawls's theory can be used to suggest the principles that should guide its distribution. (These principles are interestingly different from those that can be made to emerge from Michael Walzer's theory of justice, as will become apparent in the next chapter.)

In general, Rawls's theory of justice can make room for two of the crucial ingredients of the 'critical natural capital' conception of environmental sustainability: justice for future generations, and critical natural capital itself. Moreover, it can provide us with guidance as to what the principles of distribution for critical natural capital should be both within and across generations.

## Conclusion

At this halfway stage in our discussion of Conception A of environmental sustainability, we can draw some tentative conclusions regarding the shape of theories of justice that might legitimize this
conception. I shall outline these conclusions by reference to the
table of justice developed in Chapter 3 and captured in Table 5. Both
international and intergenerational justice are crucial aspects of this
notion of sustainability, and both forms of justice seem compatible
with only a restricted list of the characteristics of theories of justice
outlined in Table 5. In the first place, the community of justice is,
in principle, universal across time and space. We did, however,
see good reasons why moderation of this universality might be
necessary—particularly in view of the absurd conclusions to which
it can lead in the context of future generations. This moderation
might be achieved through some form of discounting, or through
following through the implications of an ethic of care. My own view
is that both these approaches make too many concessions to
the criticisms that spawn them, and that too many present activities
with adverse environmental effects in the future could be legitimized by them.

Second, the shape of the basic structure of theories of justice that
are compatible with this conception of environmental sustainability
looks quite specific too. These theories are likely to be impartial as
far as theories of the good for human beings are concerned—except,
of course, in the limiting case(s) where the putative good for human
beings entails international and intergenerational justice. Similarly,
although I have left discussion of proceduralism and consequentialism until the next chapter, we can say here that a thoroughgoing proceduralism is unlikely to be compatible with the demands
of international and intergenerational justice. Justice, here, refers to
justice in the distribution of critical natural capital, and there is a
firmer guarantee that such distribution will turn out to be just by
continually monitoring outcomes than by cleaving rigorously to
procedures and letting outcomes take care of themselves. It
does need to be pointed out, though, that consequentialism makes
little sense in the context of future generations: we cannot monitor

consequences in the future, and so from a consequential point of view we can never strictly know whether we have done justice by it. At this point, Rawls's modified just savings principle, described above, is of considerable assistance. According to this principle, consequences are written into our present actions in that these actions are subject to the constraint that a just stock of capital be passed onto future generations.

Finally, as far as the basic structure is concerned, international and intergenerational justice seem to demand the universalizability of theories of justice. The internal logic of the notion of international justice is such that it would be contradictory for norms regarding the just distribution of critical natural capital to vary across cultures—and the same logical principle applies to justice between generations. So theories of justice compatible with international and intergenerational justice are likely to be impartial, consequentialist, and universal.

The third question in Table 5 deals with the question of what is to be distributed, and in Conception A of environmental sustainability the answer to this question is: critical natural capital. In terms of the generic possibilities outlined in Table 5, critical natural capital counts as an 'unproduced good' (the adjective 'unproduced' captures its 'naturalness'), but it is also a special type of unproduced good in that it is a 'preconditional' good. This 'specialness' signals, first, that theories of justice which make room for distinctions in terms of what is to be distributed are more likely to be prima facie candidates for compatibility with Conception A than those which do not, and second, that this compatibility is likely to be enhanced if the distinctions allowed include some notion of (a) the naturalness and (b) the preconditionality of certain goods. The chances of compatibility will be maximum when some combination of these distinctions—i.e. the preconditionality of certain natural goods—is built into the theory. On this reading, Bruce Ackerman's all-purpose 'manna' looks less than useful, and Rawls's natural primary goods (as we saw above) can only be considered a step in the right direction rather than the final destination.

The fourth and final question of Table 5 refers us to the question of the principles of just distribution. I shall say more about this in the next chapter, but it seems fair to suggest now that the very preconditionality of critical natural capital points us in the direction of need as the appropriate principle for its just distribution. Again without wanting to anticipate the next chapter in too much detail, support for the principle of need in this context can be derived from either universalist or particularist sources. On the one hand, needs-meeting as an objective of social policy is prima facie connected with universalizability because the fundamental importance to the maintenance of human life of the meeting of needs means that reasons why it should *not* be universalized would have to be given, rather than the other way round. And on the other hand, pre-conditional goods like critical natural capital might just have need as a principle of distribution 'built into them' in the Walzerian fashion described in *Spheres of Justice* (1983). I shall, though, leave further discussion of this issue until the next chapter.

Finally, we are now in a position to say something about the broad relationship between justice and sustainability—at least as far as Conception A is concerned. As we have said on a number of occasions, the principal feature of this conception is its insistence on the sustainability of critical natural capital. That is to say that its prime interest lies in the sustaining of critical natural capital rather than its just distribution. So while proponents of environmental sustainability and of distributive justice might—in this context— each be talking about the same thing (critical natural capital), they ask different questions of it. This suggests that the relationship between distributive justice and environmental sustainability can only ever be a contingent one.

There are, however, at least two ways in which the relationship might be made tighter. The first would be to show that distributive justice (or a particular type of it, anyway) is functional for environmental sustainability. That is to say that if it could be shown that distributing critical natural capital according to need, internationally and intergenerationally, contributed to the sustaining of critical natural capital, then the relationship between justice and sustainability would be one of reinforcement. It goes without saying that demonstrating this is at least as much an empirical matter as a theoretical one, and this is not the place (and nor am I the person) to pursue the critical empirical element in this relationship. I shall, however, have something more to say about it in the next chapter.

The second way in which justice and sustainability might be drawn together is to say that if justice is (at least partly) about the distribution of goods which are preconditional for human life, then it is obvious that if there were no such goods (or if their supply were continually endangered), there could be no justice. It is a small step from this suggestion to the special case where preconditional goods are understood in terms of unproduced natural goods (or critical natural capital), and from there to the idea that without critical natural capital there could be no distributive justice. In this sense, environmental sustainability is a precondition for distributive justice. However, this preconditionality has nothing to say about the normative content of schemes for justice. From this point of view it is still an open question whether (in Table 5 terms) the community of justice should be open or closed, which of the six 'live' options for the basic structure is appropriate, and what the principle of distribution should be. In other words, to say that environmental sustainability is a precondition for distributive justice is to say nothing determinate about the content of justice, and so we are thrown back to the empirical point made at the end of the previous paragraph—a point which, as I say, I shall pursue a little further in the next chapter.

# 5

# 'Critical Natural Capital' and
# Social Justice (Part II)

I SUGGESTED at the end of the previous chapter that the connection between environmental sustainability and distributive justice is fundamentally a contingent one, and I want now to pursue this thought in connection with work done by Amartya Sen on human welfare, and in discussion of possible principles of distribution. My comments on Sen will show that concern for human welfare need not necessarily lead to a concern for environmental sustainability, and my comments on distributive principles will simultaneously confirm the contingency of the relationship between justice and sustainability, and open up the range of distributive principles that might tighten this relationship. In this context, distribution according to need is usually advanced as the most likely candidate, but I shall outline a case for desert too. Finally, I shall spend some time considering debates regarding the acquisition of property in natural goods, and regarding the role that property in such goods might play in strategies for environmental sustainability, before concluding with some comments on compensatory justice in this rather special context of discussion of a non-substitutable good—critical natural capital.

## *Environmental Sustainability, Human Welfare, and Principles of Distribution*

A glance at Box 4 in the table of conceptions of environmental sustainability developed in Chapter 2 will remind us that the principal reason for such sustainability in Conception A is the mainten-ance of levels of human welfare. I shall illustrate this instrumental-ity of concern for the environment by reference to the work of Amartya Sen who, as is well known, has been very influential in debates regarding welfare in developing countries. Sen's crucial or-ganizing distinction is between 'goods' and 'capabilities', and it is his stress on the importance of the latter, with the former as merely 'carriers' of the latter, that makes his connection with sustainability issues so tenuous. He writes that, 'If we value capabilities, then that is what we do value, and the possession of goods with the corre-sponding characteristics is instrumentally and contingently valued only to the extent that it helps in the achievement of the thing that we do value, viz. capabilities' (Sen 1984: 317). If we imagine the 'goods' to which he refers as potentially including items of critical natural capital, then such capital is not important in itself but only in so far as it enables (or is fundamental to) the realization of capabili-ties. To this degree, Sen's orientation is suited (just) to this concep-tion of environmental sustainability (Conception A), but wholly unsuited to Conceptions B and C where (parts of) the natural world are valued in themselves.

Indeed, I have constructed Sen's proximity to the cause of envi-ronmental sustainability by interpreting 'goods' in the way required by Conception A, but Sen's work is conspicuous for its lack of reference to the natural environment. The tenacity of his focus on distribution and consumption puts him at one remove from the *supply* of goods (like rice—Sen 1984: 316), and from the ecological preconditions for a reliable supply. This goes to show that it is possible to spend a lifetime analysing the causes of poverty without ever considering the natural environment—as indeed Sen has done—and we seem entitled to deduce that there is therefore no necessary connection at all between a concern for distributive justice and a concern for environmental sustainability.

The connection can arise, though, through arguments to the effect that environmental sustainability is affected by distributive questions, and these arguments are put—as we saw in Chapter 1—most forcefully in the sustainable development literature. It may be worth reminding ourselves of the general points again. It will be remembered that in the Brundtland Report it is claimed that 'inequality is the planet's main "environmental" problem' (WCED 1987: 5–6), and that the 'links between poverty, inequality, and environmental degradation' (WCED 1987: p. xii) imply that such degradation can only be halted by measures to eliminate poverty and increase equity. Similarly, Tim O'Riordan argues that actions at the household level that lead to unsustainability are 'essentially uncontrollable unless the structural conditions that induce poverty and desperation are altered' (O'Riordan 1993: 35), and Rosa Braidotti affirms a 'growing recognition of the connections between the crisis in development, the deepening global environmental crisis, the growth of poverty and gender inequalities' (Braidotti 1994: 3). I could go on citing the evidence interminably but it all points in the same direction: that poverty and / or inequality are seen as major causes of environmental degradation, and that therefore policies aimed at relieving poverty and / or increasing equity will result in improved environmental quality. (Referring again to themes raised in Chapter 1, I stress that this 'sustainable development' point is not the same as the 'environmental justice' point, which has it that relative levels of wealth will affect the distribution of environmental goods and bads. The question here is, rather, whether poverty relief is functional for environmental sustainability.)

In assessing the links between environmental sustainability and the distribution of wealth, it needs to be pointed out, first, that poverty and wealth can *both* contribute to environmental problems: 'Both poverty and affluence [can be] identified as the driving forces behind environmental degradation and resource depletion, sweepingly termed pollution of poverty and pollution of affluence', writes Bartelmus, 'The former refers to the pressures of growing populations in poor countries on marginal and vulnerable lands, forests and congested cities . . . In industrialized countries, on the other hand, impacts of high-level economic growth and consumption are responsible in most cases for environmental degradation' (Bartelmus 1994: 11). Simply relieving poverty, therefore, and pushing countries along development paths involving the accumulation of wealth and increasing consumption, will not in themselves necessarily result in improved environmental quality. This argument, of course, has been at the centre of green criticisms of 'industrialism' for some time now: poverty relief may be a necessary condition for environmental protection, but in the absence of a wider questioning of contemporary processes of production and consumption, it will not be a sufficient condition. Andersson has suggested the complexities involved by pointing out that the relationship between wealth increases and environmental improvement is not linear, and that 'environmental improvement' is, in any case, far too vague a term, since wealth differentials may affect the wide variety of inputs and outputs that bear upon environmental quality in different ways: 'It has been shown that as income goes up there is increasing environmental degradation up to a point, after which environmental quality improves . . . But, so far, that relationship has been seen only for a selected set of pollutants' (Andersson et al. 1995: 13).

It is almost certainly wrong, too, always to assume that poverty is a 'sign of unsustainability' (Carew-Reid et al. 1994: 17). Indeed, it is an article of faith for some political ecologists that the poor are the best conservers of the environment and the most effective recyclers of 'waste'. Perhaps the most we can say is that *under certain conditions* poverty 'produces' environmental unsustainability, and these conditions are most likely to be fulfilled when the poor have been obliged to live on (and from) ecologically fragile land. (This applies, of course, to those relatively recently forced to live in this way, as opposed to those such as the aboriginal population in Australia, which has adapted to living off ecologically fragile land over a long period of time). The practically forced migrations of people to such land happen, of course, far too often, and the causes include rapid population growth, 'land consolidation and agricultural modernization in fertile agricultural areas which pushes the poor—without the capital to invest in such modernization—from fertile to marginal land, and land tenure inequalities' (Leonard 1989: 5). In these 'poverty reservations' it is extremely persuasive to suggest that 'the need to reconcile anti-poverty and environmental improvement strategies is most urgent' (Leonard 1989: 6). This dynamic is captured by the WCED Report which argues that:

traditional shifting cultivators, who once cut forests, grew crops, and then gave the forest time to recover, now have neither land enough nor time to let forests re-establish. So forests are being destroyed, often only to create poor farmland that cannot support those who till it. (WCED 1987: 29–30)

In the terms used to define the 'critical natural capital' conception of sustainability, people inhabiting such poverty reservations on ecologically marginal land are in permanent danger of making unsustainable use of what (for them) is critical natural capital. To the extent that poverty relief mitigates this danger, there is a direct relationship between (an egalitarian form of) justice and (this conception of) environmental sustainability. But it would be wrong to jump from this to the conclusion that justice is always functional for sustainability. We will always need to ask ourselves what kind of justice?, which conception of sustainability?, and under what conditions? In particular, here, it is important to recognize that poverty is not always linked to unsustainable practices, that therefore its relief may not result in environmental improvements, and that, in any case, the poor pursue some of the most environmentally sustainable lives on earth.

These remarks lead to the conclusion that there is no necessary relationship between egalitarian forms of social justice and environmental sustainability. Bartelmus cautiously suggests that 'Possible synergisms between the redistribution of income/wealth and environmental protection could result under conditions of pollution of poverty or affluence. There is still little experience with the relevance of such synergistic effects for the combined pursuit of equity and environmental protection' (Bartelmus 1994: 111), while Mark Sagoff makes the point more directly: 'I do not think any systematic relationship exists . . . between the policies environmentalists favor and the relative well-being of the rich and the poor' (Sagoff 1988: 56). My broader point—and one which this entire book is intended to address—is that the phrases 'the policies environmentalists favor' and 'the relative well-being of the rich and the poor' both need considerable unpacking before the question of whether there is a systematic relationship between the two can be answered. 'The policies environmentalists favor' can be understood in at least the three ways represented by Conceptions A, B, and C developed in Chapter 2, and 'the relative well-being of the rich and the poor' is a notion with as many ramifications as the dimensions of justice described in Chapter 3. I pointed out in the previous paragraph that there *is* a systematic relationship between poverty alleviation and the preservation of critical natural capital where the poor are forced to subsist on ecologically marginal land, but that this relationship will become less than systematic the further one moves from its defining parameters. Outside of these parameters, social justice and environmental sustainability may even appear to be competing rather than compatible objectives, in which the best we can hope for would be the 'side-constraint' that 'approaches to justice must be environment-preserving' (Jamieson 1994: 203).

## Principles of Distribution

We can consider the issue of the (in)compatibility of justice and sustainability a little further by examining the principles of distribution in more detail; this relates to the final question of Table 5 developed in Chapter 3, where principles such as needs, desert, entitlement, equality, and so on were outlined. The 'critical natural capital' conception of environmental sustainability confronts us with two possibly competing objectives: distributive justice among human beings, and distributive justice in connection with environmental sustainability. Now the principle of distribution may be common to both objectives; for example, we might be persuaded that need is the suitable principle on which to base distributive decisions among human beings ('Global justice is the encapsulation of an ideal of a network of relations between people who are equal in their needs', Belsey 1995: 47), and we may also believe that the meeting of people's needs will lead to greater environmental sustainability. Something like this dynamic was at work in the discussion above on 'poverty reservations' and unsustainable practices.

But need may not be the only principle of distribution capable of making compatible the twin objectives of social justice between human beings and environmental sustainability (leaving aside the observation made above that it may not always make them compatible anyway). Consider desert, for example. It will read oddly to the sustainable development enthusiast brought up on the belief that need and sustainability are intimately connected that desert might be functional for sustainability (too), but it is certainly a possibility.

Sustainability can be regarded as a common objective for society (in this Conception A case, the common objective of preserving critical natural capital), and one thing we might ask ourselves is, how can we best meet that objective? Sustainable developers ask themselves that question, and their answer (as far as social justice is concerned) is: via the universal meeting of people's basic needs. But the distributive principle of desert is in fact much more closely and normally linked to the idea of society's common objectives than is need. Distribution according to need (cor)responds to the idea of the intrinsic possession by everyone of a common characteristic (equality of need, for example), while desert corresponds to the idea of people's contribution measured against some criterion extrinsic to them. Charles Taylor puts it like this:

Granted a certain view of the common good, in the sense of an indivisible good, which a social perspective necessarily offers us, since it sees human beings as realizing their potential only in a certain common structure, it may appear evident that certain people deserve more than others, in the sense that their contribution to this common good is more marked, or more important. (Taylor 1986: 44)

I think we can legitimately remove the Hegelian baggage from Taylor's remarks, translate 'common good' as 'common objective', and consequently view desert as an appropriate distributive principle in connection with the common objective of preserving critical natural capital.

Of course desert is also a very common candidate for the principle that should decide distribution among human beings, irrespective of whether it might be functional for sustainability or not. Indeed Alasdair MacIntyre considers desert to be the principle most often deployed by ordinary people to express views on justice and injustice: 'it seems clear that . . . it is the reference to desert which makes them [such ordinary people] feel strongly that what they are complaining about is injustice, rather than some other kind of wrong or harm' (MacIntyre 1985: 249), and it may be worth pointing out MacIntyre's observation that legitimacy for desert will be hard to get from Rawls and Nozick since they do not mention it seriously at all. (On the other hand, we might want to take MacIntyre's own support for desert with a pinch of salt, since his affirmation that desert is central to most people's picture of justice is derived from an imagined debate between two ideal-type characters of his own invention whose possible situations hardly cover the whole gamut of social life: store owner, police officer, construction worker, a member of the liberal professions, social worker, or some-one with inherited wealth. Above all, they are all (with the excep-tion of the last) in work—rather important when it comes to deciding principles of justice; MacIntyre 1985: 244–5.) Still, this worry about MacIntyre should not prevent us from seeing that desert is, on the face of it, as useful a principle of distribution for this conception of environmental sustainability as need—and maybe even more useful, given its usual association with reward for the accomplishment of objectives.

The recognition that the principles of distribution that are compatible with (this conception of) environmental sustainability may be multiple is important in that it opens up more routes to legitimizing such sustainability (from the point of view of social justice) than may appear to be the case. Put differently, the possibility of conflict between the objectives of social justice and environmental sustainability endangers the legitimization of either one of them. If, for example, it were shown that environ-mental sustainability could only be bought at the cost of increasing social injustice, and if it were simultaneously believed that social justice is a more desirable goal than sustainability, then sus-tainability would lose its legitimacy. The chances of such clashes are reduced, though, if the base for compatibility can be constructed widely, and my intention here has been to show that need *and* desert, rather than either one or the other, can form part of that base.

One way to think of the principles of distribution in connection with environmental sustainability, then, is in terms of their func-tionality for such sustainability. Another way is to consider them in connection with environmental goods themselves. The idea that principles might 'attach' themselves to environmental goods is sug-gested by Michael Walzer's theory of 'spheres of justice' (discarded earlier as being of not much help in the context of international justice). In the first place, the role that the natural world plays in Conception A is fully compatible with an 'environmental goods', or resource-based, view of nature. The idea is captured by Jamieson when he writes that 'Perhaps the most important idea of global environmental justice views the environment as a commodity whose distribution should be governed by principles of justice' (Jamieson 1994: 203). (This view of the natural environment is increasingly called into question in the 'irreversibility' and 'natural value' conceptions of environmental sustainability—Conceptions B and C—but even there we will find the acceptance that the reproduction of human life itself involves viewing at least some aspects of the natural environment in terms of things to be bought and sold—and distributed.)

Walzer observes that all theories of social justice have a distributive principle, and he remarks that most such theories involve *one* distributive principle—any one of those registered in Table 5. Walzer's view is that the search for one foundational principle to cover all possible benefits and burdens is a chimera. History shows this, to his satisfaction at least: 'there has never been a single criterion, or a single set of interconnected criteria, for all distributions. Desert, qualification, birth and blood, friendship, need, free exchange, political loyalty, democratic decision: each had its own place' (Walzer 1983: 4). And for the less empirically minded among us (those who might say, 'well, just because there never has been a single criterion doesn't mean that there shouldn't, and might not, be one'), Walzer convincingly uses need as an example to show that particular principles (might be made to) work for some goods, but certainly not for others: 'Marx's maxim ["from each according to his ability, to each according to his needs"; Marx 1969: 160] doesn't help at all with regard to the distribution of political power, honor and fame, sailboats, rare books, beautiful objects of every sort. These are not things that anyone, strictly speaking, needs' (Walzer 1983: 25).

Walzer turns this insight into a general rule regarding the plurality of social goods and the consequent plurality of principles governing their distribution:

I want to argue . . . that the principles of justice are themselves pluralistic in form; that different social goods ought to be distributed for different reasons, in accordance with different procedures, by different agents; and that all these differences derive from different understandings of the social goods themselves—the inevitable product of historical and cultural particularism. (Walzer 1983: 6)

Or, in other words, that 'the multiplicity of goods is matched by a multiplicity of distributive procedures, agents and criteria' (Walzer 1983: 3).

The question for us is whether there is a distributive principle that is 'attached' to environmental goods? On the face of it, the answer would seem to be no. We need to take seriously Walzer's affirmation that the principle(s) of distribution derive from different social understandings of the good(s) in question. He is at great pains to emphasize that 'Distributive criteria and arrangements are intrinsic not to the good-in-itself but to the social good. If we understand what it is,' he continues, 'what it means for those for whom it is a good, we understand how, by whom, and for what reasons it ought to be distributed' (Walzer 1983: 8–9). The distributive principle is, for Walzer, rooted in social worlds, and since social worlds are different, so too will be distributive principles—even for ostensibly the same goods: 'Goods in the world have shared meanings because conception and creation are social processes. For the same reason, goods have different meanings in different societies. The same "thing" is valued for different reasons, or it is valued here and disvalued there' (Walzer 1983: 7).

Walzer's pluralistic view responds to an intuition that many of us would share in regard to many social goods—and it may be that the intuition is most strongly shared when it comes to environmental goods. One of the reasons the green movement has made such an impact over recent years is because of the depth of disagreement among people over the value of the non-human natural world. The impact has not consisted in everyone flocking in wholesale agreement to the green banner, but in the tumultuous nature of the debates greens have sparked off—evidence, it would seem, of the pluralism of value (here, of environmental goods) on which Walzer bases his theory of justice.

But this is only half the story. As well as fierce disagreement, the green movement has also been instrumental in turning us *all* into environmentalists, at least in so far as we have all come to recognize that environmental sustainability is a precondition for human life itself. Subscribing to this view puts us—broadly speaking—in the Conception A bracket, where the preservation of critical natural capital is recognized as essential to the reproduction of human life. Surely, we might say to Walzer, while there may be disagreement over the value of the snow leopard, we will all cross-culturally agree that the thin layer of topsoil that divides humanity from starvation is of critical value.

But Walzer may *not* agree:

There is no single set or primary or basic goods conceivable across all moral or material worlds—or, any such set would have to be conceived in terms so abstract that they would be of little use in thinking about particular distributions . . . A single necessary good, and one that is always necessary—food, for example—carries different meanings in different places. Bread is the staff of life, the body of Christ, the symbol of the Sabbath, the means of hospitality, and so on. (Walzer 1983: 8)

Despite this, the suspicion that food will always be regarded as of fundamental value lingers on; it *is* a 'necessary good', and it *is* 'always necessary'—and the fact that the symbolic uses made of food to which Walzer refers are themselves so foundational merely underlines the cross-cultural importance of the thing itself. Analogously, we might suggest once again that critical natural capital can be regarded as of high cross-cultural value—and if we do, the next question is whether any particular principle of distribution can be 'attached' to it.

First of all we need to know what kind of good critical natural capital is, and I would suggest that everything we have said so far leads to the conclusion that critical natural capital can be regarded as natural capital that is preconditional for human security and welfare. Walzer's *Spheres of Justice* helpfully contains a chapter (chapter 3) entitled 'Security and Welfare' in which he discusses the principle of distribution appropriate to these features of human life, and there he comes to the conclusion that need is the principle most fit: 'every political community must attend to the needs of its members as they collectively understand those needs; that the goods that are distributed must be distributed in proportion to need; and that the distribution must recognize and uphold the underlying equality of membership' (Walzer 1983: 84). So if Walzer's theory can be made to swallow a cross-culturally positive value for critical natural capital, it might just follow that the principle of distribution associated with it is that of need. (This only refers, of course, to forms of critical natural capital that can be distributed; the ozone layer is not, for example, a case in point. I shall have more to say about this form of natural capital in the next section on property ownership.) Either way, this aspect of Walzer's theory of 'spheres of justice' looks applicable to the issue of environmental sustainability, and it points the way towards a legitimizing of need as the principle according to which environmental goods (as understood in Conception A) should be distributed. (I should stress that this is not an argument for need to the exclusion of all other principles—the remarks I made about desert earlier still stand.) Finally, I hope that this brief *excursus* into 'spherical justice' has done enough to show that, while John Rawls may have enjoyed the lion's share of the attention as far as environmentalist thinking about justice is concerned, Michael Walzer's contribution is as suggestive here as it has been in other contexts.

## Property Ownership and Sustainability

The legitimacy of private property, the uses to which it can be put, and its extent are questions that partitioned the political landscape long before the issue of environmental sustainability came to our attention. Our interest in it here, though, takes two principal forms. The first is whether the ownership of critical natural capital can be justified, and the second is whether the possession of private property is functional for sustainability. These questions are of considerable importance to us since, as we saw in Chapter 2, the absence of property rights in nature is often advanced as a cause of unsustainable behaviour, with their conferral being the corresponding remedy (Table 4).

I am aware that the issue of property ownership is not exhausted by a discussion of *private* property ownership, and that *common* property resources are a fascinating source of reflection in the context of sustainability. I have chosen not to pay this form of ownership the attention it would otherwise deserve, though, for the pragmatic reasons that private ownership has made the most ideological and controversial headway, and because detailed discussion of all forms of property regimes would result in unhelpfully thin coverage, given the space available. Similarly, the apparently simple question of the functionality of property ownership for sustainability dissolves into myriad further questions: ownership of what? (land, sea, air, tradeable pollution rights, species, genetic resources, and so on); on what principle of distribution? (equality, entitlement, utilitarian, and so on). Once again these are large questions, and I can only gesture here at their shape.

Of all attempts to justify the ownership of what I shall continue anachronistically to call natural capital, John Locke's reflections are of vital importance, both in themselves and because they have given rise to influential modern versions of the 'entitlement' theory of justice as found, for example, in the work of Robert Nozick (1974).

Nozick views things like this:

If the world were wholly just, the following inductive definition would exhaustively cover the subject of justice in holdings.

1.  A person who acquires a holding in accordance with the principle of justice in acquisition is entitled to that holding.
2.  A person who acquires a holding in accordance with the principle of justice in transfer, from someone else entitled to that holding, is entitled to that holding.
3.  No one is entitled to a holding except by repeated applications of 1 and 2. (Nozick 1974: 151)

What happens to critical natural capital when submitted to these principles of acquisition and transfer?

Locke himself points out that the idea of 'just acquisition' is a problem because although everyone has property in their 'person', 'the earth and all inferior creatures [are] common to all men' (Locke 1690/1924: 130). How, then, can private property of what was previously held in common be justified (I shall refer to the seabed as an example below)? Locke's answer runs as follows:

Whatsoever . . . [a man] removes out of the state that Nature hath provided and left it in, he has mixed his labour with it, and joined to it something that is his own, and thereby makes it his property. It being by him removed from the common state Nature placed it in, it hath by this labour something annexed to it that excludes the common right of other men. For this 'labour' being the unquestionable property of the labourer, no man but he can have a right to what is once joined to, *at least where there is enough, and as good left in common for others.* (Locke 1690/1924: 130; my emphasis)

As Nozick (and others, e.g. Simon 1984: 190) have pointed out, this 'labour' theory gives rise to a number of questions, such as, 'What are the boundaries of what labour is mixed with?' and, 'Why does mixing one's labour with something make one the owner of it?' (Nozick 1974: 174). Despite the fact that these problems have been referred to in the environmental context (see e.g. Simon 1984: 191) I shall leave them aside here and focus instead (as have others) on the so-called 'proviso' contained in the italicized words in the quotation from Locke, above.

And I shall begin by pointing out that there are in fact two provisos in Locke. This first is the one just referred to, and the second takes its cue from (and includes) the possible objection that the principle outlined above would seem to legitimize the accumulation of enormous amounts of personal property. The second proviso, then, runs like this:

It will, perhaps, be objected to this, that if gathering the acorns or other fruits of the earth, etc., makes a right to them, then any one may engross as much as he will. To which I answer, Not so . . . As much as any one can make use of to any advantage of life before it spoils, so much he may by his labour fix a property in. Whatever is beyond this is more than his share, and belongs to others. (Locke 1690/1924: 131)

Locke drives his point home with an example: 'if the fruits rotted or the venison putrefied before he could spend it . . . he invaded his neighbour's share, for he had no right farther than his use called for any of them' (Locke 1690/1924: 135).

Let us call these two provisos the 'extravagance' and the 'sufficiency' provisos respectively. These provisos, as they stand, have very different implications for human impact on the natural environment. The extravagance proviso allows for considerable appropriation of natural objects, at least on cornucopian assumptions, while the sufficiency proviso limits such appropriation to a great degree. Tim Hayward draws the sensible conclusion, indeed, that a stringent interpretation of Locke's sufficiency proviso 'would seem to support quite a radical ecological approach to justice whereby any individual or group would be entitled to satisfy their immediate needs, subject to their doing so with ecological sensitivity and regard to like needs of others, but not to pursue unlimited acquisition' (Hayward 1994: 134).

If we take the sufficiency proviso in isolation Hayward has a point, but in the context of Locke's wider reflections on just acquisition this proviso pretty quickly gives way under the assault of money. Locke begins this part of his argument by pointing out the variable wastage rates of natural objects. He first repeats the sufficiency proviso established above by saying that 'the exceeding of the bounds of [a man's] property [does not lie] in the largeness of his possession, but [in] the perishing of anything uselessly in it', before going on to affirm that, given this general proviso, if the man in question 'bartered away plums that would have rotted in a week, for nuts that would last good for his eating for a whole year, he did no injury' (Locke 1690/1924: 139). The amount of legitimate possession is therefore a function of the wastage rate of the natural object in question—the longer the natural object lasts, the more of it one may legitimately possess.

The terminus of this argument is not hard to guess, even for those unfamiliar with Locke's trajectory. For as Locke says next: 'And thus came in the use of money; some lasting thing that men might keep without spoiling, and that, by mutual consent, men would take in exchange for the truly useful but perishable supports of life' (Locke 1690/1924: 139–40). By this point, the sufficiency proviso has collapsed back into the extravagance proviso since the 'fruits and venison' whose rapid spoilage rate Locke used earlier to illustrate the sufficiency proviso are now exchangeable for unspoilable coinage. The way to unlimited (in principle) accumulation is now only barred by the first proviso: that there be 'enough and as good left for others'.

The implications of this proviso are in turn affected by the variables of supply and demand. As Locke himself says, in conditions of plenty (high supply and low demand) the proviso is easily met:

And thus considering the plenty of natural provisions there was a long time in the world, and the few spenders, and to how small a part of that provision the industry of one man could extend itself and engross it to the prejudice of others, especially keeping within the bounds set by reason of what might serve for his use, there could then be little room for quarrels or contentions about property so established. (Locke 1690/1924: 131)

This is turned on its head, though, in the alternative case of low supply and high demand, in which the proviso on accumulation of leaving enough and as good for others would limit legitimate appropriation considerably. As Nozick says, by way of Hastings Rashdall's example, 'a person may not appropriate the only water hole in a desert and charge what he will' (Nozick 1974: 180; Rashdall 1915). Extrapolated to the wider arena of critical natural capital this would indicate that where it is scarce, limitations on its appropriation are justified by invoking Locke's first, 'extravagance', proviso.

But again, these limitations on appropriation are only justified if we accept a particular interpretation of 'enough and as good'. In the Rashdall/Nozick example, the limitation on appropriation only comes into play because there is just one water hole in the desert, and because the natural capital represented by the water hole is, as well as being critical, also not replaceable by any other type of human or natural capital. If there were more water holes in the desert, then the appropriation of one might still leave 'enough' for others, and/or if the function provided by water (liquid for life) could be carried out by a human-made substitute, then the appropriation even of the only water hole might leave 'as good as' for others. In either case, appropriation of the water hole would be legitimized—even taking account of Locke's 'extravagance' proviso.

It should be clear from all this that the 'as good as' part of Locke's proviso is absolutely crucial, and it can be read as an early intimation of what we have been calling 'substitutability'. If high degrees of substitutability are allowed, then Locke's proviso is relatively easy to meet since, as Nozick points out in a different language, 'Someone whose appropriation otherwise would violate the proviso still may appropriate provided he compensates so that their situation is not thereby worsened' (Nozick 1974: 178). The point about

Conception A of environmental sustainability, though, is that critical natural capital cannot be substituted for—that, indeed, may be
(under some circumstances) what makes it critical. In this context,
Locke's extravagance proviso leads to the conclusion that the appropriation of critical natural capital can legitimately be limited: there
may be nothing here that is 'as good as' (and this point takes on even
greater significance in the context of the 'irreversibility' and 'natural
value' conceptions of environmental sustainability, as will become
clear in Chapters 6 and 7).

   From this point of view, then, the issue is not that Locke's proviso
'once held and no longer does' (Nozick 1974: 175), but that the
proviso does not hold in certain areas—areas of non-substitutable
critical natural capital. Under conditions of scarce and non-substitutable critical natural capital, the proviso does what environmentalists
would probably want it to do: prohibit the irresponsible appropriation of critical natural capital. There is therefore more succour
in Locke for supporters of this conception of environmental
sustainability than, for example, Brian Barry (1991c.: 246) and
William Ophuls (Hoffert 1986: 8–10) suggest, and some modern
European farmers might be taken to task for violating Locke's
proviso since their 'unquestioned property "rights"' have led to
'prescriptive entitlements' in the policy arena, such as compensation
for not producing, even when production itself 'results in redundant
commodities, in chemical contamination of food and rural
water supplies, in accelerated soil erosion, or in rural landscapes
cleared to make way for larger machinery' (Bromley and Hodge
1990: 200).

   One controversial area in which we might expect Locke's just
acquisition principles to give us some guidance is that of unowned
resources that lie outside national boundaries—for example minerals on the seabed. Locke's theory would suggest that 'only those
who actually appropriate the resources found there are entitled to
the resulting benefits' (Simon 1984: 181), a point of view which
Simon has dubbed 'global libertarianism'. As Simon points out, the
effects of such a principle are disadvantageous for those without the
necessary capital and technology to make and exploit seabed discov-
eries: 'In a world of vastly unequal opportunities, where some are
born into relative affluence and others into a subsistence economy

or worse, to view natural resources as the exclusive property of those who exploit them perpetuates and extends the initial inequalities' (Simon 1984: 197–8). (Given, of course, that we have not yet encountered a clinching argument that inequality is bad for sustainability, Simon's point is more relevant for those concerned with egalitarianism than for those concerned with sustainability.)

Intuition suggests that we should be looking for transformative rather than conservative principles of justice here, and John Rawls provides us with an alternative to Locke. Imagine that in the original position behind the veil of ignorance we were deprived of the knowledge as to 'which state we inhabit in the real world'. In that case, 'what principles for appropriation of resources might we adopt if we were in ignorance of whether we lived in a more affluent, technologically developed society or a less affluent, technologically underdeveloped society'? (Simon 1984: 199; and see also Pasek 1994: 886). The chances are that we would adopt something close to what Simon calls 'resource egalitarianism'. This does not involve everyone ending up with equal incomes or wealth, but states rather that everyone has 'an equal prima facie right to benefit from the exploitation of resources found outside national boundaries' (Simon 1984: 194).

In a sense this amounts to the suggestion that everyone should have equal prima facie ownership rights in these resources, and such a position squares with the increasingly popular view in developing countries that each person on earth should be allocated (i.e. should own) an equal amount of environmental space. Those who occupy less than their allotted space (in terms both of sources and sinks) would be entitled to sell their spare capacity to those who exceed their allotment. Such a scheme of tradeable permits in environmental space would clearly benefit people in developing countries who exist at levels of source and sink use considerably beneath any notional permitted ceiling. Juan Martínez-Alier gives an example of this:

In Rio [the 'Earth Summit' of 1992], the Rich saw the $CO_2$ absorption facility provided by the oceans and . . . vegetation as basically a free access good on a first come first served basis. Some well-informed and intelligent voices from the Poor argued for ownership rights to this $CO_2$ sink function to be instituted, and to be shared equally by all of humankind, in such a way that poor people making little use of it (because of their low $CO_2$ emissions) could sell their unused part to the Rich. (Martínez-Alier 1993: 98)

This would, of course, amount to an international distribution of wealth, and it must be said that a similar result can be got from Locke's just acquisition principle, provided that his proviso is cashed out in full. Let us recall Nozick's observation that on a Lockean reading, 'Someone whose appropriation otherwise would violate the proviso may still appropriate provided he compensates so that their situation is not thereby worsened' (Nozick 1974: 178). From this point of view, the appropriation by an international undersea mining company of ore on the Atlantic seabed could be justified so long as compensation was paid—and so long as such compensation was considered 'as good' as the original unowned resource. This is the conclusion that Simon comes too, indeed: '*limited ownership rights* for the developers, but it would also *require* them to pay the equivalent of a tax for the benefit of the globally disadvantaged' (Simon 1984: 202; emphasis in the original). In this way, Rawls and Locke get us to the same place from different starting points, and in both cases it seems that an underlying and in-principle equality in the ownership of critical natural capital is appropriate—where it is appropriate to own it at all.

There is thus no simple answer, in Locke at least, to the question of whether (critical) natural capital can be justly owned or not. However, if we take Locke's theory as the one most likely to produce an affirmative answer (given that his express intention was to legitimize the ownership of private property), and if we find there that an in-principle prohibition on private ownership can be generated for certain forms of natural capital under certain conditions, then it would seem that no inductive theory will produce the universal legitimization that some might look for. Of course it also needs to be pointed out that even where the appropriation of natural goods is legitimate, this does not necessarily confer on the owner(s) the right to do whatever they will with their property: property ownership and regulation may not be entirely comfortable bedfellows but their cohabitation is of course quite common. Then there remains the possibility that the ownership of natural capital might be justified for performative reasons, i.e. that it contributes to the objective of environmental sustainability. Let me turn now to the debates that surround this sort of claim.

There are five sets of reasons which, individually or collectively, might sustain the argument that private ownership of natural capital will contribute to environmental sustainability. The first is that it promotes stewardship, and this is linked to the second: that natural capital can produce profits for the owner, but only if it is properly cared for. So, as Elizabeth Brubaker has pointed out, 'complementing those who protect the environment out of the goodness of their hearts are the myriad others who conserve their lands and resources for economic gain. Property owners are learning that it often pays to create habitat and protect wildlife' (Brubaker 1995: 193). Robert Nozick makes a similar point in the context of policies to reduce pollution and improve conservation:

the clearest examples of misdirected activity have occurred where there are no clear private property rights: on *public* lands denuded by timber companies and in oil fields under separately held pieces of land. To the extent that future people (or we later) will be willing to pay for the satisfaction of their desires, including trips through unspoiled forests and wilderness land, it will be in the economic interests of some to conserve the necessary resources. (Nozick 1974: 81)

This has been a particularly potent argument in the area of genetic resources where, although developing countries have consistently opposed the idea of germplasm ownership (Sedjo 1988: 307), it has been suggested that such countries would benefit from ownership of such resources through them being able to sell them on to pharmaceutical companies in the 'developed' world. In addition, it is argued that the conservation of genetic resources and the environment on which their survival depends would be enhanced through such ownership because any decline in environmental quality would threaten the resource, and therefore the profit. In this vein Roger Sedjo highlights 'the role that property rights for species does and could play in protecting genetic resources directly and, in many ways more importantly, the role property rights could play in providing incentives to protect and maintain the types of natural and wild habitats in which currently unknown genetic resources may reside' (Sedjo 1988: 294).

The same argument has been applied in the context of endangered species, where Michael 't Sas-Rolfes observes that trade in rhinoceros horns goes on unabated despite the fact that 'all five species of rhinoceros' are listed in CITES (Conference on International Trade in Endangered Species) Appendix 1, which 'effectively banned all trade in them or their products' ('t Sas-Rolfes 1994: 10). 'T Sas-Rolfes says that 'Most conservationists argue that the ban on the trade in rhino horns has not been effective because it has been insufficiently enforced' ('t Sas-Rolfes 1994: 11), but he has other ideas. 'Since rhino horn can be removed without killing the animal, and even grows back at an acceptable rate', he says, 'perhaps we could harvest horn on a sustainable basis, and sell it legally' ('t Sas-Rolfes 1994: 12). So 't Sas-Rolfes is willing to give a cautious affirmative answer to his own question: 'can we protect species by simply privatising them?' ('t Sas-Rolfes 1994: 11), although he also enters four caveats against the general rule. The privatization of species should not be pursued in situations where communal forms of tenure have proved to be successful, when species have no commercial value, when species have a 'very slow biological or reproductive growth rate', and privatization may not be successful where the political context is uncertain and unstable, since private companies may not feel secure enough to invest ('t Sas-Rolfes 1994: 12). Since the habitats of endangered species (of the 'flagship' variety, at least) are often to be found in regions of considerable political instability, this last caveat is likely to be of greater relevance than might appear at first sight.

These reservations notwithstanding, 'sustainability-through-privatization' seems a serious option, and its perverse attractiveness in our general context of justice and sustainability is only enhanced by Mark Sagoff's mischievous suggestion that some of the profits gained from 'environmental assets' could be redistributed to the poor (Sagoff 1988: 57). The objections to the privatization strategy, though, take us some way beyond 't Sas-Rolfes's rather tentative caveats noted above, and I shall discuss these objections shortly.

It is part of 't Sas-Rolfes's rhinoceros argument that the privatization of species and the legal trading in them would avoid the famous Tragedy of the Commons, and this is the third argument often entered in favour of environmental property. As he says, the rhinoceros's being wild means that it has been 'traditionally regarded as an open access resource by humans . . . [which] . . . leads to the so-called Tragedy of the Commons', and he points to a fundamental difference between cattle (which have survived) and bison (which have not): 'the former were privately owned and controlled and the latter were not' ('t Sas-Rolfes 1994: 11). This also forms part of Roger Sedjo's argument, referred to above, that genetic resources should be privatized: 'Given the lack of well-defined property rights to natural plant germplasm, resource economists would expect that many of the difficulties associated with the so-called "common property problem" and the resulting "tragedy of the commons" would apply to genetic resources as well' (Sedjo 1988: 295). (Strictly speaking, it is more usually open access than common property that leads to the tragedy of the commons since common property regimes nearly always have mechanisms for regulating the exploitation of the resource in question.)

The classic open access situation leading to the tragedy of the commons is in the oceans, and Elizabeth Brubaker has pointed out that,

A number of countries have assigned property rights to inland and ocean fisheries. In some of the most successful ocean fisheries cases, the rights have taken the form of individual transferable quotas (ITQs) that allocate to individual fishermen a percentage of the total allowable catch . . . Confident that their rights to fish are secure, fishermen need not waste money building bigger boats and equipping them with more advanced gear in a race to catch fish. (Brubaker 1995: 211)

In soundbite mode, Kent Jeffreys of Washington's Competitive Enterprise Institute sums up the Brubaker argument as follows: 'privatisation can halt the tragedy by eliminating the commons' (Jeffreys 1994: 9). It is worth noting that tradeable rights of this sort assume a considerable degree of centralized decision-making and enforcement. In the first place, the allowable total catch (in the case of fish) has to be decided upon, and then regular policing of fishers and their boats is required to ensure that no one exceeds the quota she or he has been allocated (or has bought from other fishers). One would have thought that if the aim is to prevent the temptation to overfish through guaranteeing each fisher a quota, then this could be achieved 'simply' through allocating quotas and policing the resulting fishing. Both of these are already part of the Brubaker proposal, but the rigmarole of doling out ITQs would be avoided.

The penultimate argument put in favour of privatizing the environment is that environmental groups can 'lease or purchase lands or waters they wish to preserve' (Brubaker 1995: 194), and in my own recollection this takes the form of hundreds of people buying tiny plots of land so as to jam the inevitable avalanche of compulsory purchase orders that results if the land in question stands in the way of (for example) a new road. Finally, ownership enables the property holder to take legal action if the property is degraded in any way. This sort of action can take many forms, but one illustration would be that many fisheries in Britain are in private hands, and polluters (factories, farmers) have sometimes been taken to court and ordered to pay compensation for degrading the fisheries.

There are, then, a number of arguments that have been put in favour of environmental property rights, and they are performative arguments in the sense that the legitimacy of ownership rests on the extent to which it (ownership) can be shown to contribute to environmental sustainability. In presenting these arguments I have already hinted at some of the difficulties associated with them, and now I would like to tease these out a little further.

Enforceability is a perennial problem here. It is obvious in the Brubaker fisheries case above that a successful ITQ system depends on enforcing the quotas adequately, but there is also the problem involved in enforcing the property rights themselves. This is of particular importance in cases of pollution, such as those referred to at the end of the previous paragraph. As Brubaker herself says: 'Property rights, to be meaningful, must be enforceable. If a victim can't successfully sue a polluter that has harmed him, his property rights are of little value' (Brubaker 1995: 177). There are a number of reasons why attempts to sue might fail—or might not get off the ground at all. Robert Nozick points out that the transaction costs involved in taking legal action can constitute a powerful deterrent against even beginning it. Consider, he says, a situation in which 'individual polluters have widespread and individually minuscule effects . . . it will not pay any one person to sue, despite the great total cost involved' (Nozick 1974: 80). And the same is true in reverse: 'If many persons similarly impose tiny costs on each individual, the total costs may then be significant. But since no one single source significantly affects one individual, it still will not pay any individual to sue any individual polluter' (Nozick 1994: 80). To this we might add the difficulties involved in identifying polluters in the first place, so in sum Nozick seems to have it half right when he concludes that 'It is ironic that pollution is commonly held to indicate defects in the privateness of a system of private property, whereas the problem of pollution is that high transaction costs make it difficult to *enforce* the private property rights of the victims of pollution' (Nozick 1974: 80). I say 'half right' because the transaction costs problem is one that seems endemic to private property solutions to environmental problems, at least where these involve court action. It is hard to see how the system could be improved to the point where transaction costs were even nearly eliminated, and therefore equally hard to avoid the conclusion that this constitutes a substantial defect in private property approaches to environmental problems.

Another batch of problems for such approaches relates to the issue of assigning private property rights in environmental goods. This is not the 'in-principle' question referred to in the discussion of Locke above, but the practical question of establishing the boundaries necessary for the assignment of ownership rights. Recall, for example, Robert Sedjo's plan for the protection of plant genetic resources through the bestowal of property rights; as Sedjo himself says: 'An obvious necessary condition for such a system is that it be possible to describe a plant with sufficient specificity so that the clear and unambiguous assignment of property rights is possible' (Sedjo 1988: 309). The amount of information required to make property rights a realistic proposition across the entire range of genetic possibilities beggars the imagination. Similarly, market and property enthusiast Kent Jeffreys says, 'Even I must admit that we cannot privatise the global oceans (or the atmosphere, a similar conceptual difficulty)' (Jeffreys 1994: 8–9). Some have responded directly to the apparently impossible challenge implicit in Jeffreys's remarks; Elizabeth Brubaker, for example, has written that:

As increasing scarcity makes the establishment of property rights in the fisheries more pressing, technological developments will make their enforcement increasingly feasible. Satellite technology is a case in point. Assigning property rights to ocean fisheries has traditionally been hindered by the difficulty of keeping out trespassers. Satellites make 'fencing' the oceans possible. In the United States, NASA has experimented in policing the oceans, with satellites that can identify boats by the unique 'fingerprints' in their exhaust. (Brubaker 1995: 293)

By this point, environmental sustainability has taken off into the realms of science fiction, but even back here on Earth, and in circumstances where boundaries might be relatively easily established (livestock, for example), it is extremely important to bear in mind the uses to which property rights can be put. These uses are by no means always benign: 'Just as economically dependent or relatively powerless humans are at risk of harm from the exercise of property rights by other humans, so, too, are non-human animals which live within human social relations and practices involving property rights, such as intensive livestock farming' (Benton 1993: 145). We shall have cause to come back to Benton's far-reaching analysis later.

The final difficulty with 'sustainability-through-privatization' suggestions that I want to mention here relates to the supposed profits that developing countries might make from selling their renewable environmental assets (e.g. germplasm), assuming property rights in them were established. The problem has been flagged by Juan Martínez-Alier who points out (in an argument designed for the context of the worldwide allocation of tradeable emission permits, but which is, *mutatis mutandis*, applicable to environmental assets understood more widely) that the poor are likely to 'sell cheap' (Martínez-Alier 1993: 102). This is, he says, because:

market valuations depend partly on the distribution of income at present and therefore environmental policies based on markets will not be the same if the distribution of income changes. The chrematistic valuation of environmental resources and services 'owned' by the Poor in ecologically-extended markets will change income distribution, and it is therefore opposed by the Rich, but, *if the poor sell cheap*, then there is no reason to expect that such valuation will be an effective instrument in environmental policy. (Martínez-Alier 1993: 102; emphasis in the original)

Martínez-Alier believes that the poor *will* sell cheap, (*a*) because of the likelihood of the poor competing among themselves to sell their environmental assets, and (*b*) because what looks like a high price to poor people is a low price to rich people (Martínez-Alier 1993: 102). This is not to say that the poor are stupid, but that their poverty is linked to a weaker bargaining position compared with wealthier nations. The potential effectiveness of 'sustainability-through-property' may therefore be blunted on two fronts; first, because the prices paid to developing countries for their assets may not be more than they could get through immediate exploitation rather than sustainable use, particularly when these assets often return to developing countries in the form of hugely expensive pharmaceutical products; and second, because the relatively low prices 'developed' countries are likely to have to pay for these assets will not act as an incentive to careful use of them. Martínez-Alier concludes with the following:

I have argued that the establishment of new property rights over environmental resources and services might work to the benefit of poor sections of the population, although perhaps their very poverty will lead to a low valuation of such resources and services on the ecologically-extended markets. (Martínez-Alier 1993: 117)

If Martínez-Alier is right, then the assigning of property rights in environmental assets in an unequal world is likely both to consolidate injustice and to undermine policies for sustainability. This suggests, in turn, that the success of 'sustainability-through-property' policies has as its precondition a more equitable global redistribution of wealth.


## Compensatory Justice and Substitutability


The issue of compensation was particularly present in the discussion of Locke and his proviso, above. The proviso states that assets held in common can legitimately be made private property as long as 'enough and as good' is left for others. The 'as good' section of the proviso evidently depends on the possibility and acceptability of compensation. So in the seabed case discussed above, the appropriation of seabed minerals previously held in common might be held to be acceptable provided compensation (perhaps in the form of a redistributive tax) were paid. In this case, the tax receipts would be deemed 'as good as' the original minerals. It may be worth quoting Robert Nozick on this subject for the third time: 'Someone whose appropriation otherwise would violate the [Lockean] proviso still may appropriate provided he compensates so that their situation is not thereby worsened' (Nozick 1974: 178).

The problem with this idea in the environmental context comes in two distinguishable but connected forms. First, justice may be done, but without any contribution to environmental quality or sustainability. So grievances over rights in property being aggressed through pollution, for example, can be recompensed financially without environmental quality being improved. The second form appears when we reduce Elizabeth Brubaker's reflections on the issue *ad absurdam*. She says that 'Expropriations are fair only if, through compensation, they leave all affected parties as well off as they were before' (Brubaker 1995: 188). Everything depends, of course, on what is being expropriated, and some things are not compensable. In effect these things are not compensable because they are not substitutable, and the interest of this to us here is that a belief in the non-substitutability of (some forms of) critical natural capital is a defining feature of Conception A of environmental sustainability. From this point of view, doing justice through the medium of compensation for loss of critical natural capital is not an option.

Put the other way round, a Brubaker belief in the possibility of wholly compensatory forms of environmental justice depends on a belief in the possibility of infinite substitutability across human-made and natural capital. This, though, would imply that no form of natural capital could ever be regarded as scarce since it could always be substituted for by human-made capital—yet this would run counter to a fundamental feature of this conception of environmental sustainability: that some types of critical natural capital are non-substitutable. This suggests that wholly compensatory forms of justice are incompatible with environmental sustainability. Another way of putting this is to say that Brubaker's compensation thesis entails that a fundamental circumstance of justice is missing in the context of natural capital: the circumstance of scarcity. Brubaker herself implies that this conclusion is absurd, since conflicts over property arise precisely under conditions of scarcity:

Historically, property rights have evolved in response to growing demand, be it for agricultural land, minerals, timber or fish. As long as there has been plenty to spare, there has been no need for property rights. As resources have grown scarce (and increasingly valuable), property rights have become needed and resource users have become more willing to bear the costs of establishing and enforcing them. (Brubaker 1995: 211)

Under some circumstances, of course, justice in the environmental context just has to be seen in compensatory terms, and this is particularly the case in regard to future generations and non-renewable resources. Brian Barry says in this context that 'It might appear at first blush that the only equitable solution is to ensure that future generations face the same stock of resources as we do. This, however, would obviously mean that no non-renewable resources should ever be used' (Barry 1991b: 259). He puts the challenge for justice as follows: 'We must come up with a criterion that allows for some exploitation of non-renewable resources even when that is going to mean that, other things being equal, future generations will inherit a diminished stock' (Barry 1991b: 259), and his solution looks like this: 'We can, I suggest . . . stipul[ate] that future generations are owed compensation in other ways for our reducing their access to easily extracted and conveniently located natural resources' (Barry 1991b: 259). The compensation, he continues, should be in the form of 'improved technology and increased capital investment' (Barry 1991b: 260), giving rise to an equality across the generations of 'productive potential' (Barry 1991b: 263).

One objection we might enter to this is that reducing everything to the *numéraire* of 'productive potential' gives us no guidance as to how most appropriately to exploit our non-renewable resources today. Put differently, viewing justice in terms of the transfer of productive potential alone could legitimize the passing on to future generations of despoiled and dangerous landscapes. Something like this point emerges when Bruce Ackerman's intrepid astronauts (see Chapter 3) are confronted not with infinitely fungible 'manna' but with a world that

contains two kinds of good. On the one hand, there is the Grand Canyon, which can be used in only one of two ways, as a source for uranium or as an object of natural majesty. On the other hand, there is a slightly modified form of manna that is capable of producing anything except natural majesty upon the command of its rightful owner . . . finally . . . there is no way of mining the Canyon's uranium lode without destroying its natural aspect—mining and majesty don't mix. (Ackerman 1980: 213)

Ackerman asks us to imagine a situation in which both present and future generations are content to have the Canyon mined for its uranium deposits as long as the price is right—a situation in which conservationists (both present and future) 'find their share of the profits from energy use too good to refuse' (Ackerman 1980: 214). In this case, the responsibilities of what Ackerman calls 'trusteeship' that bind generations together can be fulfilled by the present generation through 'compensating investment' in research and development of energy production (Ackerman 1980: 214). This is very similar to the conclusion reached by Barry, above.

Imagine, though, with Ackerman, a situation in which 'the two generations differ as to the best use of the Canyon':

While generation one would prefer to fulfill its trusteeship obligation by making up the megawatts it has consumed, the second generation wants trusteeship defined in terms of the Canyon's majesty. When different generations disagree about the best use of a nonfungible good, which generation's characterization should dominate the interpretation of trusteeship? (Ackerman 1980: 214–15)

This 'nonfungible' situation is precisely the one present in all three of our conceptions of sustainability, and the impasse it represents in respect of working out just what we should try to pass on to future generations is captured in Ackerman's metaphorical throwing up of hands: 'Is it *really* impossible to permit *some* Canyon mining without retaining *some* of the place's majesty?' (Ackerman 1980: 216; emphasis in the original). Ackerman's own answer to the broader question of what to pass on the future generations revolves around what he calls 'crystal ball gazing', in which we try to second guess what future generations will want. He says that history, for one, is a rough guide: 'the dominance of a value structure in the past suggests that, ceteris paribus, its reemergence is a serious possibility. A single generation of atheists should not be permitted to transform all Christian shrines into parking lots' (Ackerman 1980: 217). Second, we should attend to 'the overall pattern of objects protected under trusteeship: Does it reflect a sense of the rich variety of possibility that the future may have in store?' (Ackerman 1980: 217). Third, he says, 'there is the simple passage of time: If a thousand years were to pass without a single generation placing a higher value on the Canyon's majesty than its energy, the possibility that even this irreplaceable object represents an "easy" case for energy development must be seriously confronted' (Ackerman 1980: 217). Whatever else these three rough guides tell us, they signal that wholly compensatory forms of justice, based on total fungibility of natural 'resources', are not an option in the context of environmental sustainability. As Mark Sagoff says, 'There are few decisions favorable to our wishes that cannot be justified by a likely story about future preferences. Even a nasty strip mine or a hazardous-waste dump produces energy that will strengthen the industrial base left to future generations' (Sagoff 1988: 60–1).

I shall pursue this point in the next chapter, and for now we just need to bear in mind that while Barry's compensation strategy will end up forming part of the larger picture, it needs to be set alongside the warning implicit in Conception A that improved technology and increased capital investment cannot compensate for (some) critical natural capital since such capital is unsubstitutable and therefore non-compensable. 'Oil is oil is oil', says Barry sagely (Barry 1991*b*: 267), but in that (relatively) happy case, oil can be substituted for by other forms of energy. 'Critical natural capital is critical natural capital is critical natural capital' is a far less elegant mantra, but the non-substitutability implicit in it is in this case real rather than apparent. Robert Nozick refers us to three types of situation in which, or reasons why, a system of compensation is not always appropriate: first, where the 'fairness of the exchange price is very hard to compute' (Nozick 1974: 65); second, 'A system that allowed assaults to take place provided the victims were compensated afterwards would lead to apprehensive people, afraid of assault, sudden attack, and harm' (Nozick 1974: 66); and third, 'a system permitting boundary crossing, provided compensation is paid, embodies the use of persons as means' (Nozick 1974: 71). I have no quarrel with any of these, but Conception A of environmental sustainability suggests the addition of a fourth area of exception: non-substitutable critical natural capital. From this point of view, Barry's objective of securing an equality of productive potential across the generations is best reached by a combination of compensation and preservation/compensation for that which is compensable (e.g. some non-renewable resources), and preservation of that which is not (i.e., here, non-substitutable and non-renewable critical natural capital).

The solution to the question of what to pass on to future generations is very often couched in terms of something vague like 'opportunities'. What this discussion shows is that this is a rather weak and unhelpful formulation. At best it only gets us to first base. The crucial question is what these 'opportunities' might consist in, or what might be required for their fulfilment. Our investigation so far suggests that an ineliminable element of 'real stuff' (or 'critical natural capital', in our present language) needs to be passed on, and to talk only of passing on 'opportunities'—or even 'productive potential'—is to be in danger of missing this fundamental point. Finally, the point at which the two 'sets' of non-renewable resources and critical natural capital meet (i.e. the Venn diagram area where they have elements in common) is the point at which the train of sustainability hits the buffers of the Second Law of Thermodynamics; the end of the line is a symmetrical and very cold universe in which human aspirations to sustainability and justice have long since vanished from view.

## Conclusion

We have seen nothing in this chapter that makes a substantial difference to the tentative conclusions established at the end of the last one. That is to say that the broadly universalistic (both in terms of the community of justice and the normative reach of theories of justice) characteristics of a theory of justice likely to be compatible with this conception of environmental sustainability still hold. Likewise, a basic structure involving impartiality, a degree of consequentialism, and universalism is likely to be a feature of such a theory. Above all, we have seen confirmation here of the contingency of the relationship between justice and sustainability. The principal reason for striving for environmental sustainability, according to the 'critical natural capital' conception, is its importance for human welfare. However, concern for human welfare does not in itself lead to concern for environmental sustainability, as our consideration of the work of Amartya Sen showed. At the very least, one would need to construct arguments designed to show Sen that his analysis of the conditions for human welfare is incomplete as long as it does not refer to environmental sustainability as a precondition for such welfare. This, then, echoes the argument from preconditions for linking justice and sustainability that I flagged in the conclusion to the last chapter.

In that conclusion I also suggested that the preconditional argument can have nothing to say about the determinate content of theories of justice, and that such content could only be given if it could be shown that a particular combination of the features of theories of justice outlined in Table 5 gave rise to environmental sustainability. But my discussion of the principles of justice towards the beginning of this chapter suggested that much more empirical work will need to be done before any firm conclusions regarding the functionality of distributive justice for environmental sustainability can be drawn. From the point of view of environmental sustainability, therefore, it will not be enough to attend to just relations between people and assume that critical natural capital will thereby be sustained. It seems apparent that one needs to keep a special eye open for critical natural capital, as it were, and theories of justice (or aspects of them) which do not encourage this—or, worse, which prevent it—are prima facie unsuitable for linking with environmental sustainability. This is the case, as we saw, with theories which rely on compensation to do justice, both in the present and for the future. Another way of making this same point is to say that the substitutability feature of conceptions of environmental sustainability plays an important part in determining the likely compatibility between theories of justice and conceptions of sustainability—and as we shall see in the chapters that follow, this role is even more crucial in connection with other conceptions of sustainability.

# 6

# 'Irreversibility' and Social Justice

THE distinguishing feature of this second conception of environmental sustainability (Conception B) is its focus on the sustaining of irreversible nature. As I pointed out in Chapter 2, irreversible nature may also be critical natural capital, but not necessarily so. Critical natural capital is capital critical for the maintenance of human life, while irreversible nature is irreversible in the sense that once it has gone it cannot be recovered. Some irreversible nature—a determinate species, for example—may be critical for human life, in which case it will straddle Conceptions A and B, and the reasons for sustaining it will be drawn from either column (this conclusion is represented in Box 5 of Table 2 by including human welfare as a reason for sustaining irreversible nature). But other species may confidently be said not to be critical for the maintenance of human life, and so their disappearance will not be a cause for concern within the confines of Conception A. In Conception B, though, 'duties to nature' make their first appearance as a reason for sustaining (irreversible) nature—that is, we may want to sustain it irrespective of whether it is functional for human welfare or not. Up to now I have referred to 'duties to nature' rather than 'obligations to nature', or 'justice to nature', because these last two descriptions would imply that nature somehow has a claim upon us in respect of obligations and/or justice. Such an implication would require substantiation of a sort which it is not my intention to provide here, although I shall spend some time in what follows discussing to what extent the language of justice—and particularly distributive justice—is applicable to the non-human natural world.

This last remark indicates that we shall be largely concerned here with the first row of the distributive justice table developed in

Chapter 3—the row that deals with the community of justice. But as
I indicated at the end of the last chapter we will also be confronted
with questions relating to the basic structure of theories of justice.
Remember that the overriding objective here is to assess theories
of justice for their compatibility with the intentions that lie
behind the various conceptions of environmental sustainability
we have identified. In this sense, the impartial/substantive,
procedural/consequentialist, and universal/particular distinctions
outlined in Chapter 3 give us a backdrop against which to place
our conceptions of sustainability so as to judge compatibilities
and incompatibilities. Without wanting to give too much away
now, I can say that the impartial/substantive distinction will be of
particular interest to us here since the issue of 'the good' is raised
here in an acute and interesting form. Let me begin, though, by
discussing to what extent our putative duties to nature might
be regarded as duties, or obligations, of justice. (To begin with, at
least, in what follows, I shall not discriminate between particular
'parts' of nature, although it will become clear that it is important to
do so.)

## Justice to Nature?

Arguments for leaving the natural world out of the equation of
justice usually proceed by stipulating conditions for inclusion that
the natural world fails to meet. The 'heavyweights' of liberal justice
theory, at least, seem agreed that justice is for humans only. Rawls,
for example, refers to 'the basis of equality, the features of human
beings in virtue of which they are to be treated in accordance with
the principles of justice', and asks himself, 'On what grounds . . . do
we distinguish between mankind and other living things and regard
the constraints of justice as holding only in our relations to human
beings?' (Rawls 1973: 504). And he goes on,

The natural answer seems to be that it is precisely the moral persons who
are entitled to equal justice. Moral persons are distinguished by two features: first, they are capable of having (and are assumed to have) a concep-

tion of their good (as expressed by a rational plan for life); and second, they are capable of having (and are assumed to acquire) a sense of justice . . . Thus equal justice is owed to those who have the capacity to take part in and act in accordance with the public understanding of the initial situation . . . one should observe that moral personality is here defined as a potentiality that is ordinarily realised in due course. (Rawls 1973: 505)

I shall come back to Rawls's last remark a little later, but for now we need simply point out that only human animals have (or can have) a conception of the good and a sense of justice, so, by his own lights, Rawls draws the justifiable conclusion that 'Our conduct towards animals is not regulated by these principles [of justice]' (Rawls 1973: 504).

Michael Walzer also underpins his theory of justice with a notion of the equality of human beings, and, like Rawls, he asks himself, 'By virtue of what characteristics are we one another's equals?' (Walzer 1983: 314). And he answers: 'One characteristic above all is central to my argument. We are (all of us) culture-producing creatures; we make and inhabit meaningful worlds' (Walzer 1983: 314). Once again, so far as we know, only human animals are 'culture-producing', so as long as that is the criterion for membership of the community of justice, non-human animals and the rest of the non-human natural world will remain outside it.

Much earlier in the same text he asks himself the same questions—'In what respects are we one another's equals? And by virtue of what characteristic are we equal in those respects?' (Walzer 1983: p. xii)—and gives answers which neatly summarize the strategy of exclusion that he, Rawls, and others practise:

This entire book is an answer of a complicated sort to the first of these questions; the answer to the second I don't know, though in my last chapter I shall suggest one relevant characteristic [the one referred to in my previous paragraph—A.D.]. But surely there is more than one: the second question is more plausibly answered with a list than with a single word or phrase. The answer has to do with our recognition of one another as human beings, members of the same species, and what we recognise are bodies and minds and feelings and hopes and maybe even souls. For the purposes of this book I assume the recognition. (Walzer 1983: p. xii)

'Recognition' can obviously take place at many levels and in virtue of many characteristics. Walzer's list of characteristics (bodies, minds, feelings, hopes, souls) is supposed to amount to a collection only possessed by human beings, and it is this that justifies restricting the recognition of equality to 'human beings, members of the same species'. But the first three items on his list—bodies, minds, and feelings—are indisputably also possessed by many non-human animals, so a slightly different list (leaving off the last two items) would have produced an entirely different community of justice. And if we accept (as many people do or have done) that non-human animals may possess souls too, then the only characteristic in Walzer's list that stands between him and admitting Noah's Ark to the community of justice is hope. (Is it too Derridean to suggest not only that Walzer deploys 'hope' to keep animals out of the community of justice, but also that he 'hopes' he can do so? I shall come back to this in the context of Robert Nozick below.)

All this simply goes to show that (some of) the characteristics which underpin equality (which in turn underpins the beings to whom—or to which—we owe justice) can be made to cross the species boundary. Just which characteristics are chosen is clearly crucial, but there seems no indisputably determinate way of choosing 'accurately'. The best Charles Taylor (for example) can do is to base the choice on intuition: 'Our intuitions about distributive justice are continuous with our basic moral intuitions about human beings as beings who demand a certain respect . . . It is because people ought to be treated in a certain way, and thus enjoy a status not shared by stones and (some think also) animals, that they ought to be treated *equally* in collaborative situations' (Taylor 1986: 36; emphasis in the original). Of course the point is that people's intuitions vary regarding the status of animals, and as I suggested above it can anyway be shown to be rationally inconsistent to exclude some animals from considerations of justice. This is the issue to which I now turn.

The alternative strategy is based on attempts to demonstrate the existence of a continuum, rather than a series of breaks, between species: 'whatever the crucial determinant of moral concern—happiness, rights, sentiment—the argument is that it is irrational to

restrict such concerns to human beings, since the differences between ourselves and some other species which would alone justify
such a restriction simply do not exist' (Cooper 1995: 139). Cooper's
gloss on the argument is particularly appropriate for those at either
end of the species spectrum—children (human) and adult rhesus
monkeys (primate), for example. In these 'limit cases', the determinant of moral concern may often be possessed by both parties,
or sometimes even possessed more obviously by the 'subordinate'
species.

Rawls himself refers to limit cases during his discussion of 'the
features of human beings in virtue of which they are to be treated in
accordance with the principles of justice', to which I referred above.
Very small children do not possess either of the features which he
regards as crucial (a conception of the good and a sense of justice),
but our intuitions balk at leaving them out of the community of
justice, so Rawls avers that having the 'capacity' for these features is
sufficient. Moreover, this rider enables him to maintain the boundaries which separate humans from other species since as far as we
know no non-human animal has even the capacity to entertain a
conception of the good or build on a sense of justice.

Rawls admits, however, that there are more awkward limit cases,
such as those regarding people 'more or less permanently deprived
of moral personality' (Rawls 1973: 510). These, he says, 'may
present a difficulty', although he 'assume[s] that the account of
equality would not be materially affected' (Rawls 1973: 510). This is
perhaps an unwise assumption to make, given that it is precisely
such limit cases that have led philosophers such as Tom Regan,
Peter Singer, and Mary Midgely to point to the inconsistent
manœuvres undertaken to maintain distinctions at the human/non-
human margins. Rawls himself at one point unwittingly assists those
who would include at least some animals in the community of
justice by declaring support for the 'Aristotelian Principle [which]
characterizes human beings as importantly moved not only by the
pressure of bodily needs, but also by the desire to do things enjoyed
simply for their own sakes' (Rawls 1973: 431). In a footnote he
observes that 'This seems also to be true of monkeys' (Rawls 1973:
431 n. 22), thereby recognizing the possibility, at least, that characteristics often thought to be specific to humans are in fact shared by

some non-human animals too. To then make those characteristics determinants for moral concern, and to grant moral concern to humans while withholding it from relevant animals, would amount to what has come to be called 'speciesism'.

Making use of the limit cases to which I referred above, Donald Vandeveer has performed an immanent critique of Rawls with the intention of showing that a rigorous application of his own rules would lead him (Rawls) to include all sentient beings in the community of justice. Vandeveer recalls Rawls's view that only moral persons are owed justice—that is, persons capable of a sense of justice and of possessing a conception of the good. He also recalls Rawls's observation, referred to above, that not all persons are moral in the required sense, so strictly speaking they are not owed justice. At this point, as we have seen, Rawls says that it would be 'unwise in practice' (in Vandeveer 1979: 369) to withhold justice from these persons, and Vandeveer asks the obvious question: why should we extend just treatment to beings that are not strictly owed it?

The answer is simply that, on reflection, we want to owe them justice and so we find a way of doing so that is consistent with the principles of the original theory. But Vandeveer's point is that this consistency leads to a further inconsistency, in that if we make room for the severely retarded we ought also to make room for other sentient creatures whose characteristics are similar to them. Vandeveer points out that it is fundamental to Rawls's theory that people behind the veil of ignorance 'choose a principle [of justice] designed to secure certain benefits for the least advantaged'. 'Surely', he continues, 'the category of the least advantaged would include not only badly off "moral persons" but those so seriously incapacitated as to be sentient yet *not* moral persons, e.g., the severely retarded' (Vandeveer 1979: 371). Once the severely retarded are included, it is a relatively small step to the inclusion of sentient animals whose cognitive particulars are similar (or even superior) to theirs. Vandeveer concludes that, 'If . . . the original position were fully neutral, its participants would not only have to be ignorant of the [*sic*] race, sex, or social position qua participants [in the just society], it would seem that they would have to be ignorant of their species membership as well' (Vandeveer 1979:

372–3), with the implication for Rawls's Difference Principle that justice would 'prohibit inequalities among sentient beings except in so far as they maximise the benefits of the least advantaged sentient creatures' (Vandeveer 1979: 373).

Vandeveer's proposals bring with them difficulties of their own, of course. Some have asked whether it is actually possible to imagine oneself as a veal calf or a parakeet—although is it any easier to imagine ourselves being severely retarded? Others have argued, more particularly, that we cannot know what is good for veal calves or parakeets, and therefore there is no way of making the Difference Principle work in these (and other) cases—just what would 'inequalities' mean in these contexts? Still others will say that treating all sentient creatures as if they were moral persons would severely curtail the instrumental use we might legitimately make of them, and that as a consequence the production and reproduction of human life could grind to a halt. From the other end, as it were, it might be objected that Vandeveer's immanent critique of Rawls robs Rawls's original position of much that is interesting about it. If all we are required to do behind the veil of ignorance is to consider the lowest common denominator interests of other beings, then the relatively sophisticated thinking that leads to the two principles of justice need never take place. Vandeveer might side-step these concerns and emphasize his two basic theses: first, that by his own lights Rawls is inconsistent in excluding sentient animals from the community of justice; and second, that we know enough about sentient animals and their basic needs to see that even a less-than-perfect application of the Difference Principle would substantially alter our relationship with them.

Rawls's reluctance to pursue this line of thought is striking, and his evasion compares interestingly with the confused honesty one finds in the little remarked passages devoted to animals in Robert Nozick's own seminal contribution to justice theory (1974). Nozick pursues this issue in the context of a discussion on 'side constraints', the idea of which he conveys as follows: 'In contrast to incorporating rights into the end state to be achieved, one might place them as side constraints upon actions to be done: don't violate constraints C. The rights of others determine the constraints upon your actions' (Nozick 1974: 29). This last sentence leads him to consider the position of animals: 'Are there any limits to what we may do to animals? Have animals the moral status of mere *objects*? Do some purposes fail to entitle us to impose great costs on animals? What entitles us to use them at all?' (Nozick 1974: 35). Nozick rehearses the kind of 'thought experiment' questions which have become so familiar to us as debates about animal rights have gathered pace and sophistication: 'Can't one save 10,000 animals from excruciating suffering by inflicting some slight discomfort on a person who did not cause the animals' suffering?' (Nozick 1974: 41), and these questions lead him in turn to the same sort of enquiry regarding 'equality of condition' flagged above in the context of Rawls and Walzer: 'in virtue of precisely what characteristics of persons are there moral constraints on how they may treat each other or be treated?', and then, significantly and with admirable honesty, he says that, 'perhaps, we want these characteristics not to be had by animals; or not to be had by them in as high a degree' (Nozick 1974: 48). (This is the sentiment I wanted to mention in connection with Walzer's putative postmodern 'hoping' that animals might be left out of the community of justice, referred to above. Nozick, here, recognizes the possibility of such an unspoken desire.)

Nozick's last remark, in any case, captures the a priori intention of keeping animals out of the justice game—an intention apparently present in so many theories of justice. His own list of characteristics (unoriginal, as he himself emphasizes) looks like this: 'sentient and self-conscious; rational (capable of using abstract concepts, not tied to responses to immediate stimuli); possessing free will; being a moral agent capable of guiding its behaviour by moral principles and capable of engaging in mutual limitation of conduct; having a soul' (Nozick 1974: 48). Nozick then bypasses the question of whether these characteristics are possessed by beings other than human beings, and asks the even more radical question of why possession of these features should lead to constraints by others in their conduct towards the features' possessor at all. He believes that, 'Leaving aside the last on the list, each of them seem insufficient to forge the requisite connection' (Nozick 1974: 48). This reiterated importance of the soul as the determining characteristic is interesting (remember Walzer's insistence on it, above), not least because it can open the door to the community of justice to a number of animals in a number of cultures where possession of a soul is not restricted to human beings.

The similarity between Walzer and Nozick is not limited to their quasi-religious reliance on the soul as the marker of justice; they both also suggest that it is a collection of characteristics, rather than any single one, that marks the boundaries of the community of justice. This is Nozick's version of the idea: 'In conjunction, don't they all add up to something whose significance is clear: a being able to formulate long-term plans for its life . . . ?' (Nozick 1974: 49). But still Nozick is not satisfied: 'Why not interfere with someone else's shaping of his own life', he asks (Nozick 1974: 50). Even his last attempt to found inviolability—'I conjecture that the answer is connected with that elusive and difficult idea: the meaning of life' (Nozick 1974: 50)—meets with a final dose of scepticism: 'But why shouldn't my life be meaningless?' (Nozick 1974: 50). His parting shot is an inconclusive, 'I hope to grapple with these and related issues on another occasion' (Nozick 1974: 51).

What are we to make of Nozick's stream-of-consciousness reflections on the community of justice? In the first place, he seems at a loss to identify any feature of human life that irrevocably leads to the conclusion that we owe justice to members of our own species. This might mean that we owe them no justice at all, or it might mean that we owe them justice on some ineffable and inexplicable basis. If it is the second (as seems to be the case), then we may plausibly owe a duty of justice to beings other than human beings, and this conjecture is supported by Nozick's own affirmation that 'Animals count for something. Some higher animals, at least, ought to be given some weight in people's deliberations about what to do'—even though 'It is difficult to *prove* this' (Nozick 1974: 35).

Second, the questions with which we began this discussion of Nozick—'Are there any limits to what we may do to animals?' (Nozick 1974: 35)—apparently innocently asked, may look quaint to us today in that now at least we possess philosophical frameworks within which to try to answer them, and had Nozick been aware of these frameworks his discussion of the position of animals in his theory of justice might have been more conclusive. In this context, a rather forlorn footnote is significant: 'After my discussion of animals was written, this issue was raised in an interesting essay by Peter Singer, "Animal Liberation", *New York Review of Books*, April 5th 1973' (Nozick 1974: 338 n. 11). One wonders what Nozick's theory of justice would have looked like had he (Nozick) been armed with Singer's fully worked out theory of animal liberation, and also with Tom Regan's case for animal rights. It is tempting to surmise that if Nozick had prepared his text a few years later, then his would have been the only major theory of intra-human justice to have emerged from contemporary Western political theory which systematically incorporated obligations of justice to (some) sentient beings as well. (Although it is almost more tempting to surmise that any theory of justice that incorporated justice for even a very re-stricted set of non-human animals would immediately be regarded as a second division theory. Is this what happened to William Galston (1980)?) Whether the first hypothesis is correct or not, what does seem certain is that determined attempts to keep animals out of the community of justice, represented here by Rawls, Walzer, and to a lesser extent Nozick, appear equivocal. Rigid frontiers are hard to place and even harder to police: wherever we erect them, infiltrators will find their way in.

Perhaps the most determined and sophisticated recent attempt in the context of justice to talk of continua rather than frontiers is Ted Benton's *Natural Relations: Ecology, Animal Rights and Social Justice* (1993). Benton's continuum derives from two observations. The first comprises a form of 'naturalism':

According to this view, humans are to be thought of as a form of natural being, as part of the order of nature, rather than as ontologically privileged beings, set apart from, or even against, the rest of nature. A naturalistic approach to understanding the relation between humans and other animals gives centre stage to what humans share with animals in its account of the nature and well-being of humans themselves. More specifically, it focuses on organic embodiment, in all its consequences and requirements, as basic to any such account. Health, physical security, nutrition, shelter are all as indispensable to human well-being as to the well-being of any other animal species. But to recognise this is also to see that in these aspects of their lives it is true not just that humans and other animals have much in common, but also that they are materially independent. (Benton 1993: 17)

The species frontier is breached here with the observation that humans and other animals have similar organic needs as far as the production and reproduction of their lives are concerned, and Benton's last sentence points to the second feature of his naturalism: the idea that humans depend on animals for their livelihoods, and vice versa. For example: 'One aspect of human embodiment—our requirement for food—engages us in social relations and practices which inescapably include animals: as partners in human labour, as objects of labour, and of consumption, as well as competitors for habitats and common sources of food' (Benton 1993: 18). In sum, says Benton, 'the broad framework of thought which informs my approach . . . is one which shares this emphasis on the significance of [human] social relations [for animals], but which at the same time takes seriously the "human/animal continuum" which is presupposed in the animal rights literature' (Benton 1993: 16). Benton's naturalism provides the basis for his continuum, and the focus on animals that interact most obviously with human beings gives him a way of setting limits on the animals to whom he thinks we may owe duties of justice.

As far as our table of dimensions of justice is concerned, Benton's continuum evidently provides for a wider community of justice than that provided for in unmodified versions of Rawls's, Walzer's, and Nozick's theories of justice, but it also leads him to endorse a specific principle of justice as most appropriate for this widened community—the principle of need, which he refers to in what follows as a 'socialist principle of distributive justice'. The appropriateness of this principle lies in its being transferable across species boundaries. It is hard (although not impossible) to make sense of entitlement as a principle of distribution as far as non-human beings are concerned, and it is even more difficult to do so with desert (a favourite option for Alasdair MacIntyre, as we remember). On behalf of need, Benton says that

there is no ontological obstacle to its extension beyond species boundaries. Though, I have argued, the case for attributing rights to non-human animals faces severe intellectual obstacles, their 'neediness' as natural beings is a feature shared with human animals. Moreover, a needs-based view of justice has the further advantage of extending the scope of cross-species moral concern beyond the narrow circle of species whose

individuals satisfy [Tom] Regan's subject-of-a-life criterion. Need understood in terms of conditions necessary for living well or flourishing is a
concept applicable not only to all animal species, but to plant-life as well.
(Benton 1993: 212)

What might this mean in practice? Benton suggests that, as far as the
use of animals for labour or food is concerned,

If animal husbandry is tolerable at all, these considerations tell in favour
of husbandry regimes which preserve opportunities for animals to
establish and maintain the broad patterns of social life which are peculiar
to their species. Where physical and psychological development requires
more-or-less prolonged relationships between juvenile animals and
adults, conditions for these relationships need to be provided. (Benton
1993: 172)

Such a rule of thumb would presumably proscribe the slaughter of
calves for veal meat, and the overall conditions associated with
factory-farming would immediately be ruled out of court:

Production regimes such as these [factory-farming] impose massive
constraints and distortions on the mode of life of species of non-human
animals caught up in them. Their lives are sustained solely to serve
purposes external to them, conditions and means for the acquisition
and exercise of their species-powers are denied to them, and, more
specifically, their social needs and capacities are systematically denied and
suppressed. In short a good deal of the content of Marx's contrast between
fulfilled and emancipated human life, and a dehumanized, estranged
existence can also be applied in an analysis of the conditions imposed
by intensive rearing regimes in the case of non-human animals. (Benton
1993: 59)

   But Benton seems equally clear that human and animal interests
cannot and should not weigh equally in the balance of justice. As far
as I can see the nearest he gets to determining relative weights is
through the distinction between 'justice as equality of treatment and
as equivalence of treatment' (Benton 1993: 213)—a distinction he
illustrates in the following way: 'there are great species-specific
differences in their [human and animal] patterns of need and modes
of satisfaction . . . To be prevented from practising her religion may
reduce a human to utter misery, but can have no meaning as a harm
for a horse or a dog' (Benton 1993: 214). This illustration does not

take us very far, though, since it incorporates no direct conflicts of interest between humans and animals, and this is precisely where the rules ordering relationships of justice between human and animals will be most obviously tested. Similarly, we might say that Benton has not provided us with a full theory of justice since, as we saw Michael Walzer pointing out in Chapter 3, need as a distributive principle only works for some goods: 'Marx's maxim doesn't help at all with regard to the distribution of political power, honor and fame, sailboats, rare books, beautiful objects of every sort. These are not things that anyone, strictly speaking, needs' (Walzer 1983: 25). However, Benton's general point must be that if the satisfaction of need across species boundaries were taken seriously, human–animal relationships would be fundamentally altered, and changes of this sort will be the aim of any transformative theory of justice. Something like Benton's theory of justice and the ontology that underpins it, indeed, would seem the most likely route to legitimizing the so-called 'five freedoms' referred to by Britain's Animal Welfare Council: 'freedom from thirst, hunger or malnutrition; appropriate comfort or shelter; prevention, or rapid diagnosis and treatment, of injury and disease; freedom to display most normal patterns of behaviour; freedom from fear' (in Johnson 1995: 166).

In any event, this discussion regarding the community of justice surely shows that Michael Walzer was right to say that 'The community is itself a good—conceivably the most important good—that gets distributed' (Walzer 1983: 29). With the introduction of potential communities of which Walzer was only inconclusively—if at all—aware, such as the international community, future generations, and non-human beings, the sustainability agenda merely heightens the stakes of the distribution of community membership. Indeed, in the light of what has been said so far, we are entitled to conclude that Walzer pointed out an essential truth about distributive justice and then forgot to follow it as far as he should. I should like to pursue this thought a little further now.

Consider Walzer's 'open-ended distributive principle', which reads as follows: 'No social good x should be distributed to men and women who possess some othe good y merely because they possess y and without regard to the meaning of x' (Walzer 1983: 20; sentence emphasized in the original, but not here). This principle underpins Walzer's notion of 'complex equality', according to which (as we saw in Chapter 4),

> no citizen's standing in one sphere or with regard to one social good can be undercut by his standing in some other sphere, with regard to some other good. Thus, citizen X may be chosen over citizen Y for political office, and then the two of them will be unequal in the sphere of politics. But they will not be unequal generally so long as X's office gives him no advantages over Y in any other sphere—superior medical care, access to better schools for his children, entrepreneurial opportunities, and so on. (Walzer 1983: 19)

The way this works can be seen, for example, by letting y be money and x political power in Walzer's general principle. The principle would then read: 'Political power should not be distributed to men and women who possess money merely because they possess money and without regard to the meaning of political power.' Many of us would agree with Walzer that 'This is . . . an attractive picture' (Walzer 1983: 17).

Now what happens if we let y be 'membership of the community of justice' (a hypothesis which, as far as I know, Walzer never explores)? The principle will then read: 'No social good x should be distributed to men and women who possess membership of the community of justice merely because they are members of the community of justice and without regard to the meaning of x.' This principle appears to undermine the very organizing theme in Walzer's work with which we began: that membership of the community is primordial. As we saw above, Walzer's view is that 'The community is itself a good—conceivably the most important good—that gets distributed' (Walzer 1983: 29)—but now we can see that community membership is irrelevant as far as the distribution of social goods is concerned, since 'No social good x should be distributed to men and women who possess membership of the community of justice merely because they are members of the community of justice.' Membership of the community of justice—however defined—entails nothing as far as the distribution of other benefits and burdens is concerned.

As we saw in Chapter 4, Walzer's theory looked to be of limited value as far as international justice is concerned, since his radical particularism appeared to rule out the possibility of a precondition for there being such a thing as international justice, namely an international community. But a strict application of his own open-ended distributive principle in the context of membership of the community of justice seems to show that community membership is (and should be) irrelevant as far as the distribution of other goods is concerned. This then opens the way to the distribution of such 'other goods' on some other basis than 'membership of the community', and therefore to a universalism which might in principle embrace the international and non-human communities.

In one way, this (re)interpretation of Walzer is wholly opposed to the spirit of his work, which is to follow through the implications of his belief that 'Goods in the world have shared meanings because conception and creation are social processes. For the same reason, goods have different meanings in different societies. The same "thing" is valued for different reasons, or it is valued here and disvalued there' (Walzer 1983: 7). But in another way, we might regard our reinterpretation as saving Walzer from himself. He states his overriding intention as follows: 'My purpose in this book is to describe a society where no social good serves or can serve as a means of domination' (Walzer 1983: p. xiv). If, once again, we take the social good in question to be 'membership of the community of justice', it is clear that leaving parts of the international community or parts of the non-human natural world out of the community of justice inevitably turns possession of this particular social good into a means of domination. It seems clear that as far as the particular case of the non-human natural world is concerned, Walzer was unaware of these difficulties when he wrote that 'The primary good that we distribute to one another is membership in some *human* community' (Walzer 1983: 31; my emphasis). In this sense, the only way to realize Walzer's stated purpose is to make community membership irrelevant as far as the necessary entailing of other social goods is concerned, and this is what we achieved via the strict application of his open-ended distributive principle above. Another way of expressing the same conclusion is to say that membership of the community of justice should in principle be as wide as possible, so that it cannot serve as an instrument of domination—and we are left with the ironic and rather surprising thought that Walzer's apparently radically particularistic theory of justice might just contain the resources to enable us to widen the community to the desired degree. If this is right, then Walzer's theory can be used to recommend the provision of security and welfare across both the human and non-human communities, since 'Membership is important because of what members of a political community owe to one another and to no one else, or to no one else in the same degree. And the first thing they owe is the communal provision of security and welfare' (Walzer 1983: 64). In this way, and by a different and rather circuitous route, we are enabled to reach the same kind of 'security and welfare' conclusion as that expressed by Benton above: 'If animal husbandry is tolerable at all, these considerations tell in favour of husbandry regimes which preserve opportunities for animals to establish and maintain the broad patterns of social life which are peculiar to their species' (Benton 1993: 172).

## Rights

The question of whether the 'duties to nature' flagged in this conception of environmental sustainability are obligations of justice may turn on whether rights can be ascribed to (parts of) the non-human natural world. The question of whether they can be so ascribed is a large one, and it has been asked and answered in a variety of ways in a huge and ever-increasing number of texts devoted to the subject. It would be inappropriate and impossible to give anything more than a flavour of the debate here, but it is important that something be said, since 'Those who think it appropriate to regard animals and, perhaps, plants as possessing rights are likely to be most happy with that vocabulary [i.e. the vocabulary of justice]: for it is common practice to describe violations of rights as acts of injustice' (Cooper 1995: 140). In other words, if one believes that even some animals have rights, then it behoves anyone who leaves those animals out of their scheme of justice to explain why they have been left out. Once again, I leave until later the question of whether, even if animals are appropriate subjects for rights-talk, this can take us very far in our context here of justice to 'irreversible nature'.

The easiest way to avoid this obligation of explanation is to refuse rights-possession to anything other than human beings. This seems to be Rawls's tactic: 'the meaning of equality is specified by the principles of justice which require that equal basic rights be assigned to all persons. Presumably this excludes animals; they have some protection certainly but their status is not that of human beings' (Rawls 1973: 505). Note that Rawls is not precluding concern for animals, it is just that he thinks such concern cannot be motivated by reasons of justice.

Others disagree. In an essay that has become justifiably central to the debate, Joel Feinberg (1981) argues in favour of rights for some animals. He agrees that animals cannot have duties, but asks why that should mean that they cannot possess rights either. Sometimes, he says, it is argued that they cannot possess rights because they cannot claim them, but this is countered by the existence of proxies who act on behalf of children—unable to claim their rights, of course, but undoubtedly in possession of them. Then it may be said that proxies always act as representatives of their charges' interests, and that animals do not have interests, so to speak of the proxy representation of their rights (read 'interests') is absurd. This seems to Feinberg to be simply wrong: 'Many of the higher animals at least have appetites, conative urges, and rudimentary purposes' (Feinberg 1981: 143), and can therefore have an interest in having these fulfilled. He concludes that, 'in general, animals *are* among the sorts of beings of whom rights can be meaningfully predicated and denied' (Feinberg 1981: 143; emphasis in the original), and that this conclusion emerges from a general principle that runs as follows: 'the sort of beings who *can* have rights are precisely those who have (or can have) interests' (Feinberg 1981: 143; emphasis in the original).

So now the extent of the community of rights-holders—and thus the extent of the community of justice, providing we accept that rights are a 'central concept' in justice (Almond 1995: 8)—depends upon who or what can be said to possess interests. Once again, the ascription of the characteristics that are said to determine interest possession is crucial, and the nuances can be very important. Feinberg's own list above—'appetites, conative urges, and rudimentary purposes'—is, as he says, most obviously applicable to the 'higher animals', but the charmed circle can be considerably widened by making reference to another of his lists which reads as follows: 'latent tendencies, direction of growth, and natural fulfillments' (Feinberg 1981: 142). On the basis of his first list Feinberg says that trees (for example) do not have interests (Feinberg 1981: 144), but deployment of his second list would suggest that they might.

We saw Robert Goodin developing his 'vulnerability' thesis in Chapter 4 in the context of future generations, and he piggybacks on Feinberg's work, too, to apply his thesis to the case of environmental protection in general and animals in particular. Goodin's notion is that 'what gives rise to our special duties to protect animals from pain and suffering is their peculiar vulnerability to us' (Goodin 1985: 181), although he struggles to take this much further than (some) animals since, '[A]s we move down the order of nature from animals to vegetables to rocks, it becomes increasingly doubtful that the objects in view can have interests of their own which command our respect' (Goodin 1985: 182). In the wider environmental context, indeed, Goodin's view is quite similar to that of Bryan Norton: that the environment is best protected indirectly through protecting what future generations of human beings 'will (or even might) come to value' (Goodin 1985: 184). This indirect protection is not what we are concerned with here so I shall leave it to one side for the moment. It will, though, figure more centrally in the Conclusion.

The importance of 'line-drawing' is clear, then, and the point is that wherever we draw it, those on the 'right' side of it might well benefit from being there. The conferral of legal standing on inanimate and natural objects for the purposes of including them in the justice game has been promoted by a number of people, and most notoriously by Christopher Stone (1974). Something of the flavour of the effect this might have emerges from exchanges during the case of the *Sierra Club* v. *Morton, US Secretary of the Interior*, et al., in the US Supreme Court on 19 April 1972. The case turned on the proposed development of the Mineral King Valley in California's Sierra Nevada mountains by Walt Disney Enterprises, opposed by the Sierra Club but confirmed by the court. Mr Justice Douglas dissented from the court's opinion, arguing for legal standing for the valley. He pointed out that

Inanimate objects are sometimes parties in litigation. A ship has a legal personality, a fiction found useful for maritime purposes . . . The ordinary corporation is a 'person' for purposes of the adjudicatory processes, whether it represents proprietary, spiritual, aesthetic, or charitable causes . . . So it should be as respects valleys, alpine meadows, rivers, lakes, estuaries, beaches, ridges, groves of trees, swampland, or even air that feels the destructive pressures of modern technology and modern life. (in Hoban and Brooks 1996: 195)

This does not amount to the absurdity of preferring estuaries to human interests, as some have alleged. It merely amounts to the request to allow estuaries a legitimate place in the court's proceedings, with the outcome being determined by 'due process of law'. There is, in other words, no guarantee that granting legal standing to ecosystemic features would protect them any better than at present—and this points us to the second part of our discussion of rights.

Implicit in this discussion so far is the suggestion that most of the debates regarding the rights of non-human beings and/or objects revolve around whether such objects and/or beings can be said to possess rights, and if so, which ones. A less visible but equally important dimension of the debate concerns the very usefulness of the rights discourse and of rights possession. Mark Sagoff argues that 'only individuals, that is, particular plants or animals, could possess rights or interests, but it is collections, such as species, communities, and ecosystems, that environmentalists are concerned to protect' (Sagoff 1988: 156). This is particularly serious for our current conception of environmental sustainability, which has at its heart a determination to preserve and sustain what we have called 'irreversible nature'. The classic and most readily recognizable examples of irreversible nature are species: once they are gone they are gone forever. If Sagoff is correct in saying that rights can only attach to individuals, then the rights discourse looks an unlikely way of arriving at species protection.

The question of whether rights can attach to communities is a complex one, and it has been tied in for some time now with debates within liberalism—debates which have steered the group rights question in specific directions. As Will Kymlicka has put it: '[T]o many people, the idea of group-differentiated rights seems to rest on a philosophy or world-view opposite to that of liberalism. It seems more concerned with the status of groups than with that of individuals' (Kymlicka 1995a: 34). The challenge for liberals, therefore, has been to try to square group-differentiated rights with liberal principles, and much of the debate about such rights has taken place within that context. The details of this context, though, are not generally applicable to the environmental case. For instance, for liberals, group rights are a problem because they are potentially in tension with the rights of the individuals who make up the community. This is not such an issue for defenders of our present conception of environmental sustainability because of their focus, precisely, on the interests of the community over the individuals that comprise it. Nevertheless, Kymlicka, writing from within the liberal tradition, does make a distinction that helps us to identify the kind of group or collective right that environmentalists will want to endorse. He distinguishes between collective rights involving 'internal restrictions' and those relating to 'external protections'. The first are rights invoked by a given community to 'protect [it] from the destabilizing impact of *internal dissent*' (Kymlicka 1995a: 35; emphasis in the original), and the second are rights 'intended to protect the group from the impact of *external decisions*' (Kymlicka 1995a: 35; emphasis in the original). The first kind is irrelevant to our present context for obvious reasons, and so it is the second that has some purchase: this is the idea of protecting species 'from the impact of external decisions' by assigning them rights. This still begs the question, of course, of whether rights can be so assigned, and many will disagree that they can (e.g. Hartney 1995), but the debate within political philosophy on this point is sufficiently open for environmentalists to be able to find the resources in it they require if they so wish.

Another way into the question, anyway, is to suggest that, in our particular context, Sagoff underestimates the extent to which the substantiation of individuals' rights depends on nurturing the conditions in which those rights can be exercised. This view has it that the well-being of species, communities, and ecosystems (to use Sagoff's examples) can piggyback on the well-being interests (the rights) of individual organisms, in that the latter depend at least in part on the former. Still, the direction of ethical dependency here (wholes on parts) runs in the opposite direction to biological dependency (parts on wholes), and this leaves room for ethical concern to be dropped when the ties of biological dependency are weak. It is possible to subscribe to the piggyback idea, for example, and still to countenance the deaths of a great many members of a given species on the grounds that the individuals left alive are surrounded by enough of their number to ensure the substantive exercise of their 'rights' as individuals.

The importance of Ted Benton's contribution to this aspect of the debate needs to be recognized. Benton's concern about the rights discourse is not so much directed at whether the discourse is appropriate for the kinds of natural 'objects' with which environmentalists are normally concerned, but at their political usefulness. Socialist critiques of a liberal understanding of rights point to the distinction between the formal possession of rights and the substantive enjoyment of them. It is, in other words, one thing to possess a right and another to be able to exercise it, and the gap between the latter and the former can only be bridged by supplying the (often material) conditions necessary for the potential to become actual. Benton puts it like this:

the most influential statements of moral concern for non-human animals have (often for strong reasons) adopted established and widely-held moral theories—utilitarianism and liberal-rights theory especially—and then gone on to show how such theories cannot be consistently confined within the species boundary. This is a good *ad hominem* strategy if it can be assumed that the opponents of the 'extended circle' are already persuaded by the established moral theories in their paradigm application to the human case. (Benton 1993: 2)

The problem with the application of the rights discourse even in the human case, though, is that rights are, 'merely formal, and so [i.e.

therefore] ineffective in the protection of individuals, as long as the profound social and economic inequalities of capitalist societies persist' (Benton 1993: 120). Of course, those who accept Benton's point but still want to hold on to rights as a lever for change will respond by saying that the list of rights should be extended to include the social and economic rights necessary for the substantive enjoyment of political rights. Benton anticipates this response: 'I have . . . suggested that the liberal-individualist discourse of rights has responded to these criticisms by moving towards a positive rather than a negative conceptualization of rights and by adding social, economic and cultural rights to the early modern list of rights of "man and citizen".' But, he goes on, 'in the absence of profound alterations in social and economic relations, these advances in the discourse of rights serve only to render more evident the gap between aspiration and reality' (Benton 1993: 121). The discourse of rights, then, will always come up against the practice of exploitation: 'rights are unlikely to be effective in practice unless those who have the power to abuse them are already benevolently disposed to their bearers . . . Where humans gain their livelihood from a practice which presupposes a "reification" of animals, or gain pleasure from sports which involve systematic animal suffering, it seems unlikely that a rational argument that this treatment is unjust to the animals concerned would be sufficient to make the humans concerned change their ways' (Benton 1993: 94). The crucial thing, he concludes, is to take into account 'the socio-economic and cultural positions and formations of the human agents concerned' (Benton 1993: 94).

In this way, Benton builds up a socialist critique of animal rights theory and an ecological critique of socialist theory. The first 'highlights the social-relational preconditions that enable individuals (whether human or animal) to acquire and sustain those attributes and abilities in virtue of which they are held to have inherent value' (Benton 1993: 172), while the second 'exposes an important limitation in the socialist-radical critique of rights: its focus on social-relational conditions . . . at the expense of more broadly ecological ones . . . [because] if habitat protection is demonstrably necessary to any strategy for preserving the well-being of non-human animals, why should this not follow in the human case?' (Benton 1993: 173–4).

From this latter point of view, Benton might say that Juergen Habermas's notion that 'the integrity of individuals cannot be preserved without the integrity of the lifeworld that makes possible their shared interpersonal relationships and relations of mutual recognition' (Habermas 1993: 98) is too restricted in its stress on the human and social intersubjectivity of the lifeworld. This 'lifeworld' (Lebenswelt) should surely include the non-human natural world, and the importance of this to us is heightened when we see that Habermas makes these remarks in the context of a critique of Rawls. How, asks Habermas, 'can Rawls motivate his audience to place themselves in the original position at all', given that, 'from the point of view of those involved, the fictive agreement in the original position lacks any moment of insight that would point beyond the calculation of their own interests'? (Habermas 1993: 91).

Habermas says that there is no answer to this in unmodified versions of Rawls's original position, and that the only way to solve the 'motivation problem' is to recognize a pre-existing disposition to justice in people. This disposition, says Habermas, is grounded in 'solidarity', in that 'Justice conceived deontologically requires solidarity as its reverse side' (Habermas 1993: 98), and this solidarity, in turn, is grounded in an ontology of socialization: 'persons . . . can be individuated only via the route of socialization. They are formed as individuals only by growing into a speech community and thus into an intersubjectively shared lifeworld' (Habermas 1993: 97). In other words, a lifeworld is the condition for justice itself since without it there would be no motivation for justice—or no 'solidarity', which is the precondition for justice. If we now think of the notion of the lifeworld in the context of the non-human natural world, we can see both that 'solidarity' must now include solidarity towards at least those aspects of the non-human world that contribute to our individuation, and that a sustained and sustainable non-human natural world is a precondition even for Habermas's intersubjective (human) speech community.

Of course, the non-human natural world cannot be mapped directly onto Habermas's notion of the lifeworld because the former both contains, and goes beyond, the 'speech community' that Habermas regards as constitutive of the lifeworld. Nevertheless, the 'individuation' of which Habermas speaks surely has to be regarded as taking place in a lifeworld that contains all of life, and that which sustains it, rather than just the part capable of speech. In this way, an application of the second arm of Ted Benton's critique (that which takes the social-relational position to task for paying too little mind to the ecological preconditions for the exercise of rights) reveals limitations in Habermas's own critique of Rawls. From a Bentonian point of view, all the signs point to the need to include (aspects of ) the non-human natural world in theories of justice, both as an object of justice and as a precondition for justice itself.

In our context, Benton's general idea is extremely important. It may not be enough for those who understand environmental sustainability in terms of the sustaining of irreversible nature to try to protect it by working it into the traditional rights discourse. Species are eradicated with particular rapidity in the species-dense regions of the tropical rainforests, and while we know that this happens for a number of reasons, not all of them connected with issues of justice, it is certainly true that some clear-felling is carried out by landless peasants, forced by the landholding regimes of extensive cattle agriculture to eke out a precarious existence on ecologically sensitive land. In this kind of case, where ecological degradation (the loss of irreversible nature) is systematically bound up with economic exploitation, the employment of the liberal rights discourse on behalf of *either* the human or non-human species involved is likely to fall short of the mark.

Some will say, though, that the detail of Benton's argument is not so appropriate for arguments for sustainability. Robyn Eckersley points out, for example, that 'Benton's discussion of animal welfare is essentially confined to the individual welfare of those animals that are brought directly within human social and economic relations' (Eckersley 1994: 168). Neither of the conceptions of sustainability with which we have been concerned so far has focused on individuals: Conception A dealt with 'critical natural capital', which we understood as the life-sustaining aspects and processes of the non-human natural world, and Conception B is about irreversible nature, whose archetypes are species. How can a concern for 'the individual welfare of those animals that are brought directly within human social and economic relations' generate the protection of the kinds of nature with which these two conceptions of environmental sustainability are concerned?

Benton's answer might begin with a remark Eckersley herself makes, where she points out that the similarity between socialist and ecological critiques of animal rights theory (pre-Benton) is that they both focus on 'the *contextual conditions* which may impede or promote individual or collective well being' (Eckersley 1994: 168; emphasis in the original). To the extent, then, that the individual welfare of animals depends on the 'contextual condition' of critical natural capital (Conception A) and/or irreversible nature (Conception B), arguments for their sustaining can be generated from a Bentonian concern for individual animals. This is certainly true of human beings, says Benton:

The human/animal comparison, then, draws our attention to the extent to which humans, as living organisms, depend for their organic well-being on their (socially mediated) relation to their ecological conditions of life. If such basic requirements can ground rights, at least in the human case, then we are led to postulate appropriate environmental conditions for organic well-being as itself a right which ought to be acknowledged alongside, and presupposed by the rights to freedom of worship, of speech and so on. (Benton 1993: 175)

Given Benton's naturalism, referred to above, it seems fair to assume that the right to the 'environmental conditions for organic well-being' is due to relevant animals as well, in which case some aspects, at least, of the kind of nature which is of interest to proponents of Conceptions A and B can be granted protection on the grounds of concern for individual animals.

But, Eckersley might respond, Benton's focus on 'animals that are brought *directly within human social and economic relations*' (my emphasis) will be too restrictive for the taste of most environmentalists, (*a*) because it invites concern for too limited a range of animals, and (*b*) because this limitation results in another one: a limitation on the 'environmental conditions' with which we are entitled to be concerned—only those that affect the 'animals that are brought directly within human social and economic relations'. The proof of this, says Eckersley, is that, 'although he [Benton] occasionally discusses habitat protection, he pays scant attention to the general problem of the erosion of biodiversity' (Eckersley 1994: 168). Put differently, Eckersley might say that the only biodiversity with which Benton can consistently be concerned is that which provides the environmental conditions for the organic well-being of animals that are brought directly within human and social economic relations. If these glosses on Benton and Eckersley are correct, the stage is now obviously set for an exchange regarding the range of animals that are implicated in the production and reproduction of human life. It would, though, be inappropriate to develop an imaginary account of that exchange here; suffice to say that it would amount to yet another contribution to the contested issue that has animated much of the discussion in this chapter so far—the extent of the community of justice.

Alert readers will have noted that there has been something of a slippage during this discussion, from 'social justice' to 'justice as such'. If justice as such is concerned with 'giving each their due', then we can see that social justice is a particular sort of justice in that it is about giving a particular sort (or sorts) of due—it is not concerned, for example, with giving offenders their due punishment. The point of this distinction here is that the communities of justice as such and social justice may not be the same, in that the internal meaning of the terms may include (or preclude) particular memberships. We would not normally, for example, include animals in the community of legal justice since we do not believe that they have the kind of responsibility for action assumed by such justice (but see Evans 1987). So what about distributive justice, properly speaking? Is there anything about distributive justice that makes it inapplicable to the non-human natural world? Marcel Wissenburg has subjected this question to illuminating analysis, and he concludes that 'It all depends on whether we are dealing with rational, with sentient, or with living and inorganic nature, and on the different roles that nature can play in the distributive justice language game: those of distributor, distributed good, and recipient of whatever is distributed . . . I shall argue that there are sound reasons for treating different types of nature differently' (Wissenburg 1993: 6).

As suggested in the previous quotation, Wissenburg goes on to distinguish three types of nature: 'rational, sentient, and living or

inorganic nature' (Wissenburg 1993: 6), and he points out that while
only 'mankind' can distribute benefits and burdens, other parts of
nature might be regarded as legitimate recipients of such benefits
and burdens (this distinction is represented in the bifurcated an
swers to the 'What is the community?' question in Table 5). Assuming that human beings are themselves legitimate recipients in the
game of distributive justice, Wissenburg says that 'The idea of distributive (in)justice towards the rest of nature—which we, in so far
as we are Greens, intuitively feel to exist—apparently cannot be
built into a green political theory unless we find . . . characteristics
of man which make humans morally relevant, which they share
with other beings, and which can thus make these other beings
morally relevant as well' (Wissenburg 1993: 10).

Sentience is an obvious place to start, but it will not do on its own,
says Wissenburg, because it does not take the differences between
human beings and other sentient animals seriously enough—a
careless application of sentience in its utilitarian guise might lead
us, for example, to underwrite 'the sacrifice of some humans for
the temporary (and soon forgotten) happiness of some animals,
or the extinction of humanity for the future happiness of all
other animals' (Wissenburg 1993: 10). So Wissenburg suggests a
compromise in which 'The conscious experience of pleasure or
pain . . . [is] . . . seen as a (one) necessary element in every rational
plan of life, an element that is not the whole story of man's moral
importance. The rest of the story—morality, rationality, the content
of plans for life—still makes us humans, to an as yet undefined
degree, more important than animals' (Wissenburg 1993: 11). The
community of legitimate recipients of distributive justice is then
defined as containing those beings which can 'consciously'
(Wissenburg 1993: 12) receive benefits and burdens (I take this to
mean that they are capable of consciousness, not that they are
conscious of notions such as 'recipience', or 'benefits', or 'burdens').
By these lights, plants cannot be recipients of distributive justice
since, while they share life with human and other sentient beings,
'Life is a necessary but not a sufficient condition for being a
moral subject or for deserving moral treatment as a subject'
(Wissenburg 1993: 12). Wissenburg concludes that, 'plants and
organic nature cannot play any part in theories of distributive justice

other than as resources' (Wissenburg 1993: 12), where 'resources' are understood as a generic answer to the question 'What is distributed?' in Table 5.

What are we to make of Wissenburg's analysis in our context? First, he clearly believes that the language of distributive justice is applicable to parts of the non-human natural world. Second, though, this language may not be applicable to the feature of the non-human natural world that is important to our present 'irreversibility' conception of environmental sustainability. This is because Wissenburg's conception of justice seems to be paradigmatically concerned with relationships between individuals, while irreversible nature is most often conceived of in terms of collections of individuals. It may not be stretching Wissenburg too far on the rack, though, to suggest that if he is happy with the idea of distributive justice between social classes or nation-states, then he may also be able to entertain the idea of justice between species.

Third, Wissenburg's analysis makes crystal clear a point where arguments for sustainability seem necessarily to clash with the demands of distributive justice, and this is the point at which the *recipients* of justice potentially become *resources* for distribution. Let us assume, with Wissenburg, that at least some sentient non-humans can be regarded as belonging to the community of justice. It is also clear that, as things stand at present, these sentient non-humans may be used as resources by humans for labour or food. Can we make sense of the idea of sentients as simultaneously recipients of, and resources for, justice? The apparent difficulty emerges if we think of this in terms of human beings: surely part of what doing justice to human beings is about is not regarding them as resources?

But, of course, human beings *are* used as resources—not for food, perhaps, but certainly for labour. Doing justice to them in this context consists in recompensing them for their labour. Arguments of justice here turn not on whether human beings should labour at all, but how much they should be paid for it. The point is to remember Kant's dictum that human beings be treated as ends in themselves and not as means only. So if justice is about giving members of the community of justice their due, we may appropriately square the idea of non-human sentients as simultaneously recipients and resources by giving them their due according to their species life. This naturally invites debate about the *extent* to which non-human sentients may be regarded as resources, and to what ends. Meat-eaters, vegetarians, and vegans will each have different views on this, but the point here is that each of these views can properly be interpreted in terms of distributive justice.

Even the more specific language of distributive justice (more specific, that is, than the language of justice in general), then, seems applicable to a community of justice wider then the human community. The problem of applicability in our context therefore seems not to derive from the specificity of the language of justice, but from the specificity of the language of this conception of sustainability. Remember that the guiding principle here is the sustaining of irreversible nature, so our question must be whether this objective can be defended in terms of distributive justice. An answer to this question will turn on whether irreversible nature is the kind of thing of which justice can be predicated, and the only way to answer *this* question is to consider examples of irreversible nature. Is the anthropogenic elimination of (some) species a prima facie act of distributive injustice? I think that it is, on the grounds that (some) species can be properly regarded as recipients of justice in terms of the provision and maintenance of their conditions for/of life. Is the consumption of oil (which can only be renewed over millions of years and can therefore to all intents and purposes be regarded as irreversible nature) an act of distributive injustice (to oil)? I think not, on the grounds that oil is not the kind of thing of which justice can be predicated.

In sum, Wissenburg has it practically right. He begins his analysis with the question, 'Given a necessary course of action directed towards the environmental crisis, can we defend it in terms of distributive justice?' (Wissenburg 1993: 3), and his answer is a 'qualified "yes"' (Wissenburg 1993: 6). Wissenburg's 'yes' is qualified (as we saw above) by his differentiation between various parts of the non-human natural world. I concur with this, but would add the significant rider that we need to qualify our 'yes' not only in terms of the community of recipients (the first question of Table 5), but also in terms of the basic structure of theories of justice (the second question). Some theories seem better able to cope with the idea of a 'necessary course of action' than others, and it is to this large question that I now turn.

## The Basic Structure

I closed Chapter 5 with some remarks on basic structure, and it will help to recall them here. I suggested that of all the 'live' basic structure options outlined in Table 5, the one that seemed most incompatible with the 'critical natural capital' conception of environmental sustainability was that which combined impartiality, proceduralism, and universality. This was fundamentally because a procedural theory of justice cannot guarantee any outcomes—and certainly not the outcome of the preservation of critical natural capital.

I then pointed out that substantive theories of justice might also be a problem—if the theory of the good life to which they cleave involves the destruction rather than the sustaining of critical natural capital. This, though, can work both ways, since the substantive theory of the good in question might involve, precisely, the maintenance of critical natural capital through renewing, substituting for, and protecting it. If one could guarantee the 'right' kind of substantive theory of the good, then, the substantive/consequentialist/universal combination might be the most appropriate one for the conception of environmental sustainability with which we dealt in the last chapter.

The stakes of this debate are rather higher for our present conception (B) of environmental sustainability because here our reasons for sustaining irreversible nature can be regarded as reasons of justice to (some parts of) nature. There is, then, a more direct relationship between the basic structure of theories of justice and the objective of Conception B than in the case of Conception A, where reasons for maintaining critical natural capital were prudential rather than justice-based (as far as the natural world is concerned).

We need, of course, to distinguish between two types of consequence; first, the actual outcome of decisions, and second, the way in which decisions may (or may not) contribute to the realizing of a particular view of the good for human beings. The first meaning is captured by 'proceduralism/consequentialism' in Table 5, and the second by 'impartiality/substantiveness'. Both are contained in the following quotation from Rawls, where he notes that:

utilitarianism is a teleological theory whereas justice as fairness is not. By definition, then, the latter is a deontological theory, one that either does not specify the good independently from the right, or does not interpret the right as maximising the good. (It should be noted that deontological theories are defined as non-teleological ones, not as views that characterize the rightness of institutions and acts independently from their consequences. All ethical doctrines worth our attention take consequences into account in judging rightness. One which did not would simply be irrational, crazy). (Rawls 1973: 30)

Rawls here autodefines his theory as impartial ('non-teleological') and consequentialist—although as I pointed out in Chapter 3 this is not to say that Rawls believes that *only* consequences matter. And while we are in definitional mode, Rawls helps us with what 'the good' might mean: 'a conception of the good normally consists of a more or less determinate scheme of final ends, that is, ends that we want to realise for their own sake' (Rawls 1993: 19). Without stretching the point, the objective of our present conception (B) of environmental sustainability—the sustaining of irreversible nature—looks to be a conception of the good (or at least a part of one), in a way that the objective of Conception A—the sustaining of critical natural capital as a means to satisfying human welfare—is not. This, again, is one of the reasons why the issue of the basic structure of theories of social justice is so important to us here.

If, as I suggested above, the impartial/procedural/universal combination looked inappropriate for Conception A, then it looks likely to be even more inappropriate for Conception B given the substantive conception of the good present in it. This hypothesis can only be tested, though, against a theory of justice that can justifiably be regarded as uniting these three terms. Rawls's theory, which we might have regarded as a candidate, is ruled out by Rawls himself (among others), as we saw above. The latest volume in

Brian Barry's developing treatise on distributive justice has a title, though, that points us in the right direction: *Justice as Impartiality* (Barry 1995*a*). Barry's justice as impartiality looks more procedural than the Rawlsian picture on which it is based (but which it goes beyond):

[There] are cases where the theory of justice as impartiality reaches de-finite conclusions about what justice requires. But as far as the great bulk of contemporary legislation and policy-making is concerned, justice as impar-tiality will have things to say about *how* the legislation or policy can be framed consistently with the demands of justice, but it is silent on *what* the content of the legislation or policy should be. (Barry 1995*a*: 143)

Barry underlines this conclusion by comparing justice as impartial-ity with utilitarianism:

Utilitarianism has a criterion that is (in principle, anyway) able to give an answer to every question about what is the right public policy. Justice as impartiality can in many cases do no more than set the outer limits of what is acceptable, and in other cases all it can do is specify that the decision must be made by a fair procedure. (Barry 1995*a*: 144)

Barry's 'impartiality' is clearly on a par with Rawls's 'deontology'— that is, both theorists regard substantive theories of the good as incompatible with defensible theories of justice. But Barry appears willing to endorse heavier doses of proceduralism than Rawls, so it seems reasonable from the point of view of testing the hypothesis I outlined above (that the impartial/procedural/universal combina-tion looks particularly inappropriate for Conception B) to look at Barry's theory in some detail. This decision seems even more sens-ible when we see that Barry provides us with a decision-making example (whether or not to build a dam) that contains a number of the elements that interest us here.

'Let us . . . suppose', says Barry, 'that the issue before the polity is whether or not to build a dam that would, if built, destroy the habitat of an endangered species of fish—for convenient reference, call it the snail-darter' (Barry 1995*a*: 145). This is an example that squares well with our present concerns in that the construction of the dam in question would threaten the survival of a feature of 'irreversible nature'—the snail-darter. Proponents of Conception B of environmental sustainability, then, will want the snail-darter preserved and, according to the hierarchy of priorities outlined in Box 11 of Table 2, the only thing that could prima facie override the snail-darter's preservation would be the satisfaction of present generation human need. How will justice as impartiality cope with this?

Right at the outset, Barry says that we should reckon that it has been 'determined that building or not building the dam is the kind of issue that is not settled by the criteria of justice as impartiality' (Barry 1995a: 149). But a decision still has to be made, and the question is what role the various competing conceptions of the good should play in the decision. So, 'Suppose you have an ecocentric conception of the good', continues Barry, 'and on the basis of this you vote against construction of the dam. Now let us assume that when the votes are tallied it turns out that there is a majority in favour of building the dam. How should you react to this?' (Barry 1995a: 149).

Barry's answer is that if 'you endorse the theory of justice as impartiality . . . [you must] . . . accept that the right thing is for the dam to be built' (Barry 1995a: 149), and this is because if 'justice as impartiality endorses this procedure [i.e. majority voting in a refer-endum], then it also indirectly endorses the outcome as just' (Barry 1995a: 151). Of course, 'If the referendum had gone the other way . . . then it would have concluded that the opposite outcome was just' (Barry 1995a: 151). Importantly, says Barry, none of this obliges you to change your view of the good: 'Unless you change your mind about the ecological ethic or its implications for the case in hand, you must continue to regret the way the wrong decision was made . . . The outcome is, as far as you are concerned, legitimate but bad—bad in the precise sense that it offends against your conception of the good' (Barry 1995a: 150).

The question for the 'irreversibility' conception of environmental sustainability, then, is whether it can support an endorsement of justice as impartiality, and the answer would seem to be no. The protection, maintenance, and/or sustaining of irreversible nature is the *raison d'être* of this conception, and to the extent that this forms part of a conception of the good, impartiality between conceptions of the good is alien to it. By the same token, proponents of the 'irreversibility' conception will be wary of a theory of justice that sets such store by procedures when they might lead to consequences that undermine the very core of the conception itself.

On the other hand, theories of the good are not proscribed by justice as impartiality—it is simply that justice should not be seen as being in the service of this or that theory of the good. Barry might ask ecocentrics just how they propose to choose between the policies associated with competing conceptions of the good. In ceding to democratic procedures, Barry allows conceptions of the good their legitimate voice, but arrives at decisions in a way that does not (obviously) depend on coercion or violence, and which respects what he sees as a 'fatal objection' to the idea of a duty to pursue the good—an objection which consists in 'the existence of an unresolvable dispute about what the good consists in' (Barry 1995a: 12). Barry expands on this last idea in a personal vein:

I am myself quite strongly attracted to an ecocentric ethic and would favour sacrificing a good deal of human want-satisfaction (especially if the sacrifice were equitably distributed) in pursuit of the ecological conception of the good. I think that arguments can be made for it by showing as vividly as possible the implications of following it or not and by appealing to a kind of sentiment that is ultimately, I believe, of the same nature as that which supports many religions. But I do not see how its claims can be presented in such a way as to show that it would be unreasonable to adopt a different view, and I take it that any other conception of the good is subject to the same liability. (Barry 1995a: 171)

Ecocentrics may reply to this on three levels, corresponding first and second to the procedural/consequentialist and impartial/substantive dimensions of the basic structure of theories of justice, and finally to the way in which they will want the debate over justice to develop—a form of debate which appears disabled by the ground rules of justice as impartiality. First, then, they will say that procedures cannot be allowed to hold sway to the point where they produce manifest injustices. Aside from the question of whether ecocentrism is a theory of the good or not, the destruction of one of the last habitats of an endangered species of fish will look like an injustice to ecocentrics, however the decision to build the dam is arrived at. Second, in the impartial/substantive context, ecocentrics will say that ecocentrism *is* a theory of the good, and that justice should serve its ends. Moreover (and this is the third point), they will seek to generate a debate which takes place at the level of theories of the good and not at the level of the expression of preferences, which is where the proceduralism of referenda inclines us.

This surely is the point behind Alasdair MacIntyre's assessment of the 'liberal order' as disabling (for 'liberal order' read 'justice as impartiality', although I shall make reference to Barry's own assessment of himself and his theory as liberal below—Barry 1996: 341–2):

a liberal order [writes MacIntyre] . . . is one in which each standpoint [on the human good] may make its claims but can do no more within the framework of the public order, since no overall theory of the human good is to be regarded as justified. Hence at this level debate is necessarily barren: rival appeals to accounts of the human good or of justice necessarily assume a rhetorical form such that it is as assertion and counterassertion, rather than as argument and counterargument, that rival standpoints confront one another. (MacIntyre 1988: 343)

The first part of this quotation, in which MacIntyre suggests that a liberal order 'is one in which each standpoint [on the human good] may make its claims but can do no more within the framework of the public order, since no overall theory of the human good is to be regarded as justified', seems a fair paraphrase of what Barry sees as happening in his example of how the decision to build the dam or not is taken in the context of justice as impartiality. The question is why MacIntyre should claim that debate of this sort is barren, at least as far as rival conceptions of the good are concerned, and whether he is right to make such a claim.

At least part of the answer seems to be that the systematic subordination of debates regarding the human good to the dictates of procedure desensitizes citizens to arguments regarding the human good, and dehabituates them to arguing in the mode and language which they demand. One might even suggest that a belief in 'the existence of an unresolvable dispute about what the good consists in' is a kind of self-fulfilling prophecy: such rigorous cleaving to the rules of justice as impartiality, on the grounds of certainty that such disputes are unresolvable, discourages any practice at resolving

them. On this reading, the failure to arrive at substantive conclusions regarding the good for humans is not so much because it is
impossible to do so, but because liberal impartiality will not allow us
to try. MacIntyre puts it like this:

What has become clear . . . is that gradually less and less importance has
been attached to arriving at substantive conclusions and more and more to
continuing the debate for its own sake. For the nature of the debate itself
and not of its outcome provides underpinning in a variety of ways for the
fourth level at which appeals to justice may be heard in a liberal individu-
alist order, that of the rules and procedures of the formal legal system. The
function of that system is to enforce an order in which conflict resolution
takes place without invoking any overall theory of the human good.
(MacIntyre 1988: 344)

MacIntyre's critique of both proceduralism and impartiality in this
passage is bound up with his belief—shared by others such as
Michael Sandel and Charles Taylor—that liberal impartiality
produces, and is produced by, a particular sort of individual. This
individual inhabits and propagates a disenchanted universe, devoid
of meaning and lacking an objective moral order. Sandel puts it like
this:

Bound up with the notion of an independent self is a vision of the moral
universe this self must inhabit. Unlike classical Greek and medieval
Christian conceptions, the universe of the deontological ethic is a place
devoid of inherent meaning, a world 'disenchanted' in Max Weber's
phrase, a world without an objective moral order. Only in a universe
empty of telos, such as seventeenth-century science and philosophy
affirmed, is it possible to conceive a subject apart from and prior to its
purposes and ends. Only a world ungoverned by a purposive order leaves
principles of justice open to human construction and conceptions of the
good to individual choice. In this the depth of opposition between
deontological liberalism and teleological world views most fully appears.
(Sandel 1984b: 168)

Ecocentric thinking is not teleological but it certainly dabbles in
'enchantedness', and its belief in thoroughgoing interconnectedness
stands in some tension with the idea of an independent self. But
Sandel's important point is that this independent self brings a moral
universe with it, and ecocentrics will be concerned about this moral

universe not because it does not contain ecocentrism (because it does), but because it delegitimizes any debate regarding the good for humans, believing resolution of such debate to be impossible. In this universe ecocentrics will encounter people who believe them to be 'mad', according to John Rawls at least: 'Human good is heterogeneous because the aims of the self are heterogeneous. Although to subordinate all our aims to one end does not strictly speaking violate the principles of rational choice . . . it still strikes us as irrational, or more likely as mad. The self is disfigured and put in the service of one of its ends for the sake of the system' (Rawls 1973: 554). Coincidentally, at the time of writing these words, Britain's *Guardian International* newspaper (24 Feb. 1997: 4) revealed the national popularity of 'Swampy', a roads protester in Britain who has become famous for his tunnelling exploits during attempts to stop road construction. It is hard to think of Swampy as doing anything other than 'subordinating all his aims to one end', and even in terms of the 'fanaticism' to which Rawls refers in the sentence immediately preceding the passage quoted above. Whether this makes Swampy an 'irrational', 'mad', or 'disfigured' individual is worth more than a moment's contemplation, but the important thing here is to see Sandel's and MacIntyre's point that liberal impartiality's moral universe will foster the view that his (Swampy's) behaviour is pathological rather then sensible. 'To be educated into the culture of a liberal social order', writes MacIntyre, 'is . . . characteristically to become the kind of person to whom it appears normal that a variety of goods should be pursued, each appropriate to its own sphere, with no overall good supplying any overall unity to life' (MacIntyre 1988: 337). To the extent that this liberal social order disables ecocentrism, the latter will be at odds with the former. And to the extent that, in the context of social justice, this order is founded on impartiality between notions of the good and favours procedures over consequences, the 'irreversibility' conception of environmental sustainability will sit uncomfortably with a basic structure involving impartiality and proceduralism. My conclusion as far as justice is concerned, then, is that this conception of environmental sustainability is most compatible with theories of justice that are substantive, consequentialist, and universal.

From a liberal point of view this plumping for substantiveness is bound to be controversial. It amounts to coming down very firmly on one side of the fence in the context of what Charles Taylor has called 'the first major meta-ethical issue, whether ethical theories should be procedural or substantive' (Taylor here uses 'procedural' where I have been employing the word 'impartial'; Taylor 1994: 27). Brian Barry's view is that 'no conception of the good can justifiably be held with a degree of certainty that warrants its imposition on those who reject it' (Barry 1995a: 169), but there may be an intermediate position—that some versions of the good life are *ruled out* by what Barry himself refers to (as we saw) as the 'implications of following it [an ecocentric ethic] or not' (Barry 1995a: 171). This possibility is captured by Benton:

to think through the implications of human 'embodiment' or 'embeddedness' is to reduce the range of defensible visions of the good life in ways which may begin to offer the possibility of an ordered but still plural social life beyond the material unsustainabilities and social oppressions of the present. (Benton 1993: 104)

At the very least, then, ecocentrism's wish will be to expose the impossibility and undesirability of living cornucopian versions of the good life, but it will only be able to do so in the context of a moral universe which endorses debates of this sort, and encourages them to flourish. It will not be enough to point, with Barry, to the mere existence of these debates in the universe of liberal impartiality, for there they are devalued and unpractised.

The implications for justice of the endorsement of substantiveness are considerable, since justice and the good are now linked in precisely the kind of way that impartial theories of justice believe to be impermissible. 'What is the good human life?', asks Taylor, and he continues: 'This question . . . is part of the background of a conception of distributive justice. Differences about justice are related to differences about the nature of the good' (Taylor 1986: 36). For example, 'The Aristotelian metaview . . . is that principles of distributive justice are related to some notion of the good which is sustained or realized or sought in the association concerned' (Taylor 1986: 37). So once we endorse substantiveness we also seem to endorse the idea that principles of justice are at the service of—or at least connected to—the substantive view of the good in question. Barry puts the point most clearly:

utilitarianism and Thomism differ substantively at almost every point [but] they agree that justice and morality are cut from the same cloth . . . In both cases we start with a conception of the good that is to be achieved, as far as possible. We then assess potential rules of justice by their conduciveness to the achievement of that good. Principles of justice have a purely derivative status. (Barry 1995a: 76)

In our present context, the conception of the good involves (among other related things) the sustaining of irreversible nature as an end in itself. The proceduralism and impartiality involved in Barry's theory of justice entail both the lack of a guarantee that policies will lead to this end, and a moral universe in which 'ends in themselves' are looked upon, with one or two exceptions, with suspicion. Everything points, then, to consequentialism and substantiveness as being most compatible with the 'irreversibility' conception of environmental sustainability.

The stakes for ecocentrics of the choice between substantiveness and impartiality are high in another sense too. In the context of impartiality there is always the chance that the ecocentric view will emerge victorious: that the dam will not be built or that the wetland will be preserved. But what if ecocentrics find themselves inhabiting a world in which cornucopian conceptions of the good are not only dominant but systematically imposed? The reverse side of the coin of the fanaticism about which Rawls is concerned is that one might be on the receiving end of it, and in our context this would mean the thoughtless and thoroughgoing destruction of irreversible nature— the willing, even wilful, eradication of species, and the deployment of principles of justice designed to achieve maximum benefits for the present human generation. Arguably it is precisely our living in conditions of liberal plurality that permits us the luxury of endorsing a universe in which substantiveness takes precedence over impartiality.

Finally, it may be that the impulses which inform ecocentrism come from too far back to be able to have any purchase on the modern world. In the context of comments on MacIntyre, David Miller writes that 'MacIntyre's thesis . . . cannot help us in our search for a conception of justice to guide the development of modern societies', because 'the Thomist view presupposes an ordered community within which people occupy well-defined positions whose respective contributions to the common good can be meaningfully compared' (Miller 1994: 261–2). Ecocentrism's cleaving to what sometimes looks like a conception of the good based on a re-enchantment of the natural world is susceptible to similar criticism, although MacIntyre himself resists the idea of the total irrecoverability of older forms of thought:

This does not mean that . . . one cannot be a Humean outside the specific hierarchically ordered relationships of eighteenth century England . . . What it does mean is that . . . only insofar as those features of the social order in terms of which Hume framed his accounts of justice and of action can be reproduced that one can actually *be* a Humean. (MacIntyre 1988: 391)

Part of ecocentrism's task, then, may be to identify those features of the social order necessary for its conception of the good to be viable—and one of those features, precisely, may be a moral universe in which arguments over conceptions of the good are fostered. Once more, ecocentric substantiveness seems at odds with liberal impartiality.

   All of this raises another larger and important question, at which I can only gesture here. The question is whether procedural theories of politics, more widely, are compatible with the objectives of environmental sustainability (or at least with this present conception of it). An obvious way of rephrasing this question is to ask whether liberalism—and not just liberal theories of justice—is compatible with sustainability. Mark Sagoff puts the dilemma in a nutshell:

Liberals strive to prevent 'moral' majorities from imposing ethical views and religious beliefs on minorities, for example, with respect to abortion, homosexuality, and school prayer. Environmentalists, however, may be said to constitute a moral lobby, if not a moral majority, of a sort, insofar as they advocate laws that embody ethical and perhaps even religious ideals concerning the way we ought to treat our natural surroundings. If the laws and policies supported by the environmental lobby are not neutral

among ethical, aesthetic and religious ideals but express a moral conception of people's appropriate relation to nature, can environmentalists be
liberals? (Sagoff 1988: 150)

Not all the laws proposed by the environmental lobby are non-
neutral in respect of ethical ideals for nature, of course. We were
able to resist the idea during our discussion of Conception A of
environmental sustainability, for example, that the conception entailed a view of the good for human beings—in relation to the
natural world, at least. This was because arguments in favour of
sustaining natural capital were framed in terms of human welfare.
In Conception B, though, a particular ethical view regarding parts of
the natural world underpins the defence of irreversible nature, and
to this extent we are in the presence of a form of sustainability that
is not 'neutral among ethical, aesthetic and religious ideals'. Is, then,
Conception B of environmental sustainability compatible with
liberalism?

Sagoff's own answer to the question is rather gnomic. He says
that liberals are not prevented 'from endorsing even those environmental policies that are based on particular ethical, cultural, or
aesthetic conviction', provided, first, 'These convictions [do not]
infringe on the right of every citizen to make his or her intimate
decisions', and second, that liberals remain neutral regarding
'institutional arrangements' (Sagoff 1988: 166). Quite what these
'intimate decisions' might be is not made clear, but to the distinction
Sagoff draws here between the right and good, Brian Barry
adds another: that between 'citizen' and 'exponent of justice as
impartiality' (Barry 1996: 341). As a citizen, Barry has views about
the right things to do, and these may be based on strong ethical
convictions. But the fact is, says Barry, that while 'justice as impartiality is compatible with the outcomes I favour . . . it is also compatible with their opposites' (Barry 1996: 341). Barry refuses to give
in to the temptation 'for anyone with strong views about public
policy to seek to circumvent first order debate about the pros and
cons' (Barry 1996: 341). The centrality of a view of the good to
our present conception of environmental sustainability renders it
incapable of juggling citizenship and impartiality successfully,
and it is this that, in the end, looks likely to underpin continuing

tensions between liberalism and (some forms of) environmental sustainability.

## Conclusion

The distinguishing features of Conception B of environmental sustainability are its focus on the sustaining of 'irreversible nature', and the concomitant belief that substitutability between human-made capital and irreversible nature is not always possible. As far as distributive justice is concerned, and in terms of the vocabulary established in Chapter 3 and collected together in Table 5, the theories of justice most likely to be compatible with this conception of sustainability will be those which can entertain the idea of all human beings as (potential) dispensers of justice, and of the full range of groups from present generation human beings to future generation non-sentients as potential recipients. It is not impossible for theories which have an 'agent-affected' sense of the community of justice to be similarly compatible, but there would be something odd about tying the apparently universal injunction to sustain 'irreversible nature' too closely to the particularisms of agent-affectedness. The injunction is to sustain irreversible nature wherever it is found, and not just if it happens to be on the agent's doorstep. This is not a case of YIMBY (yes in my backyard), but of EOPE (everywhere on planet Earth). Another form of compatibility, of course, would be that where a particular regime of distributive justice could be shown to be functional for the sustaining of irreversible nature, and I shall say something more about this below.

It is also worth pointing out that, contrary to the way things might look at first sight, the injunction to sustain irreversible nature does not entail a necessary clash with human interests. In the first place, sustaining irreversible nature might well be in the interests of human beings, and, second, human beings (as a species) can themselves be regarded as an exemplar of irreversible nature. So the injunction to sustain irreversible nature is also an injunction to sustain the human species. This does not mean, of course, that there will never be clashes of interest between the interests of (some parts of) 'irreversible nature' and human beings, and I shall spend some time in the concluding chapter discussing the question of the compatibility of theories of justice *across* these three conceptions of sustainability (A, B, and C), as well as *within* them.

Perhaps the most signal shift of emphasis compared with Conception A, though, takes place in the 'basic structure' element of theories of justice. A glance at Table 5 will remind us that the basic structure contains three pairs of alternatives: impartial or substantive (in terms of a notion of the good for human beings), proceduralism or consequentialism (in terms of judging the justice of any distributive situation), and particularism or universalism (in terms of the prescriptive reach of a given theory of justice). As far as the first of these pairs is concerned, we remember John Rawls defining the good in the following way: 'a conception of the good normally consists of a more or less determinate scheme of final ends, that is, ends that we want to realise for their own sake' (Rawls 1993: 19). It is my view that Conception B's driving idea—that irreversible nature be sustained—can comfortably be read in terms of a conception of the good (or at least a part of one) as Rawls defines it. That is to say that this conception of environmental sustainability has a notion of the good for humans at its very heart. The principal implication of this is that Conception B is likely to be incompatible with theories of justice that are driven by the desire to be impartial between theories of the human good. This is not to say that impartiality is *necessarily* inimical to Conception B, because it is obvious that, even under impartiality, decisions might be arrived at that contribute to the 'final end' of sustaining irreversible nature. However, those who conceive of the good for humans as being about—at least in part—the sustaining of irreversible nature will be concerned at the lack of guarantees regarding the realization of that good under a regime of impartiality. Perhaps more importantly, they will also be concerned that the assumption that agreement on the nature of the good for humans cannot be reached delegitimizes attempts to do so. At the very least, they will say, regimes of impartiality are unlikely to encourage the kind of language and habits of thought that first-order debate regarding the good for humans will probably involve.

We could jump from this to the conclusion that Conception B's apparent connection with theories of the good severs its relationship with justice since it is not so much concerned with the distribution of benefits and burdens as with the protection of something (irreversible nature) that cannot be properly described as either a benefit or a burden. The language of distributive justice looks inappropriate here. I would caution against such a conclusion at this stage, although things might look different at the end of the next chapter. First, as I discussed earlier, debates surrounding the sustaining of irreversible nature can be read as distributive debates: what is being distributed here is membership of the community of justice. Second, it is not that a theory headed up by a substantive notion of the good for humans has nothing to do with justice, but rather that justice occupies a quite particular place in such a theory. Justice, in such a theory, is at the service of the realization of the human good, and its content is to be understood in terms of the good for humans. The idea that the role of justice is to contribute to the realization of a particular end returns us to the point—flagged above—that the question of what kind of theory of justice might be compatible with the 'irreversibility' conception of environmental sustainability can only be answered in the light of practice. In this sense, compatibility would not, and could not, be determined in theoretical terms, but what we can say in advance of practice is that the regimes of justice that are compatible with Conception B will be those that contribute to the realization of B's overriding aim: the sustaining of irreversible nature.

As far as the other terms in the basic structure are concerned, consequentialism goes hand in hand with substantiveness in that proceduralism cannot provide the in-principle guarantees that the substantive end will be realized. Similarly, Conception B seems wedded to universalism as far as the prescriptive reach of theories of justice is concerned. So to the extent that we can link justice and sustainability in this context at all, the prescriptive injunction to sustain irreversible nature is a universal one. To liberals, this combination of substantiveness and universality will undoubtedly look explosive. Not only is impartiality eschewed, but it is replaced by the apparent will to export a particular view of the substantive good for humans all around the world. We have already noticed liberals' concern at the likelihood—in the Conception B context—of justice being put at the service of the good, and to this we must now add the possibility of export turning into imposition. Is there a way of realizing (most of) the goals of the 'irreversibility' conception without falling foul of the implications of its apparently substantive fundamentalism? I shall return to this question in the concluding chapter.

The two final rows in Table 5 now require concluding comment—'what is distributed?' and 'what is the principle of distribution?' As far as the first is concerned, the category in Table 5 that comes closest to Conception B's 'irreversible nature' is 'unproduced environmental goods'. However, unlike in Conception A, where it was reasonable to say that what was being sustained was also what was being distributed ('critical natural capital'), Conception B understands 'what is distributed' in terms of what is *functional for* what is being sustained ('irreversible nature'). In other words, this is a particular case of the rule we observed above: that where a substantive notion of the good is present, justice is put at its service. The same applies here in the specific context of what is to be distributed. This is to say that the first test of compatibility of this component of theories of justice with Conception B is whether the distribution of this or that good or bad, this or that produced or unproduced resource, has any bearing on securing the objective of sustaining irreversible nature. If, thereafter, it can be shown that the distribution of any particular good or bad contributes to securing that objective, then a prima facie compatibility is demonstrated (and vice versa, of course).

Conceiving 'what is to be distributed' in terms of a means to the end of sustaining irreversible nature seems to leave the question of compatibility pretty wide open—except in one exceptional case. The exceptional case is this: it is unlikely that the cause of sustaining irreversible nature will be served by thinking of what is to be sustained in terms also of something that is to be distributed. In other words, to apply the 'what is to be distributed' language of distributive justice (where the answer is 'unproduced environmental goods') may be inappropriate to Conception B in cases where unproduced environmental goods can be understood as referring to irreversible nature. This is because to view irreversible nature as something to be distributed, only, amounts to regarding it as a means to an end, only, and this is contrary to justice. The possible exception to this is the private ownership of environmental goods on the grounds that such ownership encourages good stewardship. The pros and cons of this argument were discussed at length in the previous chapter. Once more, all this appears to amount to evidence that (aspects of) the language of justice strain when placed in contact with certain conceptions of sustainability, and this in turn implies that the cause of this 'irreversibility' conception of sustainability may not be best served by employing the idiom of justice.

Having established that practically any answer to the question 'what is to be distributed?' is compatible with Conception B so long as it is functional for securing the ends of Conception B, the final issue to be resolved here is that of the appropriate principles of distribution (the bottom row in Table 5). This issue has two dimensions. First, there is the question of the appropriate principles of justice in respect of irreversible nature as an object of justice. Assuming we can think of irreversible nature in these terms (an issue I discussed at some length towards the beginning of this chapter), at least one of the principles in Table 5 is ruled out by definition: desert. It makes no sense to think of irreversible nature 'deserving' a particular distribution of benefits and burdens, as it can do none of the sorts of the things we would associate with calculating desert. Similarly, bearing in mind our remarks above concerning substantiveness and consequentialism, principles of justice associated with impartiality and proceduralism are least likely to be compatible with distributive justice for irreversible nature. So chance (obviously) and entitlement (in the Nozickean sense) are prima facie inappropriate because they pay insufficient mind to outcomes.

'Market value' seems at first to have little mileage in it, and this is because there is no market in (most aspects of) irreversible nature. But it may be worth recalling Michael 't Sas-Rolfes's argument, outlined in Chapter 5, that privatization of species might be a way of protecting them. The reason that this argument even begins to work is that there is potential profit to be made from species-protection—but it is equally obvious that if profits fall (or even decline to zero), the incentive to protect disappears (as 't Sas-Rolfes himself points out). Market enthusiasts might say, though, that as supply dwindles while demand remains buoyant, prices will rise, and it is this—precisely—that will ensure the continued protection of rare species. But of course demand is not buoyant for all species—only 'flagship' ones of the type sponsored by organizations such as the World Wide Fund for Nature. At this point we might draw the increasingly common distinction (in the context of environmental economics) between actual markets and 'shadow' markets. It is just possible that shadow market preferences would reveal a desire to protect forms of irreversible nature that are at present untraded and therefore unpriced. But—and this takes us back to point of departure—distribution of benefits and burdens based on market value is fundamentally a procedural form of distribution, and we have established (or at least argued) that there is a prima facie asymmetry between the substantive intentions of this conception of environmental sustainability and procedural forms of distributive justice. It has become increasingly popular to try to square the circle of substantiveness and proceduralism by pointing out the difference between 'revealed' and 'transformed' preferences, where the latter (developed in the light of circumstances akin to Habermas's 'ideal speech situation') are fed into the relevant procedure. Where these preferences have been 'appropriately' transformed, the 'right' outcomes will be, if not actually guaranteed, at least more likely. It is not hard to see how this line of reasoning might be applied to our market context. Contingent valuations arrived at according to unreconstructed preferences may well be different from those arrived at under 'ideal speech'-type conditions. But—and here is the rub—they may not be, and so the in-principle guarantees sought by supporters of Conception B that irreversible nature will be sustained cannot be produced from within the procedural framework.

Of the principles in Table 5 that remain—needs, equality, to the benefit of the least advantaged, utility, and 'it depends . . .'—utility has the advantage of being consequentialist, but there are too many indeterminacies in questions such as 'to the greatest benefit of whom/what?', and 'how is utility to be calculated?' to make it a front-running candidate. The circumstances under which 'equality' might be made to work are similarly difficult to pin down, since enunciation of this as a principle shakes down as a barrage of supplementary questions each of which has indeterminate answers. Equality is, though, in a family relationship with 'need', and this latter does seem to be a principle appropriate in the context of sustaining irreversible nature. Exactly what it is that irreversible nature 'needs' for its sustaining is a question to which I cannot give a determinate answer here, but we certainly can confirm that the question makes sense and, moreover, that this amounts to circumstantial evidence in support of the claim that the languages and intentions of justice and sustainability can be brought into fruitful contact. Similarly, Rawls's 'to the benefit of the least advantaged' may have some purchase here, if it can be established that irreversible nature can be thought of in this way. Marx's effective relativizing of the principles of distribution through linking them to different modes of production appears to undercut the universalism inherent in Conception B, although there is no doubt plenty of food for thought in the suggestion that some modes of production will be more likely to 'produce' the sustaining of irreversible nature than others. It is also worth remembering Marx's view that the distributive principle in communist society would be needs-based, and to the extent that this reveals Marx's preferred principle for distribution, his view squares with remarks made a few lines above. Finally, Walzer's 'it depends on the good in question' is incompatible with Conception B—at least where the 'good in question' is irreversible nature. This is because, as I pointed out above, to regard irreversible nature as a good for distribution, only, is to regard irreversible nature as a means, only, and this is contrary to justice.

So much for the first dimension to which I referred above, that where we are concerned with appropriate principles of justice in respect of irreversible nature as an object of justice. The second dimension has to do with the principles of justice that will be appropriate in the exclusive context of the relationship between human beings. At this point, the idea that justice (here) might be at the service of the good recurs. Conception B defines itself in terms of a very specific objective—that of sustaining irreversible nature. It is consistent with this self-definition that Conception B view other aspects of social life in the light of that objective—and distributive justice between human beings is no exception. This sidelines, once again, principles such as chance and entitlement which are not objective-driven, and principles such as needs and equality will only be helpful if it can be shown that meeting people's needs, or making them more materially equal in some sense, contributes to sustaining irreversible nature. As I have had cause to say on a number of occasions, these are largely empirical questions, and we do not have sufficient evidence at present in a sufficiently wide variety of contexts to be able to draw firm conclusions. All this throws into sharp relief the principle of desert. On the face of it, desert as a principle is tailor-made for an objective-driven conviction such as that represented by the 'irreversibility' conception of environmental sustainability. One is said to 'deserve' in respect of something one has done or achieved, and it is easy enough to see how rewards might be based on contributions to the goal of sustaining irreversible nature. I have already remarked how needs-meeting is the principle of distribution most often connected with environmental sustainability (or, at least, with sustainable development), but all this suggests that more attention should be paid to desert. No doubt sustainable development's aim of achieving a 'historic compromise' between development and sustainability, and the requirement of keeping poorer countries on board as this compromise has developed, has contributed to the stress on meeting needs. My own view, though, is that while needs-meeting is wholly defensible as a principle of distributive justice for a large number of very good reasons, these reasons do not (necessarily) include functionality for environmental sustainability of the type envisaged here.

In sum, the question of the compatibility of theories of distributive justice with this conception of environmental sustainability has two dimensions. First, there is the issue of whether we can talk about 'irreversible nature' as an object (a 'recipient') of this type of justice at all. If we can, then the theories of justice that are most likely to be compatible with Conception B are those which: (a) entertain a broad sense of recipience and recipients; (b) have a basic structure involving a substantive view of the human good, a focus on consequences, and a prescriptive universalism; (c) treat unproduced environmental goods as ends in themselves rather than as means only, and (d) work with distributive principles most closely linked to the idea of 'sustaining', such as the principle of need.

The second dimension is that which relates to distributive justice among human beings in the light of Conception B's main objective, which is the sustaining of 'irreversible nature'. Here, the distributors and recipients of justice are broadly coterminous: present human beings (I shall say something about future generations below). The basic structure of compatible theories of justice will be the same as that outlined in the previous paragraph—substantive, consequentialist, and universal—and the substantiveness here will colour answers to the last two questions, 'what is to be distributed?' and 'what is the principle of distribution?' In both cases, the answers must refer us back to, and contribute to, the objective of sustaining irreversible nature. As far as the first case is concerned, there seems to be no reason to think that the distribution of any thing in particular will contribute to the sustaining of irreversible nature, but in the second case, we may have cause to rehabilitate desert as a legitimate principle for distribution in the context of (this conception of) environmental sustainability.

In this concluding discussion I have followed the spirit of the 'order of concern' outlined in Box 11 of Table 2; that is to say that I have discussed justice here primarily in the context of present generation human and non-human needs. There is no guarantee, of course, that justice in these contexts will entail justice for future generations, although the very notion of *sustaining* irreversible nature contains a ground-level commitment to doing it the justice of ensuring its survival, at least. The possibility of the need for trade-offs between present and future generation justice is side-stepped in Box 11 by simply recording/asserting that present generation needs have precedence over future generation needs. There remains the intriguing possibility, however, that trade-offs need not be the order of the day anyway, and that a rigorous and primary focus on justice for future generations (even only of human beings) may generate acceptable forms of justice for the other 'objects of concern' outlined in our figure of conceptions of environmental sustainability. I shall explore this possibility in the concluding chapter, but now it is time to turn to the final 'natural value' conception of sustainability.

# 'Natural Value' and Social Justice

THE defining feature of this final conception of environmental sustainability is its focus on the sustaining of 'natural value'. It will be remembered that from Alan Holland, for example, the value of nature to which he refers derives from the history of natural objects, so what is important from the point of view of sustainability is 'maintaining enough of the particular historical forms of association and their historically particular components—all the better if they have the mark of nature upon them' (Holland 1994: 178).

The ascription of value to nature need not necessarily be based on its possession of a particular history, although as I pointed out in Chapter 2 Robert Goodin (1992) has made an important contribution to our analysis of green political theory from this point of view. It may also, for example, derive from the belief that value inheres in those parts of the human and non-human natural world 'that display the property of autopoiesis, which means "self-production" or "self-renewal"' (Eckersley 1992: 60). But the point for us here is that the 'natural value' conception of environmental sustainability is distinguished from the 'irreversibility' conception in two ways. First, the former entertains a wider frame of reference for what is to be maintained and/or sustained than the latter: the set called 'natural value' is larger than the set called 'irreversible nature': the latter may be coterminous with the former (think of a species, for example), but where it is not, we see that the latter 'nests' in the former.

Second, in the 'natural value' conception the language of substitutability is wholly eschewed, and in this way one dimension of the 'irreversibility' conception is taken as far as it will go. Substitutability is a defensible feature of the 'irreversibility' conception in so far as the loss of some forms of irreversible nature can legitimately be substituted for without offending justice—oil is a good example. But we also saw that some forms of irreversible nature are (according to the ethical view established in Conception B) in principle non-compensable. Here, the language of substitutability is inappropriate, and it is this eschewal of substitutability which is taken as far as it will go in Conception C. Indeed, rather than define Conception C in terms of what it seeks to sustain, we might more accurately characterize it in terms of its rejection of substitutability as a feature of sustainability. Simply, and by definition, the original is to be preferred to any possible substitute.

Our overall intention, of course, is to examine the relationship between justice (particularly distributive justice) and environmental sustainability, and so the questions for us here are, first, whether the sustaining of 'natural value' can be defended in terms of (distributive) justice, and second, if so, which features of theories of justice might most successfully underpin such a defence.

Let me assume—for the sake of initial argument—an affirmative answer to the first question. This allows me to take the second question first, and this would be helpful since aspects of it can be answered quite quickly due to ground covered in the previous two chapters (and particularly the last one). Let me address the question in terms of the dimensions of justice developed in Table 5. In the first place, the community of justice entertained in this conception is a wide one. Theories of justice which restrict their range of application are bound to be incompatible with this conception of environmental sustainability. I shall return to this point below. Second, all the remarks made in the previous chapter regarding the basic structure of theories of justice apply here, but with greater force. That is to say that the 'natural value' conception of environmental sustainability not only harbours a conception of the good but is headed up by one. In the previous chapter I took Rawls's generic definition of the good as a guide: 'a conception of the good normally consists of a more or less determinate scheme of final ends, that is, ends we want to realise for their own sake' (Rawls 1993: 19). It seems clear that Conception C's determination to maintain and sustain natural value comprises an end that its supporters will want to realize for its own sake, and to this extent, Conception C is defined by a conception of the good. Given this, theories of justice that trade on impartiality are likely to be prima facie incompatible with Conception C.

The same goes for theories of justice that stress procedures over consequences. The 'natural value' conception involves a very clear objective: the maintaining and sustaining of 'historical forms of association and their historically particular components'—understood particularly here in the context of the natural world. If the justice of a situation is determined by how it was arrived at rather than what it actually is, any achievement of the objectives of Conception C is more likely to be by accident than by design. To the extent, then, that the maintaining of natural value can be talked of in terms of distributive justice at all, it will be most compatible with theories of justice that deal in consequentialism.

Finally, Conception C will want the universal/particular debate resolved in favour of the former. This has been perhaps the most constant refrain throughout our discussion of the relationship between sustainability and justice. Sustainability is, it seems, a universal doctrine by definition: it makes no sense to be in favour of sustainability and not to want it universalized. The particularity, or context-sensitive, aspect of sustainability lies in its application, not in its prescriptive range; that is to say that its implementation is likely to be coloured by particular circumstances, but the normative guidance for implementation will be of universal reach. All this leads to the conclusion that as far as the basic structure of theories of justice is concerned, the 'natural value' conception will be most compatible with theories that are substantive, consequentialist, and universal—and this of course commits supporters of such sustainability to seeking to universalize their substantive conception of the good. This conclusion should not surprise us, since it might be regarded as the leitmotif of the ideology of ecologism, about which I have written elsewhere (Dobson 1995, for instance).

As far as the third question of Table 5 is concerned, the relevant goods to be distributed are those which contribute to the maintaining and sustaining of units of significance. As I pointed out at the end of the previous chapter, there may be no determinate way of filling out this part of the 'justice questionnaire', although of the categories of goods outlined in Table 5, preconditional goods seem to be the most foundational, since they will underpin the sustaining of units of significance. These preconditional goods will be a combination of produced and unproduced goods, and their very preconditionality points us—from the perspective of doing justice to natural value—in the direction of a determinate answer to the last question in Table 5: 'what is the principle of distribution?', and the relevant principle here is need. This has also been something of a refrain during our discussion of social justice and environmental sustainability. The principle of need implies the provision of goods which underpin individuals' production and reproduction of everyday life. These goods are the precondition for any sort of life at all and our intuitions tell us that, in an almost Walzerian fashion, need is the principle of distribution that is 'called up' by them. Similarly, the language of sustainability is a language of preconditionality. That is to say that a sustainable environment is a precondition for the existence of the form of life (whatever it is) with which we are concerned. There seems, then, to be a conceptual link between environmental sustainability and need as a principle of distribution, due to their shared roots in issues surrounding the preconditions for life. This is also the point at which I should reiterate that the objective-driven nature of this conception of sustainability (like Conception B) points us in the direction of desert as a potentially appropriate principle for just distribution between human beings—distribution according to one's contribution to the common task which is the sustaining of 'natural value'.

Finally, in this section, I would like to refer to a point I raised in the previous chapter regarding a potential and untranscendable clash between the languages of sustainability and of justice, because here it appears in its most acute form. I remarked that the clash between the two languages occurs at the point where potential *recipients* of social justice may also be regarded as *resources* for distribution. I also remarked that the clash may be more apparent than real, since even the beings we would most readily accept as being legitimate recipients of justice—human beings—are also used as resources for labour (for example). But being a resource for labour is not the same as being a resource for distribution. Slaves were (and are) a resource for labour *and* a resource for distribution, and what distinguishes the contracted worker from the slave is that the worker sells his or her labour, and is thereby compensated for his or her use as a resource in the process of production. Only by stretching the meaning of the words to the point of parody can we regard the contracted worker as a resource for distribution—in the special sense of distribution required by the language of social justice. In principle, as I said in the previous chapter, there is no reason why non-human beings should not be similarly compensated for their use as a resource in the process of production. This compensation might take various forms; it might, for example, involve providing farm animals with exemplary conditions in which to pursue their species life.

But the point here is that the 'natural value' conception of environmental sustainability is hostile to the language of resources itself, at least in so far as 'nature' is ever to be conceived as such. Supporters of Conception C are well aware that whatever carries 'natural value' may often form an integral part of the production and reproduction of everyday life, and in this sense they know that such carriers will be seen as potential resources. What they are concerned to do is to resist the extent to which 'nature' is regarded as a resource only, and perhaps the best-known (but obviously very underspecified) summary of this is contained in Point 3 of the George Sessions/Arne Naess 'platform for deep ecology': 'Humans have no right to reduce this richness and diversity except to satisfy vital needs' (Naess 1989: 29). All this is as much as to say that, for Conception C, justice is done to the degree that the bag labelled 'what is distributed?' is as empty as possible of carriers of natural value.

This leads us to ask not so much whether the language of (distributive) justice is *applicable* here (the question that animated much of the previous chapter), but whether it is *appropriate*. A number of commentators have suggested that it is not, and most of them take their cue from the idea that the concerns of this kind of sustainability cannot be wholly expressed through justice's terms of reference. So Mark Sagoff writes that 'equality or justice is not the only ethical or cultural goal that concerns us as citizens. We may also be concerned as citizens with . . . the integrity and beauty of the natural environment. These concerns', says Sagoff, 'can[not] . . . be entirely analyzed in terms of equity or justice' (Sagoff 1988: 56–7).

As I hope to have shown in the two previous chapters, 'equity and justice' as frameworks for the defence of the integrity of the environment can probably be pushed further than Sagoff implies, but there is still the suspicion that, as Marcel Wissenburg puts it, 'In contrast to my talk of justice, the ecologists play a totally different language game' (Wissenburg 1993: 5). 'Deep ecology', he continues, 'is not concerned with justice but with nature in relation to man' (Wissenburg 1993: 5). Once again, it is my belief that the issue of 'nature in relation to man' *can* be discussed in terms of justice in that the idea of 'giving parts of nature their due' is by no means senseless.

Of course there are technical reasons why some fundamentalist forms of environmentalism are inexpressible in terms of justice. For instance, Wissenburg is surely right to say that thoroughgoing ecological holists will struggle with justice because 'it makes no sense to talk about distributive justice when there is only one party involved . . . [I]f nature is the distributor, then it cannot distribute itself justly or unjustly to itself . . . [I]f nature is a recipient, it cannot be distributed . . . if nature is a resource, there is no one to distribute it to' (Wissenburg 1993: 7). (Note that this does not mean that holists as a whole—as it were—exclude themselves from justice talk, but only those whose 'whole' is the complete whole of aggregated 'things'.) By far the most normal thing to do, then, is to 'split nature up' and to consider the parts on their merit—and as we saw in the last chapter, this is precisely what Wissenburg does, with the effect that the language of distributive justice is shown to be both applicable and appropriate to some parts of the non-human natural world. *Mutatis mutandis*, we should not regard the situation as hopeless for Conception C either.

I am not convinced, then, that 'we should admit that there are conceptions of nature which cannot be used in theories of distributive justice, and consequently that green political theories are imaginable which cannot be defended in terms of distributive justice' (Wissenburg 1993: 14). Aside from limit cases such as the holistic one referred to above, there is a whole host of green theories that look amenable to defences in terms of distributive justice—even those which Wissenburg uses to exemplify the statement just quoted: 'theories in which nature is ascribed an intrinsic value' (Wissenburg 1993: 14). Presumably the idea here is that if something has intrinsic value then it cannot legitimately be viewed as a resource, and that this is absurd since the maintenance of human life itself requires the appropriation and use of natural resources. The point, though, is that if intrinsic value is to be interpreted in such a fundamentalist sense, then it is indefensible in *any* terms, and not just those of distributive justice. I have come to regard claims for the intrinsic value of nature as metaphorical rather than literal, but no less important for all that. It is a strategic question of turning the tables; as Warwick Fox has put it (although not in the context of intrinsic value exactly), the move 'shifts the onus of justification of one's actions from the person who wants to preserve the non-human world to the person who wants to disrupt or interfere with it' (Fox 1986: 84). In terms of a metaphor of my own, introduced above, the difference is between a bag filled with as few carriers of 'natural value' as possible, and a bag filled with none. The second is absurd, while the first expresses a very real aspiration—an aspiration, moreover, which can in principle be defended in terms of justice.

Remember Wissenburg's reason for omitting 'plants and organic nature' (Wissenburg 1993: 12) from the recipient community of justice: 'neither plants nor organic nature can consciously, let alone willingly, receive, and therefore they cannot be recipients' (Wissenburg 1993: 12). And remember also Robert Nozick's rather desperate search for reasons that would exclusively connect human beings and justice: 'each of them seems insufficient to forge the requisite connection' (Nozick 1974: 48). Wissenburg's assertion that 'Life is a necessary but not a sufficient condition for being a moral subject or for deserving moral treatment as a subject' (Wissenburg 1993: 12) will look like a similar exercise of unsubstantiable fiat to those who sympathize with the 'natural value' conception of sustainability. From this point of view, Allan Holland's 'units of significance' containing nothing more than Wissenburg's 'plants and organic nature' may be regarded by these sympathizers as belonging to the community of distributive justice, and what are due to them are the conditions they need for their sustaining and flourishing.

Part of the reason for arguing that justice is inappropriate here is a quite proper attention to the insistence on non-substitutability which underpins (indeed, which defines) this conception of environmental sustainability. As we saw in Chapter 5, there is a link between the language of substitutability and the language of compensability, and this link brings the discourses of sustainability and of justice together. The argument will run that where losses in natural capital can be substituted for by other forms of natural or human capital, then justice can be done by compensating for the loss through the provision of the relevant substitutes. Once we are confronted with a conception of environmental sustainability that explicitly eschews substitutability (as this one does), though, doing justice seems impossible since compensation for loss is ruled out.

So as Dale Jamieson points out, 'many environmental goods are irreplaceable and irreversible. When species are lost or climate changes they will never return. Nature's path has been irrevocably affected by the development of Western science and technology. It is hard to conceive what the alternatives might have been, much more how to compensate those whose preferences and ways of life have been frustrated or destroyed' (Jamieson 1994: 209). They will agree with Jamieson that 'To view the environment solely as a good to be distributed seriously misconceives our relationship to the Earth' (Jamieson 1994: 210), and they will therefore argue that justice may sometimes be done by *resisting* distribution, and that this squares with the language of distributive justice on the grounds that there is nothing about that language which *obliges* distribution.

This point can be made through taking one final look at John Locke's famous 'proviso', discussed at some length in Chapter 4. As we remember, Locke argues that private property in 'the earth and all inferior creatures' may legitimately be appropriated, provided that 'there is enough, and as good left in common for others' (Locke 1690/1924: 130). The 'as good' stipulation invites the assumption that substitutability (and therefore compensation) is possible—but of course it may not be. From a Conception C point of view, 'natural value' is by definition unsubstitutable and therefore non-compensable. But this does not mean that Locke's proviso is somehow unworkable in the Conception C context; it simply means that, in principle, 'natural value' cannot legitimately be appropriated. The point is that Locke's principle of legitimate acquisition and its attached proviso gives rise to different conclusions in the context of different conceptions of environmental sustainability: the more substitutability is allowed, the more appropriation will be legitimate, and vice versa.

I can illustrate this point by referring to a remark made by Robert Nozick when discussing Locke's proviso—an apparently casual remark as far as he (Nozick) is concerned, but of some significance to us. Nozick says that, 'If I appropriate a grain of sand from Coney Island, no one else may now do as they will with *that* grain of sand. But there are plenty of other grains of sand left for them to do the same with' (Nozick 1974: 175). Nozick assumes the substitutability of grains of sand, which seems a fair thing to do. But it would be a mistake to take this game too far, especially with pieces of land which may appear valueless but which are in fact infused with natural value.

In retrospect, Locke was ill-advised to write that 'land that is left wholly to nature, that have no improvement of pasturage, tillage, or planting, is called, as indeed it is, waste; and we shall find the benefit of it amount to little more than nothing' (Locke 1690/1924: 137). Try playing the Locke/Nozick game with the American Indian conception of land, for example. No doubt early American legislators did just that (most likely without knowing it), and came up with the answer that appropriated land could be compensated for by other land ('reservations') or—worse—by money (which typically was never handed over). None of this means, I stress, that Locke's proviso does not hold under these conditions. Quite the opposite: a strict interpretation of it would have yielded the conclusion that appropriation of sacred American Indian land was unjust. (This is a *particular* instance, in specific circumstances, of the *universal* injunction to sustain natural value.)

Locke's theory of legitimate acquisition, then, seems to 'work' even in our present context, and the same can be shown to be true of another hugely influential theory which was not originally designed for this type of territory—that of John Rawls. As we have seen, Rawls himself is firmly convinced that 'justice as fairness' will not answer the question of 'what is owed to animals and the rest of nature' (Rawls 1993: 21). There are two reasons for this, as he explained in his original *A Theory of Justice*. The first is that 'Justice as fairness is not a complete contract theory' (Rawls 1973: 17) in that it is concerned with justice only, and not with 'an entire ethical system' (Rawls 1973: 17). The second is that even if the contract theory was about 'rightness as fairness' (i.e. an entire ethical system), it would still 'fail to embrace all moral relationships, since it would include only our relations with other persons and to leave out of account how we are to conduct ourselves toward animals and the rest of nature' (Rawls 1973: 17). The implications of these comments are, first, that justice does not deal with animals and the rest of nature, and second, that the contract theory will not help us to deal with them. I think that both of these implications are misplaced, and, happily, Bryan Norton has provided us with an ingenious adaptation of Rawls against which to test these assertions.

Norton begins with a typology of four different positions on resource use, each of which he believes representative of real-life view on resource issues. These positions (or rather the people who occupy them) he calls: 'Exploitationists', 'Conservationists', 'Naturalist-Preservationists', and 'Extensionist-Preservationists' (Norton 1989: 138). The detail of these positions does not matter for now; the important thing is that Norton wants some way of deciding between their different merits, and he suggests that this would be best done by finding a 'neutral vocabulary' in which to express them, and via which some sort of objective assessment of their claims could be made. Unsurprisingly, then, he is drawn to Rawls's theoretical apparatus because of the putative neutrality of the conditions of the original position, which underpins the idea of 'justice as fairness'.

Unsurprisingly, too, Rawls's 'veil of ignorance' will need to be tailored in different ways to suit the demands of each of the four positions mentioned above. Given the characteristics of the conception of environmental sustainability with which we are concerned in this chapter, I shall focus on the fourth of Norton's positions on resource issues ('Extensionist-Preservationist') since this is the one that comes closest to the idea of sustaining 'natural value'. The Extensionist-Preservationist argues that 'environmentalism must go beyond time preference issues and also develop rules for protecting the independent value that nature has' (Norton 1989: 147). This, says Norton, will be impossible to factor into Rawls's theory as it stands because rational choosers are given no reason or incentive for taking the independent value of nature into account. The solution to this is for 'The extensionist [to] . . . insist that the hypothetical rational chooser must also be ignorant of the species into which he will be born' (Norton 1989: 151). So adapted, says Norton, 'The Rawlsian model, with ignorance extended to relevant factors as here described, can claim to represent a neutral and adequate vocabulary for environmental decision-making' (Norton 1989: 152).

So far this suggests that, contra Rawls himself, the strategy revolving around the construction of an 'original position' is applicable to the kind of case with which we are involved here—and these reasons seem stronger when we see that useful results are obtained from following through the implications of rational choosers thinking in Extensionist-Preservationist terms. Such choosers will be inevitably driven towards a set of policies that 'protects all interests of all species'. But—and this is the sting in the tail—they would soon see, says Norton, that such a set of policies would be 'impossible to operationalise' (Norton 1989: 153), since the prohibitions on the utilization of species and the economic and social cost of obligations to protect them would make the production and reproduction of human life impossible.

It is important to note for my purposes that Norton arrives at a rejection of this option not because it is impossible to think it through in Rawlsian terms, but because of the result of actually doing so. I want to stress this because I am keen to see how far the paradigm of justice can be pushed in the context of this conception of environmental sustainability. Norton's work suggests that the paradigm is appropriate here. He has passed over objections of the sort which hold that 'think[ing] ourselves into the position of an animal' (Wissenburg 1993: 17) is impossible, and he has also implicitly rejected the view that animals are beyond the purview of justice. Instead, he has adopted the idea that we can include animals in the discourse of Rawlsian justice to an extent sufficient to reach reasonable conclusions in regard of them.

Given the impossibility of operationalizing the Extensionist-Preservationist option, Norton believes that rational choosers—even those ignorant of the species into which they are born—will choose some variant of the third option, the 'Naturalist-Preservationist' option. From this point of view, the rational chooser in the original position 'must choose as if he is a *possibly existent human individual*' (Norton 1989: 150; emphasis in the original). This type of chooser, concerned for a human future rather than either solely a human present or a human/non-human animal present and future, will seek to secure the conditions for whatever future time she or he is born into. In securing a human future, non-human futures are indirectly secured too, says Norton: 'If future human interests are protected to the fullest extent possible and into the longest-term future, the naturalist believes, all species will be given some measure of protection' (Norton 1989: 154).

As it happens, this conclusion is close to that expressed by Rawls himself in his reappraisal of his theory of justice. (Although he does not, of course, get there by the same route as Norton. As we saw in Chapter 4, Rawls explicitly eschews what he calls 'a (hypothetical and nonhistorical) direct agreement between all generations' (Rawls 1993: 274).) A little earlier in the same text, Rawls considers what is owed to animals and the rest of nature, and he writes that he is content to adopt the 'traditional view of Christian Ages', according to which,

Animals and nature are seen as subject to our use and want. This has the virtue of clarity and yields some kind of answer. There are numerous political values here to invoke: to further the good of ourselves and future generations by preserving the natural order and its life-sustaining properties; to foster species of animals and plants for the sake of biological and medical knowledge with its potential applications to human health; to protect the beauties of nature for purposes of public recreation and the pleasures of deep understanding of the world. The appeal to values of this kind gives what many have found a reasonable answer to the status of animals and the rest of nature. (Rawls 1993: 245)

Norton's version of this conclusion is one that would be supported by many, and the fact that here it is arrived at through deployment of a Rawlsian apparatus, including the hypothetical inclusion of non-human species, suggests that the Rawlsian theory of justice has a more widespread application than he himself believes. The fact that there may be problems with Norton's conclusion does not diminish prima facie the applicability of the way he arrived at it. The problem to which I want to refer is internal to the theory, as it were, but it is important in that it highlights the differences between a theory of justice devoted to the interests of human beings (even future ones) and one which seeks to take non-human interests into account. The problem (in the Conception C context) is this: having rejected the Extensionist-Preservationist position on the grounds that protecting all the interests of all species is an impossibility, Norton tries to smuggle such protection back in by claiming that it will be guaranteed by the umbrella protecting future generations of human beings. The claim, to repeat, is that, 'If future human interests are protected to the fullest extent possible and into the longest-term future, the naturalist believes, *all* species will be given some measure of protection' (Norton 1989: 154; my emphasis). The fact, of course, is that *not* all species will be protected by this umbrella, and recognition of this fact is implicit in the following gloss (Norton's own) on the general lines of policy produced by the Naturalist-Preservationist position. The rational chooser here, he says, 'will opt, depending upon his degree of risk aversion, for a society that imposes some pre-emptive constraints to protect biological diversity across generations . . . limits sufficient to protect the future productivity of ecological systems on the welfare-seeking activities of each generation' (Norton 1989: 155). The idea of 'sufficient' protection here is precisely that which will leave some species out in the cold, and the mention of the probable 'redundancy' of some ecological systems (Norton 1989: 156) merely confirms that a focus on the non-human natural world as exhaustively instrumental for the maintenance of human life—even long into the future—will legitimize the sacrifice of some of those systems. I shall have more to say on all this in the concluding chapter.

What Norton's foray into Rawlsian territory does show, though, is that proponents of this present conception of environmental sustainability (C) will have to square their determination to sustain 'natural value' with the legitimate demands of other present and future human beings (which can of course also be couched in terms of justice). As we saw earlier, some carriers of 'natural value' may simultaneously be resources for distribution as well as potential recipients of distribution, and in these cases of collision, proponents of Conception C will have to make their priorities clear.

It may well be somewhere around this point that the discourses of justice and sustainability part company. Sooner or later the distinction we saw Rawls drawing above between justice and an 'entire ethical system' has to come into play, and the more we feel we are dealing with a substantive view of the good, the larger the presence of an ethical system looms. As with justice, so with ethics: the primordial question has to do with the extent of membership of the ethical community. I have tried to show how the community of justice can be expanded from the inside out, as it were, by indicating how languages and theories of justice can be expanded to include the objects of concern of environmental sustainability without those languages and theories being twisted beyond recognition.

But the idea of community can itself counterpose, as well as constitute a dimension of, justice—and it may be that this 'natural value' conception of environmental sustainability takes us beyond justice and towards community in this sense. Michael Sandel has expressed something of the flavour of this possibility:

Not egotists but strangers, sometimes benevolent, make for citizens of the deontological republic; justice finds its occasion because we cannot know each other, or our ends, well enough to govern by the common good alone. This condition is not likely to fade altogether, and as long as it does not, justice will be necessary. But neither is it guaranteed always to predominate, and in so far as it does not, community will be possible, and an unsettling presence for justice. (Sandel 1984b: 175)

By 'strangers' here, Sandel does not literally mean people who do not know each other, but rather people who do not recognize each other as partners in a common enterprise. Shared dispositions which, in the best of cases, will have been discursively agreed upon (although this is not, as I understand it, the Sandelian spirit) may reduce the space required for the practice of justice. Justice as it has been presented so far in this book is admirably described by Alan Ryan as a 'chilly virtue', which is 'appropriate to the dealings of those who are strangers to each other' (in Ryan 1993: 16). In Marxist hands this kind of view can turn into the assertion that justice as such will disappear in the properly constituted and regulated community. I prefer to assume, with Sandel, on the other hand, that justice will continue to be necessary even in communities constituted by individuals whose activities are regulated by a shared understanding of the common good. But in such cases the number of issues left to be solved according to the metric of justice will have been reduced by the prior solution of many of them in the light of the norms of the common good.

In our particular case, in a society organized around a common good containing a commitment to sustaining 'natural value' it is likely that many distributive debates relating to the sphere of present generation human wish fulfilments would be otiose. This is to say that they would have been 'solved' by prior reference to the common good, which would have indicated that they not arise as issues for debate in the first place. To my mind, the 'natural value' conception of environmental sustainability presupposes a community of the sort outlined by Sandel, but with a difference. As for Sandel, it is a community formed around a common good, and to this extent it may be a community in which people are not known to each other personally, but in which they are nevertheless not strangers. But Conception C's notion of the common good itself defines and determines the extent of the community and the particular responsibilities at work in it. Put differently, the common good in question involves the sustaining of carriers of 'natural value', and so these carriers become part of the community. This kind of common good, and the widening of the community it brings with it, cannot be arrived at via the chilly route explored by Feinberg (for example) in the previous chapter. The reciprocity involved needs, perhaps, to be pre-rational in a way hinted at by Emmanuel Levinas:

if there were only two of us in this world, I and one other, there would be no problem. The other would be completely my responsibility. But in the real world there are many others. When others enter, each of them external to myself, problems arise. Who is closest to me? Who is the Other? Perhaps something has already occurred between them. We must investigate carefully. Legal justice is required. There is need for a state. But it is very important to know whether the state, society, law and power are required because man is a beast to his neighbour . . . or because I am

responsible for my fellow. It is very important to know whether the political order defines man's responsibility or merely restricts his bestiality.
(Levinas 1989b: 247)

The pre-rational order of which Levinas speaks—and he speaks
prescriptively rather than descriptively—is (to use his own terms)
one of responsibility rather than bestiality. In this pre-rational order,
one finds oneself always already in the presence of others who call
forth an ethical response. There is no need to construct a widened
community of justice in the manner of Feinberg, for example, because the community in which one finds oneself already *is* that
community.

The Feinberg technique of arriving at wider ethical communities
has been described by David Cooper in terms of an 'expanding
circle'. The expanding circle school argue, as we saw in the last
chapter, that 'whatever the crucial determinant of moral concern—
happiness, rights, sentiment—the argument is that it is irrational to
restrict such concerns to human beings, since the differences
between ourselves and some other species which would
alone justify such a restriction simply do not exist' (Cooper 1995:
139). Cooper criticizes this approach on a number of grounds
(Cooper 1995: 140–1), the most important of which for us reads as
follows:

the [expanding circle] 'model' implies that moral progress always occurs
through recognizing that some previously excluded group . . . is similar, in
all relevant respects, to a group already included in the circle of moral
concern. But this is to ignore the possibility . . . that a species ought to
engage our concern because of the respects in which it significantly differs
from ourselves. (Cooper 1995: 141)

This last sentence—'this is to ignore the possibility . . . that a species
ought to engage our concern because of the respects in which
it significantly differs from ourselves'—provides the background
to an alternative to the expanding circle technique, and it may
be that this alternative is the one most suited to the intentions
of the 'natural value' conception of environmental sustainability.
It is likely to be hard to argue of a great number of the carriers
of 'natural value' which lie at the heart of this conception that

they are 'similar, in all relevant respects' to human beings (for example). But if, on the other hand, they 'engage our concern' because they *differ* from us, then the range of concern is widened at a stroke.

It has to be admitted that the intellectual resources at the disposal of the expanding circle school are considerably greater than those at the disposal of the 'difference' school. As Wissenburg has rightly remarked, 'The reason why we love others, according to Kant and the whole of Western philosophy since the Stoics and long before, is that we recognise ourselves in the other, or to be more specific, we recognise our essence as rational, morally free, and responsible beings with plans, aims and ends' (Wissenburg 1993: 13). But there is a subordinate tradition of ethical concern, represented by Emmanuel Levinas, and to which we have already referred, which Wissenburg also mentions (Wissenburg 1993: 16)—although he chooses not to follow the trail, believing that the demands of a Levinasian approach to ethics are altogether too demanding— even self-contradictory: 'Is it really possible to conceive of nature in terms or concepts which we, and only we understand, without epistemologically and ethically colonizing it?' (Wissenburg 1993: 16).

Despite these reservations, it is nevertheless surprising that Levinasian ethics have not received more attention from the environmental community, and particularly from those members of it looking for a way to express their intuition that the natural world (or carriers of 'natural value' in our present terms) demands ethical attention because of, not despite, its manifest, differences from ourselves. What follows should not at all be taken as a wholehearted endorsement of a Levinasian approach to environmental ethics (nor, more broadly, of a 'postmodern' approach). I simply want to signal the potential available here. Levinas's view is that difference invites 'nonindifference':

We must note that for Plato a relation may be possible between the one and the other, though they are 'dead to the world', and lack, as a result, a shared other; that a relation might be possible without a common ground, that is to say, a relationship in difference; that the difference signifies a nonindifference; that this nonindifference might be developed by Plato as ultimate justice. (Levinas 1989*b*: 244)

This reference to justice is important to us too, since it calls into question the strict demarcation between justice and a wider system of ethics sustained by Rawls (and most other thinkers in the deontological tradition). For Levinas the original question of justice refers to our immediate relation with the Other, and because there is no universal law at work here, there is no 'reading off' of responsibility for the Other from a general imperative:

The other, absolutely other, is the Other . . . The Other is not a particular case, a species of otherness, but the original exception to order . . . My responsibility for the other man, the paradoxical, contradictory responsibility for a foreign liberty—extending, according to the Talmud (*Sotah* 37b), even to the responsibility for his responsibility—does not originate in a vow to respect the universality of a principle, nor in the moral imperative. (Levinas 1989*b*: 245)

This relation with the Other is one of pre-reflective immediacy, and is both signalled yet not exhausted by the idea of 'fraternity': 'The proximity of a neighbour is my responsibility for him . . . Responsibility does not come from fraternity, but fraternity denotes responsibility for another, antecedent to my freedom' (Levinas, 1989*c*: 181). The antecedence to freedom of this responsibility for the Other is what makes it utterly alien to the idea of contractual (theories of ) justice: 'Responsibility for the neighbour is precisely what goes beyond the legal and obliges beyond contracts . . . Before the neighbour I am summoned and do not just appear; from the first I am answering an assignation' (Levinas 1989*c*: 180). If a precondition for justice is reciprocity, then Levinas's view of our relation with the other can in no way be characterized in terms of justice. His use of the idea of a 'gift' (Levinas 1989*b*: 246) is important here, since the gift in most Western cultures is symbolic of a transfer which is, by definition, non-reciprocal. The giving of a gift can just about be interpreted in the formal terms of distributive justice because it involves the transfer of a benefit (or a burden, in the case of the annual pile of inappropriate Christmas presents), but here it much more importantly signifies the character of the relationship between the giver and the receiver: one of responsibility for the Other without the expectation of reciprocal reaction.

The importance to us here of this is that this kind of relationship—'one of responsibility for the Other without expectation of
reciprocal reaction'—looks to be the one which animates this
present conception of environmental sustainability. Levinas himself
falls far short of drawing anything like environmental-ethical implications from his own thought, and Jacques Derrida has pointed out
as much in his own reflections on the obstacles to consideration of
what he refers to as 'animal, plant, or stone' (Derrida 1991: 109). We
remember that moral considerability is usually granted to beings in
virtue of their possession of a characteristic that 'calls forth' such
considerability, and Derrida's version of this characteristic (which
he states on behalf of a dominant tradition in Western philosophy)
is 'presence to self':

If we still wish to speak of the subject . . . it is first of all necessary to submit
to the test of questioning the essential predicates of which all subjects are
the subject. While these predicates are as numerous and diverse as the type
or order of the subjects dictates, they are all in fact ordered around being
present . . . presence to self. (Derrida 1991: 109)

Derrida then hints at a Levinasian solution to the problem of
overcoming the necessary condition of presence to self for
considerability:

It is necessary to question this authority of the being-present, but the
question itself neither offers the first nor the last word . . . as I have tried to
show . . . everywhere I have spoken on the 'Yes, yes' of the 'Come' or of
the affirmation that is not addressed first of all to a subject. (Derrida 1991:
109)

Derrida's ' "Yes, yes" of the "Come" ' is the analogue of Levinas's
pre-reflective responsibility for the Other, a responsibility the implications of which, Derrida observes, Levinas reserves exclusively for
the human Other:

the 'Thou shalt not kill' is addressed to the other and presupposes him. It
is destined to the very thing that it institutes . . . The 'Thou shalt not kill'—
with all its consequences, which are limitless—has never been understood
within the Judeo-Christian tradition, nor apparently by Levinas, as a 'Thou
shalt not put to death the living in general' . . . The other . . . is indeed the
other man: man as other, the other as man. (Derrida 1991: 112–13)

So long, then, as subjecthood is preconditional for the application of moral injunctions such as 'Thou shalt not kill', and so long as presence to self is the defining characteristic of subjecthood, 'the other' will always and only ever refer to 'man'. For Derrida, this ontology and the ethics this produces harbour a double violence. First, those who deny that the putting to death of an animal is murder base their denial on 'the violent institution of the "who" as subject' (Derrida 1991: 115), and second, of course, there is the death of the animal itself. The first violence legitimizes the second, and the point of calling the first into question is that the ontological and ethical boundaries it creates between the human and non-human realms are thereby shown to be insecure. This, says Derrida, is the only way to get non-human animals into the justice game:

If we wish to speak of injustice, or violence, or of a lack of respect toward what we still so confusedly call animals . . . we must reconsider in its totality the metaphysico-anthropocentric axiomatic that dominates, in the West, the thought of just and unjust. (Derrida 1992: 19)

Even if we do as Derrida says, of course, we cannot jump to the conclusion that 'putting nature to death' is always wrong: the death of some parts of 'nature' (if not necessarily of animals) is an unavoidable feature of the meeting of human beings' vital needs. Derrida's point, rather, is that once the ontological and ethical frontier between humans and other animals (and, more broadly, non-human nature) is breached, a hitherto unasked question comes into view: how should we live with the non-human natural world? Derrida puts it like this:

If the limit between the living and the nonliving now seems to be as unsure as that between 'man' and 'animal', and if . . . the ethical frontier no longer rigorously passes between the 'Thou shalt not kill' (man, thy neighbour), and the 'Thou shalt not put to death the living in general', but rather between several infinitely different modes of the conception-appropriation-assimilation of the other, then . . . the question will come back to determining the best, most respectful, most grateful and also most giving way of relating to the other and of relating the other to self. (Derrida 1991: 114)

But is Derrida talking about justice here? Is the language of respect, gratitude, bestowal, and affinity the language of justice? The most common response will be that it is not, especially if we restrict ourselves to what Brian Barry has referred to as a 'narrow' conception of justice—one in which 'some distributive consideration comes into play' (Barry 1999). We might just, I suppose, stretch Michael Walzer's point that 'The community is itself a good—conceivably the most important good—that gets distributed' (Walzer 1983: 29), and argue that the very thinking of the non-human natural world in terms of respect, gratitude, and so on amounts to a de facto 'distribution of the community' beyond its normal range, and that therefore, yes, we *are* talking about justice after all.

But this may be going too far. Derrida's reflections put me, at least, in mind of what are generally referred to as alternatives to justice: the notion of the 'good life' and the idea of 'the virtues'. As far as the first is concerned, David Cooper refers to the ingredients of 'imagination, openness [and] empathy' as constitutive of the good life (Cooper 1995: 145), and he suggests that each of these capacities might involve, or even entail, concern for the non-human natural world. In similar vein, and in the context of the virtues, Cooper says: 'There are, it seems to me, generally acknowledged virtues whose exercise requires this [concern for other species]', virtues such as 'responsibility, care, kindness, solicitude' (Cooper 1995: 146). Moreover, says Cooper in an echo of my comment above on Levinas's notion of the gift, these virtues are 'most purely exercised . . . when we have nothing to expect in return' (Cooper 1995: 147), and he concludes that this foregrounding of the virtues and the good life implies that 'the vocabulary of justice is not the most felicitous one in which to express a concern for other species' (Cooper 1995: 148). I think that it is something like this that Onora O'Neill has in mind when she writes that

the conceptual distinction between environmental justice and care for the environment that goes beyond justice is a clear one . . . Some will express care that goes beyond justice through patient cultivation of fields or care for herds, others by seeking to preserve familiar landscapes and townscapes, yet others by conserving uncultivated wilderness, by protecting endangered species or by restoring them to ancestral habitats. (O'Neill 1996: 204)

We certainly seem to have moved some distance from the 'chilly virtue' that is Alan Ryan's justice, although Brenda Almond, for one, is prepared to entertain the idea that the virtues and justice can be cut from the same cloth: 'there are no a priori considerations that prevent the incorporation of a broadly conceived and extended virtue ethics within the justice framework' (Almond 1995: 7). I think that this would be more accurately put the other way round, i.e. that virtue ethics entails a quite particular understanding of (the place of) justice. This is especially true if we agree with Almond that 'flourishing . . . is an essential aspect of virtue ethics' (Almond 1995: 7–8). 'Flourishing' entails the idea that 'every kind of object has an end or function that in a sense defines it' (Almond 1995: 7), and Almond is right to imply that the idea is central to much environmental-ethical thinking. In this context, justice will generally be regarded as instrumental for flourishing, and so the justice of transactions will habitually be judged by their consequences. These judgements, in turn, refer back to a substantive theory of the good, which in its own turn is—in the specific context of this present conception of environmental sustainability—rooted in what Rawls calls 'a theory of the natural order and our place in it' (Rawls 1973: 512). For Rawls, only such a theory of the natural order can give us a 'conception of our relations to animals and to nature' (Rawls 1973: 512), and, as we have seen, these relations, for Rawls, are not relations of justice. Those who see sustainability in terms of the sustaining of 'natural value' will probably agree with him, but for different reasons. It is not, as it is for Rawls, that we do not owe animals and nature justice, but that we owe them something else. Justice, they will say with William Galston, is not the 'sole regulator' of our actions: 'Beyond distributive justice stands supererogatory benevolence; beyond retributive or punitive justice stands mercy. We are permitted to do no less than justice; we are allowed and even encouraged to do more' (Galston 1980: 283).

## Conclusion

It may appear odd to be peppering the final stages of a book about the relationship between environmental sustainability and distributive justice with suggestions that—by this point at least—the relationship has broken down. It is my belief, though, that this is what has happened and, moreover, that there is nothing odd about it. At the outset I had no preconceived sense that there would be even the most general compatibility between them, and even if there was, I suspected that there would be no overall determinate content to that compatibility. This suspicion became more marked once multiple conceptions of sustainability and notions of justice were developed (Chapters 2 and 3): if a determinate relationship between them were hard to establish *within* individual conceptions of sustainability, then even more difficulties would be encountered *across* them. What the subsequent detailed examination has shown is that there is plenty of engagement between the languages and intentions of environmental sustainability and distributive justice in the 'critical natural capital' context, but that points of contact become fewer and further apart as we move through 'irreversibility' towards 'natural value'.

We must all along bear in mind the distinction between the functionality of justice for sustainability, and the promoting of the cause of sustainability through the language of justice. We are most familiar with the first in the context of sustainable development, where it is believed that a particular set of distributive relations between human beings can contribute to environmental sustainability. My view is that this belief can only be underpinned by exhaustive empirical research in a variety of distributive and environmental contexts. I have obviously not tried to carry out that research here, although this fundamentally theoretical enquiry suggests that the range of distributive relations functional for sustainability (and the normative positions that inform them) is wider than most sustainable development theorists and practicants suggest.

As for the second dimension, the tactic of promoting the cause of sustainability through the language of justice seems less and less effective the more one moves towards the final conception ('C') of sustainability. And if we stand back from the detail of this examination for the moment, this conclusion seems less surprising than it might otherwise appear. I pointed out in Chapter 1 that green, or environmental, politics has generally set its sights on targets other than distributive justice. I also took the opportunity provided by the discussion there of the American 'environmental justice' movement to question the movement's criticism of 'traditional' environmental activists for being 'obsessively orientated toward wilderness, public land, and natural-resource conservation' (Dowie 1995: 126). This criticism seemed (and seems) odd to me because these orientations can be taken (for the sake of argument) as defining so-called traditional environmentalism. So to ask traditional environmentalists to rein in their concern for wilderness, public land, and so on is to ask them to shift the bedrock on which they build their politics. Critics are perfectly entitled to ask them to do this, of course, but they (the critics) should also understand that if the new position they (traditional environmentalists) are invited to adopt conflicts with environmentalists' original motivations, then clashes are likely to occur. What the examination in this book has shown is not just that there is no reason to assume that the kinds of distribution advanced by environmental justice activists will lead to environmental sustainability, but that environmental activists, on the one hand, and justice activists, on the other, may often speak past—rather than to—each other.

# Conclusion

I PROPOSE to conclude in two parts. First, I shall outline and briefly describe eight theses on environmental sustainability and social justice which can be distilled from the body of this book. I shall then, second, take up a question that has ghosted the text and try to resolve it. This question derives from the way in which the discussion of the relationship between justice and sustainability has been divided up into discrete 'sections', corresponding to each of the conceptions of environmental sustainability developed and described in Chapter 2. This enabled us to establish points of distributional conflict *within* conceptions of sustainability (e.g. between present generation wants and future generation needs in Conception A), but it obscured (or discouraged) discussion of conflicts *across* these conceptions. What I want to do in the second part of this Conclusion, then, is to take up the question of whether there can be an overarching idea of social justice which will be compatible with as many of the intentions of environmental sustainability as possible. I shall pursue this question by considering the claims of two contrasting approaches to generating such an idea: that of Peter Wenz (1988), and that of Bryan Norton (1991). But first, let me outline the theses.

*First thesis: the discourses of sustainability and justice may be related in three fundamental ways: (i) the environment as something to be distributed, (ii) justice as functional for sustainability, (iii) 'justice to the environment'.*

(i) All theories of justice are about the distribution of something, and one answer to the question of what this 'something' might be is: environmental goods and bads. This is the relationship between justice and sustainability to be found at the heart of the 'environmental justice' movement, both discussed in Chapter 1 and the subject of the third thesis, below.

(ii) As a social objective, sustainability might be brought about in a number of ways, and a number of preconditions might be required for it. One part of the mechanism for bringing it about, and one of its preconditions, might be social justice. This would put social justice in a functional relationship with sustainability: more of the first means more of the second. Of course, 'social justice' might mean any one of a number of things (see the second thesis, below), but there is a widespread belief that the relief of poverty (one view of what social justice might entail) would result in greater environmental sustainability (but see the fourth thesis, below). The functional relationship between justice and sustainability is nearly always presented as a virtuous one, but what if it turned out that, under some circumstances, social and economic inequality (another version of what social justice might entail) was conducive to environmental sustainability? For many, this would force a difficult choice between sustainability and justice, and would make clear—for those who choose the former, even on the basis that its realization would demand the deepening of inequality—the subordinate nature of justice to sustainability. This subordinate position of justice in relation to sustainability is concealed by the language of 'functionality', and it only comes to light when the 'win–win' relationship commonly found in theories of sustainable development is replaced by a potential 'win–lose' relationship.

(iii) In (i), above, the environment was presented as an ingredient in doing justice (something to be distributed), but it (or parts of it) might also be regarded as a recipient of justice in its own right. Broadly, the argument here turns on whether the environment (or which bits of it) possesses the kinds of characteristics which will allow us to talk appropriately of it as a potential recipient of justice. Some of the details of this argument were outlined in Chapters 6 and 7.

*Second thesis: neither environmental sustainability nor social justice has determinate meanings, and this opens the way to legitimizing the pursuit of either of them, in terms of the other, in a number of ways.*

I began this book by assuming that both environmental sustainability and social justice are at present regarded as desirable social objectives. I also suggested that they might not always be compatible objectives, and that this may lead to problems of political legitimization. It might, for instance, be determined that a rise in the price of domestic fuel would result in reduced consumption of such fuel, and that this price rise could be legitimized in terms of environmental sustainability (a reduction in the 'greenhouse' gases contributing to global warming). This move would be, though (and was, in Britain), resisted by the social justice lobby on the grounds that price rises of this sort hit the poor hardest. The tension between the objectives of justice and sustainability in this example is clear, and though this tension is avoidable (payment exemptions might be made, for instance), the example does show that policies for justice and sustainability will not always pull in the same direction.

On the other hand, the very multiplicity of the meanings of environmental sustainability and social justice means that there are more paths to legitimization in terms of compatibilities between the two than might appear at first sight. If a policy for sustainability appears to be at odds with justice, then the meaning of either might be 'tweaked' to bring the two closer into line. The tension between justice and sustainability in the example above, for instance, derives from the assumption that to 'hit the poor hardest' is unjust. The effect of such a policy, though, will look less unjust in a society in which inequality is broadly sanctioned, and in which the provision of vital needs is regarded as the responsibility of the individual citizen rather than the state. Personally, I am far from endorsing the 'tweaking' strategy, and even further from endorsing its implications in the example outlined here. However, it is crucial to realize that the contested nature of the meanings of sustainability and justice gives governments the possibility of playing a legitimizing game, and in these days in which the 'spin' put on a policy is regarded as being as important as the 'policy itself' (whatever that may mean), we can be sure that the game will be played. For the concerned citizen, the only defence against obfuscation is a clear picture of the field on which the game is being played, and I hope to have provided such a picture in this book.

*Third thesis: the concerns of the environmental movement and movements for social justice are fundamentally different as far as the 'natural' environment is concerned, although they may sometimes coincide.*

'The environment' is a common denominator in both environmental and social justice movements, but it is regarded by each of them in radically different ways. Broadly, the environmental movement seeks to conserve, preserve, and protect the 'natural' environment, while social justice movements are concerned with how it is distributed. Given this difference, it would be surprising to find that the interests of the (social) justice and environmental movements always pulled in the same direction. The 'environmental justice' movement in the USA, for example, is not about justice *to* the environment, but about how the environment (both its good and bad bits) can be justly distributed. Environmental justice might lead to a concern for the environment outside of its role as something to be distributed, but this is more likely to be for contingent reasons than because of any intrinsic connection between the two. This is not to say that environmental activists should regard the environmental justice movement as unimportant—far from it—but rather that their support for it will not be seamlessly derivable from their environmental concerns.

*Fourth thesis: the question of whether sustainability and justice are compatible objectives can only be resolved empirically, and the range—and depth—of empirical research required to resolve this question has not been done.*

It is practically an article of faith in the sustainable development movement that social injustice causes environmental unsustainability, and that therefore greater social justice would result in greater environmental sustainability. The second thesis (above), though, indicates at the very least that the relationship between these two social objectives will be a complex one, and that it is therefore unwise to make determinate claims about them. Any statement regarding the relationship between them needs to be prefaced by an explanation of what type of social justice and what kind of environmental sustainability is under consideration. This suggests two essential tasks for the sustainable development movement. The first, in line with what I have just said, is to clarify its terms of reference; when advocates of sustainable development talk about social justice and environmental sustainability, what exactly do they mean by the terms? With which conception of environmental sustainability (Chapter 2) and which aspects of the dimensions of social justice (Chapter 3) are they working? The second task is to organize a long-term programme of empirical research aimed at clarifying the social, economic, and ecological circumstances under which social injustice *is* a cause of environmental unsustainability. The empirical work purporting to link justice and sustainability in the way required by the idea of sustainable development is thin on the ground, and the intellectual foundations of sustainable development would be much more solid if a comprehensive body of such work existed.

Another way of glossing this thesis is to say that we do not know enough to be able to say whether justice is, or is not, a necessary and/or a sufficient condition for environmental sustainability. It may be a necessary condition, but only under certain circumstances yet to be systematically explored, and it is my feeling that it is unlikely to be a sufficient condition since sustainability questions are about more than justice. In this context, Brian Barry's prediction that 'whatever redistribution among contemporaries is required by justice will also be able to observe the constraints that the interests of future generations be protected' (Barry 1991b: 269) will only be true if the goods redistributed are 'spent' on sustainable practices.

*Fifth thesis: no theory of justice can henceforth be regarded as complete if it does not take into account the possibility of extending the community of justice beyond the realm of present generation human beings.*

The environment can be regarded as sustainable or unsustainable for present generations, of course, but the idea of environmental sustainability acquires its greatest resonance in the context of future generations. I have suggested here that it is reasonable to regard passing on a sustainable environment to subsequent generations as a matter of justice. Some (perhaps many) would disagree, but the onus is surely on them to explain why they disagree. From now on future generations must play a part in theories of justice, and their putative claims must be weighed against the claims of the present. As well as future humans, the environmental movement has also potentially brought (parts of) the non-human natural world into the political frame. There is now a large and well-respected body of thought that suggests that the species boundary that separates the political realm of relationships between humans from the merely affective/instrumental realm of human–animal (and even human–nature) relationships is (at least) porous. Even if theorists of distributive justice disagree with this literature they must surely take it into 'in-principle' account, and provide arguments for why (some) animals should not be regarded as legitimate recipients of distributive justice. In sum, theories of justice should henceforth entertain an in-principle triangular conception of the community of justice, with present generation humans, future generation humans, and the non-human natural world at each of the vertices of the triangle. The actual members of the justice community at each of these vertices will vary from theory to theory, but it is increasingly hard to take seriously theories of justice whose communities of justice do not have a full complement of members at the present generation vertex, and at least some members at each of the other two.

*Sixth thesis: liberal theories of justice are broadly compatible with the most common conception of environmental sustainability.*

I take the most common understanding of environmental sustainability to be that referred to as Conception A in Chapter 2—focusing on the sustaining of critical natural capital for reasons of present generation and future generation human welfare. There are no major incompatibilities between this objective and liberal notions of justice containing such archetypal features as impartiality in respect of theories of the good for human beings, the fundamental importance of primary goods as preconditional for individuals' pursuit of the good (whatever it might be), and desert as a principle of distribution beyond the satisfaction of basic needs. This is as much as to say that governments and other agencies charged with bringing about sustainability will be able to legitimize that objective within a broadly liberal framework of justice. This thesis, though, strains at three points: first, if one regards the sustaining of natural capital for purposes of human welfare as a conception of the good (or part of one); second, if one regards it as non-liberal to determine the justice of a situation by its outcomes rather than how it is arrived at; and third, if one regards any social objective driven by need-satisfaction (as is Conception A) as a prima facie concern for liberal theories of justice, underpinned, as they most normally are, by desert as a principle of distribution. It may be asking too much of liberal theories of justice to accommodate these particular interpretations of some of the key features of this conception ('A') of environmental sustainability.

*Seventh thesis: the strains in the sixth thesis are magnified in Conceptions B and C of environmental sustainability.*

Conception B's *raison d'être* is the sustaining of irreversible nature, both for reasons of human welfare, and because of perceived 'duties to nature'. In the case of this latter reason, we are in the presence of what we can call—without abusing the term—a conception of the good. The same goes for what drives Conception C: the sustaining of natural value. It would be consistent with these objectives, seen as instances of the good, to view justice as in their service: that is, to reject the idea of justice as impartiality in favour of justice as one of the many parts of the mechanism tuned to realize a substantive view of the good. This runs counter to what is regarded by liberals as a cardinal virtue of their type of theory of justice: that it is impartial as far as conceptions of the good are concerned, and therefore these conceptions of environmental sustainability must be regarded as broadly incompatible with liberal theories of justice. Further, assuming that we can talk about 'justice to nature' at all, the distributive principle most normally associated with liberal justice—desert—is not appropriate to these two conceptions of sustainability. 'Nature' cannot properly be said to 'deserve' anything—but it can be said to 'need' that which sustains it (or parts of it), so need is the principle of distribution most obviously compatible with these conceptions of sustainability. On the classical reading that makes desert the cardinal principle of distribution associated with liberal justice, then, this observation increases the incompatibility between these two notions of sustainability and liberal theories of justice.

*Eighth thesis: the broader the compatibility between sustainability and justice, the more legitimate policies for sustainability—from the point of view of justice—will be seen to be.*

The fourth thesis suggests that, while this eighth thesis may be self-evidently true, the breadth of compatibility can only be determined empirically and is therefore not open to negotiation—either compatibility is broad, or it is not. The second thesis, though, implies that there is room to broaden or to narrow compatibility by choosing 'appropriately' from the various features of sustainability and justice outlined in Chapters 2 and 3, and captured in table form in Tables 2 and 5. The examination in this book has been organized around discussion of three distinct but overlapping conceptions of environmental sustainability, and the *difference* in the relationships between these conceptions and justice has been emphasized. Broadening the potential compatibility between justice and sustainability, though, will entail the search for an idea of justice that satisfies as many of the intentions of *each* of the Conceptions A, B, and C at the same time, rather than considering them in isolation. The eighth thesis, therefore, points to the second part of this Conclusion in which I will sketch the general characteristics of an overarching idea of justice, capable of capturing and drawing together the different constituencies of interest represented in Conceptions A, B, and C of environmental sustainability.

## *Towards an Overarching Idea of Justice-for-Sustainability: Concentric Circles or Future Generations?*

As I indicated at the beginning of this Conclusion, I shall approach the question of an overarching idea of justice compatible with as many of the intentions of the three conceptions of environmental sustainability as possible by considering two different views on the question: the 'concentric circle' idea developed by Peter Wenz, and the 'future generation' strategy deployed by Bryan Norton. Different though these approaches may be, they both share a common interest in approaching the issue from the point of view of one aspect in particular in the Table 5 'Social Justice' table: the aspect that deals with the community of justice. Clearly this does not exhaust the possible dimensions of the sustainability–justice relationship but it does focus, in line with the fifth thesis above, on the feature of justice theory that seems to influence everything else we might say about that relationship: who or what is to be regarded as belonging to the community of justice in the first place. Let me first, then, outline Wenz's and Norton's ideas as I see them.

Wenz expresses the nub of his position as follows: 'I defend a pluralistic theory in which moral relationships are pictured in terms of concentric circles . . . The closer our relationship is to someone or something, the greater the number of our obligations in that relationship, and/or the stronger our obligations in that relationship' (Wenz 1988: 316). The idea of 'closeness' in Wenz should not be understood, at the outset at least, as related to actual physical proximity. It is, rather, defined 'in terms of the strength and number of one's obligations to others', and these obligations, in turn, have 'commonly respected justifications' (Wenz 1988: 316). So, as he says, 'the closeness I am discussing is not formally tied to emotional attachments or to subjective feelings of closeness' (Wenz 1988: 316).

However, when we look at the nature of these 'commonly respected justifications' for obligations we see that they are more likely to tie in those physically close to us (in terms of actual or potential interactions), or close in terms of immediate kinship, than they are those far away. Wenz writes, in a formulation to which we had cause to refer in Chapter 4, that:

The generally respected justifications for obligations include, but are not limited to, the following: I have benefited from another's kindness or help; I am in a particularly good position to help the other; another person and

I have undertaken a project together; the other person and I are working together to realize the same goal, foster the same ideal or preserve the same traditions; I have unilaterally undertaken a commitment to another; my actions have a particularly strong impact upon the other; and I have perpetrated or benefited from a past injustice toward the other, or a past injustice which adversely affects the other. (Wenz 1988: 316)

Despite the claim that there is no formal connection between 'closeness' in a moral and in an emotional/subjective sense, Wenz evidently considers the closest concentric circles to be inhabited by our kin. This much is clear from his view of the implications of the concentric circle theory for relationships between human beings. He suggests that

Most people find appealing the idea that they generally have more obligations toward their close relatives than toward their colleagues, that they generally have more obligations toward colleagues with whom they work closely than toward colleagues with whom they do not, that they generally have more obligations toward members of their own society than toward people in other societies, and so forth. (Wenz 1988: 317)

In sum, 'Existence in a given circle is usually correlated with (but is not tied by definition to) such characteristics as family membership, personal friendship, employment, ethnicity, and physical location' (Wenz 1988: 317).

There is more to say on Wenz's concentric circle theory and I shall say it shortly. (Let me flag what I shall say by noting that so far we have only talked about the *justifications* for obligation, and not about the *nature* of obligation, once obligation is established.) As far as justifications are concerned, though, the news looks both good and bad in respect of its applicability to our environmental sustainability context. If our aim is an overarching theory of justice which will bring as much of Conceptions A, B, and C on board as possible, then we need a theory of justice that can consistently include at least some parts of the non-human world in the community of justice. Wenz's formulation of the justifications for obligation seems to allow us to do this: 'I am in a particularly good position to help the other,' 'I have unilaterally undertaken a commitment to another,' and 'my actions have a particularly strong impact upon the other' are three such justifications which are as applicable to domestic pets and, perhaps, farm animals, as they are to a parent needing a hip replacement (one of Wenz's own examples). The first and third justifications here also seem applicable to inanimate nature, as long as it is close by (and, probably, owned by me—everything from my window box to my garden, as it were), so even aspects of Conception C's 'natural value' may in principle be embraced by Wenz's concentric circles.

The big drawback, though, is that animate and inanimate nature of which these three justifications cannot be predicated (i.e. just about everything beyond my window box and my garden) will not be the object of any obligation on my part, and so I will not be constrained by any obligations of justice in my treatment of it. If it is true, as Wenz says, that, 'My obligations toward a person increase with the proximity to me of the circle on which the person exists' (Wenz 1988: 317), then the same will presumably be true (in this context of justifications for obligation rather than the nature of it) of animate and inanimate nature. The corollary, obviously, is that our obligations to persons and to animate and inanimate nature decrease the further away they are on the concentric circles, and this is unlikely to satisfy conservationists, preservationists, and so on. In brief, the *universality* which I identified as a feature of theories of justice most likely to be compatible with notions of environmental sustainability seems to be undercut by Wenz's concentric circle theory—what it gives in terms of potentially broadening the community of justice it then takes away by restricting its range of application.

The other big drawback of Wenz's theory in respect of its applicability to the sustainability context (or at least a drawback of the theory as I have presented it so far) is that it looks hard to get future generations into the community of justice. None of the 'respected justifications for obligations' noted above seem prima facie suited for generating obligations for future generations, although Wenz's 'my actions have a particularly strong impact upon the other' might just be tailored to suit present generation–future generation relations (this contains echoes of Robert Goodin's 'vulnerability' thesis, discussed in Chapter 4). Curiously, this is not the option chosen by Wenz himself from his list; he refers, rather, to the idea of our being 'in a unique position to be helpful' (Wenz 1988: 333). He elaborates on this as follows: 'We can conserve the earth's resources, and develop and use technologies that preserve natural balances, or we can do otherwise and leave them in a ruin' (Wenz 1988: 333). We can do all these things, of course, but why this capacity should result in obligations to future generations when it does not do the same for 'someone who lives in another part of the country or another part of the globe' (Wenz 1988: 318) is unclear. In sum, if a litmus test of the compatibility between a theory of justice and environmental sustainability is the capacity of the former to incorporate international justice and intergenerational justice in anything more than an 'add on' way, then Wenz's concentric circle theory of justice seems to fail the test.

But I have so far only given a first approximation of Wenz's theory, and so my assessment of it is not entirely fair. Above all I have stressed the way in which Wenz's theory can be made to look as though obligations map on to physical and/or affective distance, and it is this that undermines the 'long distance' type of obligations (in both time and space) that sustainability considerations seem to demand. But Wenz himself says (as we have seen) that 'Existence in a given circle is usually correlated with (*but is not tied by definition to*) such characteristics as family membership, personal friendship, employment, ethnicity, and physical location' (Wenz 1988: 317; my emphasis). Once this is stressed, it becomes clear that Wenz has resources in his list of justifications to generate international obligations. We saw that one of these justifications ran as follows: 'I have perpetrated or benefited from a past injustice toward the other, or a past injustice which adversely affects the other', and Wenz points out that 'The United States and other Western industrial countries are partly responsible for the poverty of people in many third world countries' (Wenz 1988: 320). He draws the conclusion that 'many of the world's poor children are in a closer concentric circle than we realize', and that we should therefore be 'more willing than we have been in the past to support their elementary education and other positive human rights' (Wenz 1988: 320).

This reference to 'positive human rights' is itself illustrative of the move—to which I have already referred—from justifications of obligation to the nature of obligation: once we see that we have obligations, what exactly are we obliged to do? Wenz approaches this question by distinguishing between positive human rights, negative (human) rights, and preferences. In general, he says, the positive rights of 'remote' people outweigh the claims to mere preference-satisfaction of those close to me (Wenz 1988: 321). Wenz's position here is very close to what we find in all three conceptions of environmental sustainability developed in Chapter 2: in slightly different language, needs are privileged over wants in each of these conceptions. By attaching greater weight to positive rights over preference-satisfaction, Wenz is able to 'jump' concentric circles in a way that did not seem possible on my first-approximation account of his theory, and this theory is accordingly brought closer into line—made more compatible—with the demands of our conceptions of sustainability.

However, if the distinction between positive human rights and preference-satisfaction, in conjunction with the idea of 'reparations' (Wenz 1988: 320), makes some notion of international justice possible, the next distinction—that between positive and negative rights—is rather less helpful for compatibility with the sustainability agenda. Wenz understands negative rights in terms of 'people's basic freedoms' (Wenz 1988: 324)—freedom of association, freedom of speech, and so on—and he suggests that

We ordinarily think of negative human rights somewhat differently from positive human rights. In the case of negative human rights, we are less concerned with a person's placement on concentric circles. (Wenz 1988: 324)

This is as much as to say that the concentric circle theory of justice is abandoned (or, more positively, is universalized) when it comes to negative human rights. The importance of this from our point of view is that it opens the door to a form of justice for (some) animals, and therefore promises the kind of widening of the community of justice that will make a theory of justice potentially compatible with (some) conceptions of sustainability.

It will be remembered, however, that sustainability—and particularly Conceptions B and C—is concerned not only with the absence of restrictions but also with the presence and provision of the conditions for life. In the context of justice, this translates broadly into the meeting of basic needs, and it is precisely this that Wenz denies to animals as a right:

It is perfectly consistent with the concentric circle approach to maintain that human beings generally have no obligations regarding the positive rights of nonhuman animals. Our obligations concerning positive rights diminish in such a way that the outer circle of human beings is the last concentric circle to which they extend. These obligations generally do not extend to animals, who 'inhabit' more remote concentric circles. (Wenz 1988: 328)

The exception to this rule, says Wenz, 'concerns domestic animals, such as domestic pets and farm animals, who are dependent upon us for the necessities of life' (Wenz 1988: 328), and while this goes some way towards meeting the demands of sustainability on a theory of justice, it does not widen the community of justice sufficiently to cope with issues such as 'irreversible nature' (Conception B), and 'natural value' (Conception C). Wenz does, though, refer to 'our obligations to the nonsentient environment' (Wenz 1988: 329), and suggests that here '[O]ur obligation is merely to avoid impairing the health of the ecosystem as a whole, because healthy ecosystems are necessary for the relevant processes of evolution' (Wenz 1988: 330). This is a very underspecified obligation, and it is not at all clear, in any case, that Wenz regards it as an obligation of justice. Also, it is hard to see how discharging this obligation could involve anything less than ensuring the maintenance of the conditions for the reproduction of the 'ecosystem' (its conditions for life), but given that Wenz has ruled out this sort of obligation in respect of animals, why should it make any more sense in the context of ecosystems?

In sum, the parts of Wenz's theory of justice that look most compatible with sustainability are the parts where concentric circles are abandoned. The initial promise of the theory—that it looked capable of broadening the community of justice, even if only in the immediate environs of potential distributors of justice—is undermined by erecting the distinction between positive and negative rights, and by denying the former to animate and inanimate nature. The idea of negative rights, which can be predicated of at least some animals according to Wenz, reopens the community of justice to these animals, but at the cost (from Wenz's point of view) of under-mining the concentric circle idea itself, and (from sustainability's point of view) of disallowing the idea of a right to the presence of the conditions for the reproduction of life. As a contribution to the question of how the community of justice might be widened to take account of the demands of sustainability, then, Wenz's concentric circle theory is suggestive but flawed. The theory produces *too many* communities of justice, and Wenz unsurprisingly finds himself drawing distinctions between them and the obligations we might owe to them so as to try to find a way through the thicket of indeterminacies that the competing claims of these multiple com-munities produce. We might say, though, that this is precisely what theories of justice are about: the reconciliation of competing claims; so to castigate Wenz for attempting such reconciliation is to casti-gate theories of justice in general. But there might just be a way through the thicket—a way, at least, of reducing the complexity of competing claims—and this is the possibility I want to explore through a brief examination of what I shall call the 'future generationism' of Bryan Norton.

It is not essential to this examination that I describe the back-ground to Norton's work in this area, but it might assist neverthe-less. Norton's belief is that the arguments between different wings of the environmental movement are more apparent than real, and he has worked to find a standpoint that will satisfy the demands of as many parts of the movement as possible. Given my intention in this Conclusion to point to the possibility of an overarching theory of justice that will bring on board as much of Conceptions A, B, and C of environmental sustainability as possible, Norton's project seems prima facie worth looking at. More particularly, Norton ar-gues that the gulf between anthropocentric and ecocentric defences of the non-human natural world can be bridged by attending not to the reasons each side may give for such defences, but rather to the policies they propose. More particularly still (although Norton does not put it like this), what is required is the 'right sort' of anthropocentrism—one that is not bound to act in the interests of the present generation only, but in the interests of future genera-tions too. Norton's view is that an interest of future generations of human beings lies in the protection of biological diversity and the maintenance of ecosystem health, and so he says (as we saw in Chapter 2) that:

introducing the idea that other species have intrinsic value, that humans should be 'fair' to all other species, provides no operationally recognizable constraints on human behavior that are not already implicit in the generalized, cross-temporal obligations to protect a healthy, complex, and autonomously functioning system for the benefit of future generations of human beings. Deep ecologists, who cluster around the principle that nature has independent value, should therefore not differ from longsighted anthropocentrists in their policy goals for the protection of biological diversity. (Norton 1991: 226–7)

Put more aphoristically, Norton's point is that 'Environmentalists believe that policies serving the interests of the human species as a whole, and in the long run, will serve also the 'interests' of nature, and vice versa' (Norton 1991: 240). In Rawlsian terms, Norton is suggesting that as far as the maintenance of biological diversity is concerned, there is no difference between being placed behind a generational and a species-ignorant veil of ignorance. For someone behind either of these veils, 'Not knowing his generation, it is best to save all species, even at considerable cost; not knowing his species, ditto' (Norton 1991: 226). It is worth noting here that Norton is not the only one who would endorse the claims of a future generationist approach to protecting the natural environment. Robert Goodin, for one, has written that: 'if there is a chance that we or any of our successors will come to regard an object as irreplaceable, one for whose loss they could not be compensated, then in purely want-regarding terms it is prima facie wrong to destroy it . . . Understood broadly, that principle can have roughly the same practical implications as a principle of protecting the natural environment in its own right' (Goodin 1985: 184). As far as the environmental movement itself is concerned, Norton calls this the 'convergence hypothesis'— the convergence between future generationist anthropocentrists and deep ecologists.

What are the implications of all this for the search for an overarching theory of justice that will cater for as many of the demands of our three conceptions of environmental sustainability as possible? The obvious initial attraction is that if Norton is right, then doing the right thing by future generations of human beings will also mean doing the right thing by those aspects of the non-human natural world that are important to these three conceptions—even Conceptions B and C (namely 'irreversible nature' and 'natural value'). Supporters of these conceptions, though, will post at least four objections—three of which can be partly accommodated by the future generationist position, while the fourth is open to perhaps continual debate.

The first objection—drawn principally from the 'critical natural value' conception of environmental sustainability—will turn on whether Norton is papering over important cracks with his idea of 'the interests of the human species as a whole' (above). We might just accept that the human species as a whole has an identifiable common interest (if we take it as being something at a high level of generality like 'survival'), but the big question is how the burdens associated with achieving the common interest are to be shared out. Different sections of currently existing members of the human species have different interests, for a start, and it is by no means obvious—as we saw in Chapter 4—that the interests of current and future generations will coincide. What this means is that adopting future generations as the overarching community of justice might leave the present generation unprotected, and given that burdens generally fall hardest on the weakest and most vulnerable, we might well find that justice for future generations is bought at the cost of injustice for the present poor and vulnerable.

We might try approaching this from the other end, arguing that doing justice by the present poor will coincide with doing justice to future generations but, once again, it is by no means obvious that the two *do* coincide. In December 1997, nations from around the world met in Kyoto, Japan, to try to hammer out an agreement on reductions in greenhouse gas emissions. Fairness to future generations was obviously at the root of the determination to reach an agreement, but this has to be balanced against fairness in the present. Consequently, developing nations are to have no reductions imposed upon them so as not to put a brake on their development, even if future generations suffer as a consequence. Either way, it is obvious that future generationism on its own cannot cover all our intuitions regarding distributive justice, and so it will only make sense if we adopt something like the lexical ordering of interests found in Box 10 of Table 2, where the needs of the present generation have precedence over the needs of future generations.

The remaining three objections come from another source—that which is concerned for doing the fair thing by nature rather than (or as well as) by present generation human beings. These objections, then, have their origins in Conceptions B and C of environmental sustainability rather than in Conception A. The second objection is that future generationism abandons attempts to do direct justice to the non-human natural world, and that this amounts to the environmental movement admitting defeat in its efforts to alter the anthropocentric worldview which—so the movement (or a part of it, at any rate) claims—has been at the root of the wilful and thoughtless exploitation of non-human nature. This objection is true—any 'justice' done to the non-human natural world through future generationism is indeed indirect—but the future generationist position is a self-confessedly political one, aimed at bringing together a coalition within the environmental movement which can make a practical difference. It might even have the virtue of bringing people into the coalition from outside the movement—those who are persuaded by the claims to justice of future generations—since if the future generationist position about protecting biodiversity and so on is broadly correct, then even non-environmentalists might unwittingly (as it were) be got to subscribe to environmental ends through their commitment to justice for future generations. Our intention in this Conclusion is to seek an overarching theory of justice that will accommodate as many of the intentions and objectives of the three conceptions of sustainability as possible, and this implies some degree of compromise. On this reading, future generationism squares with the sense that developed throughout Chapters 6 and 7 that justice (and particularly distributive justice) might not be the language through which to express best the various aspirations of sustainability, not least because of the difficulties of predicating justice of the non-human natural world. These difficulties counsel against trying to 'reach' the unconvinced through the idea of doing justice to nature. The notion of doing justice to future generations is controversial enough, and some would say

that there is no political sense in adopting even this route to mobilization. But I regard future generationism as a form of 'practical
radicalism': radical in that it asks much more of us and of justice
than hitherto, and practical because it builds on accepted—even
if anthropocentric—precedent. I also think that policy decisions
reached in the light of the interests of future generations really
would be significantly different in terms of their regard for the non-
human natural world than is at present the case.

The third objection that might be made to future generationism
is that relegating the protection of nature to an indirect effect of
protecting the interests of future generations will leave too much of
nature unprotected. In other words, the only parts or aspects of non-
human nature that will be protected will be those that can be said to
be of interest to the welfare of future generation human beings. But
this is evidently a movable feast, and the screws of constraint on
present activity can be tightened or loosened depending on how the
'welfare of future generation human beings' is construed. Norton
himself provides us with three variables which can be 'tweaked' to
give different outcomes as far as constraints are concerned. With
reference to the 'rational, individual chooser' (RIC) behind a
Rawlsian generational veil of ignorance,

The extent and degree of pre-emptive constraints imposed on current
activities will depend on three factors:

  (i) the extent of substitutivity that RIC believes to exist for raw mate-
      rials in production . . .
 (ii) the extent to which he believes ecosystems to be redundant. If RIC
      believes that many species can be lost without significantly decreas-
      ing ecosystem functioning and without curtailing the opportunities
      of future generations to enjoy the full range of values associated
      with diverse biotic systems, he will insist upon lesser restraints on
      the macro-policy level.
(iii) the degree of risk-aversion he feels. (Norton 1989: 156)

So if, in turn, the possibilities for substitution are believed to be low,
few (if any) ecosystems are believed to be 'redundant', and the
desire for risk-aversion is high, then non-human nature will be
protected maximally. On this reading, and in the spirit of compromise and practical radicalism, environmentalist objectors to future

generationism might seek to tighten the screws on these three variables (or even introduce others) as much as possible, rather than
reject the idea altogether.

To my mind, the bits of nature that will be left unprotected by
future generationism are not generally the bits that worry
sustainability enthusiasts, driven as they generally are by the desire
to maintain 'wholes' such as species, rather than 'parts' such as
individual members of species. This much is made clear by Norton's
treatment of a conversation he had with a little girl on a beach who
was piling up sand dollars (sea urchins) that her mother and sister
had excavated with industrial efficiency from the seabed. Neither of
the principal languages available to Norton—'aggregationist' and
'moral' (Norton 1991: 5)—enabled him to say what he wanted to
say, that 'while it was not wrong for the girl to take a few sand
dollars, she should put most of them back'. The aggregationist view
would have it that the value of sand dollars can be exhaustively
expressed in money terms, and if they (the sand dollars) can be
converted into money (by being used to make trinkets, for example), then there can be no objection to the little girl and her
family taking them all. On the 'moralist' view, though, Norton
would 'have to decry the treatment of sand dollars as mere resources; I would have to insist that the little girl put *all* of them back'
(Norton 1991: 5–6). In sum, 'the aggregationist approach to valuing
sand dollars would prove too little, and the moral approach would
prove too much' (Norton 1991: 6).

There seems no way in which future generationism on its own
can get Norton off the horns of this dilemma. However tight one
screws down the three variables mentioned above, the conclusion
has to be that the little girl and her mother and sister were doing
nothing wrong in taking all the sand dollars. Take the variables one
by one: sand dollars are not a 'raw material' for 'production', so the
issue of substitutability is irrelevant; '[S]and dollars are by no means
an endangered species' (Norton 1991: 5), so there is no danger to the
species if the girl's family takes all the sand dollars in that particular
lagoon; and there is no obvious risk factor to be taken into account
here, so the 'degree of risk-aversion' constraint does not come into
play. On this reading, as I say, the fate of that lagoon's sand dollar
population, at least, looks sealed.

There may be a way out, though, in connection with the first of Norton's variables—the one that deals with the issue of substitutability. If we learnt anything in Chapter 2 it was that conceptions of sustainability can be classified according to their views on substitutability. Conception A argued that some 'critical natural capital' may not be substitutable, and this is pretty much the idiom in which Norton is talking in the context of the substitutability of 'raw materials for production'. The lagoon's sand dollars will get no protection from this notion of substitutability. Conception B talked about the unsubstitutability of 'irreversible nature'—and given that, as we observed, the sand dollar species is not put in danger of extinction by the little girl's excavations, the lagoon's sand dollars are left high and dry (literally) by Conception B too. Conception C, however, talks about 'natural value', and the very contestability of what carriers of 'natural value' might actually be leaves open the possibility for a defence of the lagoon's sand dollar population—or some of them, at least. The carrier of 'natural value' in this case might be the lagoon itself, and the lagoon stripped of its sand dollars would not be significant in the same way as it is in their presence. We could presumably legitimately say that the lagoon would not be deprived of the characteristics that lend it its natural value if the girl took a few sand dollars for observation—especially if this resulted in the girl attaining 'an interest in biology, eventually becoming a marine biologist who works to protect echinoids' (Norton 1991: 5)—so Norton's intuition that 'while it was not wrong for the little girl to take a few sand dollars, she should put most of them back' (Norton 1991: 5) has some substantive backing.

Does not, though, this backing come from Conception C's interpretation of substitutability, and not from the principles of future generationism? And if so, does this not still mean that too much of non-human nature will find itself unprotected by future generationism's protective umbrella? I do not think so. The point is that substitutability is part of the language in which our concern for future generations is expressed, so debates about the meaning and extent of substitutability are always already debates about future generations. Precisely the advantage of adopting a multiple view of conceptions of sustainability is that it opens up the contested nature of its component parts (e.g. substitutability), and makes possible a debate about what concern for future generations might involve. A 'natural value' interpretation of Norton's first variable—the substitutability variable—leads to a more rigorous protection of parts of the non-human natural world (in this case, most of the sand dollar population in this particular lagoon) than future generationism seems likely to produce at first sight.

My concrete suggestion, then, is that Norton's first variable should simply read: 'the extent of substitutability'. His own version implies that arguments over conceptions of sustainability have already been resolved in favour of Conception A, since Conception A's interpretation of substitutability is the one he deploys. Opening up the first variable in the way I suggest, though, will enable a broader range of conceptions of sustainability to take part in the debate over what future generationism might imply—particularly in the context of trying to maximize the protection of the non-human natural world.

These first three objections to future generationism can, then, I think, be met—and the second two can be met in ways which strengthen both the idea itself and the way in which it might entail protection of the non-human natural world. The final objection, though, is less amenable to treatment. This one meets Norton's position head on by claiming that the reasons for doing something do make a difference—that is, here, that reasons for the protection of the non-human natural world drawn from intrinsic value arguments will be different in a way that makes a difference from arguments derived from future generationism. And this will be the case in at least two ways. First, most obviously, and similar to the second argument above, the fact that future generationism gives only indirect protection to non-human nature means that some parts of non-human nature are likely to go unprotected. However tight the constraint screws are made, and however each of the three variables is construed, 'justice to future generations' will never map exactly onto 'protection of nature'. This much is true and has to be admitted.

Second, it will be argued that objectives and the reasons for them cannot be separated as neatly as Norton wants them to be. Those whose principal objective is the defence of the natural world may say that that objective partly comprises changing the reasons associated with the objective—or, in other words, that changing our relationship with the non-human natural world means changing ourselves. At this point, the defence of nature seems to be irrevocably bound up with the cultivation of something like 'ecological virtue', and this is something that future generationism in its most hard-nosed form might find hard to incorporate. On the other hand, and in line with the argument about substitutability put above, particular forms of future generationism might well entail the cultivation of ecological virtue (sensitivity to sand dollars), in which case reasons are brought back into line with objectives, even in the case of future generationism. On the other hand again, and this time finally, the suspicion that has ghosted the whole of this book is that the justice and sustainability agendas are different, and it may also be that the agenda for the defence of non-human nature is different from both of these. There will inevitably be points at which all three agendas intersect, but everything here suggests that it would be a mistake to take common interest for granted.

# REFERENCES

ACKERMAN, BRUCE (1980), *Social Justice in the Liberal State*, New Haven: Yale University Press.

ADAMS, J. (1993), 'The Emperor's Old Clothes: The Curious Comeback of Cost–Benefit Analysis', *Environmental Values*, 2/3: 247–60.

ALMOND, BRENDA (1995), 'Rights and Justice in the Environmental Debate', in Cooper and Palmer (1995).

ANDERSSON, T., et al. (1995), *Trading with the Environment*, London: Earthscan.

ANTONIO, W. d', et al. (eds.) (1994), *Ecology, Society and the Quality of Social Life*, London: Transaction Publishers.

APFFEL-MARGLIN, F., and SIMON, S. (1994), 'Feminist Orientalism and Development', in Harcourt (1994).

ARNOLD, R. (ed.) (1988), *The Wise Use Agenda*, Bellevue: Center for the Defense of Free Enterprise.

ATTFIELD, ROBIN (1995), 'Development and Environmentalism', in Attfield and Wilkins (1995).

——and BELSEY, ANDREW (eds.) (1994), *Philosophy and the Natural Environment*, Cambridge: Cambridge University Press.

——and WILKINS, B. (eds.) (1995), *International Justice and the Third World*, London: Routledge.

BAIRD CALLICOTT, J. (1991), 'The Wilderness Idea Revisited: The Sustainable Development Alternative', *Environmental Professional*, 13: 225–47.

BARBIER, E. (1987), 'The Concept of Sustainable Economic Development', *Environmental Conservation*, 14/2: 101–10.

BARRY, BRIAN (1989), *Theories of Justice*, London: Harvester Wheatsheaf.

——(1991a), *Liberty and Justice: Essays in Political Theory*, Oxford: Clarendon Press.

——(1991b), 'The Ethics of Resource Depletion', in Barry (1991a).

——(1991c), 'Justice between Generations', in Barry (1991a).

——(1991d), 'Humanity and Justice in Global Perspective', in Barry (1991a).

——(1995a), *Justice as Impartiality*, Oxford: Clarendon Press.

——(1995b), 'Spherical Justice and Global Injustice', in Miller and Walzer (1995).

BARRY, BRIAN (1996), 'A Commitment to Impartiality: Some Comments on the Comments', *Political Studies*, 44/2 (June): 328–42.

——(1999), 'Sustainability and Intergenerational Justice', in Dobson (1999).

BARTELMUS, PETER (1994), *Environment, Growth and Development: The Concepts and Strategies of Sustainable Development*, London: Routledge.

BARTON, J., and CHRISTENSEN, E. (1988), 'Diversity Compensation Systems: Ways to Compensate Developing Nations for Providing Genetic Materials', in Kloppenburg (1988).

BECKERMAN, WILFRED (1994), 'Sustainable Development: Is it a Useful Concept?', *Environmental Values*, 3/3: 191–209.

——(1995), 'How Would you Like your "Sustainability", Sir? Weak or Strong?', *Environmental Values*, 4/2: 169–79.

BELSEY, ANDREW (1995), 'World Poverty, Justice and Equality', in Attfield and Wilkins (1995).

BENTHAM, JEREMY (1789/1948), *The Principles of Morals and Legislation*, New York: Hafner (1st pub. 1789).

BENTON, TED (1993), *Natural Relations: Ecology, Animal Rights and Social Justice*, London: Verso Press.

BOTTOMORE, T., and RUBEL, M. (1961), *Karl Marx: Selected Writings in Sociology and Social Philosophy*, Harmondsworth: Pelican.

BOWERS, J. (1990), *Economics of the Environment: The Conservationist Response to the Pearce Report*, Northampton: British Association of Nature Conservationists.

BRAIDOTTI, ROSA, et al. (1994), *Women, the Environment and Sustainable Development: Towards a Theoretical Synthesis*, London: Zed Books.

BROMLEY, D., and HODGE, I. (1990), 'Private Property Rights and Presumptive Policy Entitlements: Reconsidering the Premises of Rural Policy', *European Review of Agricultural Economics*, 17: 197–214.

BROOKS, D. (1992), 'The Challenge of Sustainability: Is Integrating Environment and Economy Enough?', *Policy Sciences*, 26/4: 401–8.

BROWN, L., and KANE, H. (1995), *Full House: Reassessing the Earth's Population Carrying Capacity*, London: Earthscan.

BRUBAKER, ELIZABETH (1995), *Property Rights in the Defence of Nature*, London: Earthscan.

BULLARD, R. (1994), 'Anatomy of Environmental Racism', in Hofrichter (1994).

BURKE, EDMUND (1790/1982), *Reflections on the Revolution in France*, Harmondsworth: Penguin.

CADAVA, E., et al. (1991), *Who Comes after the Subject?*, London: Routledge.

CAMPBELL, TOM (1988), *Justice*, Houndmills: Macmillan.

CAREW-REID, J., et al. (1994), *Strategies for National Sustainable Development*, London: IUCN/IIED/Earthscan.

CARLEY, M., and CHRISTIE, I. (1993), *Managing Sustainable Development*, Minneapolis: University of Minnesota Press.

CARROLL, J. (1995), 'Envisioning Ecological Sustainability: The Need and a Method', *Environmental Values*, 4/2: 167–8.

COMMONER, BARRY (1993), 'Population and Poverty', in Fisk (1993).

CONWAY, G., and BARBIER, E. (1990), *After the Green Revolution: Sustainable Agriculture and Development*, London: Earthscan.

COOPER, DAVID (1995), 'Other Species and Moral Reason', in Cooper and Palmer (1995).

—— and PALMER, JOY (eds.) (1995), *Just Environments: Intergenerational, International and Interspecies Issues*, London: Routledge.

CORNELL, D., ROSENFELD, M., and CARLSON, D. (eds.) (1992), *Deconstruction and the Possibility of Justice*, New York: Routledge.

COSTANZA, ROBERT (ed.) (1991), *Ecological Economics*, New York: Columbia University Press.

—— and DALY, HERMAN (1992), 'Natural Capital and Sustainable Development', *Conservation Biology*, 6: 37–46.

COWEN, T., and PARFIT, D. (1992), 'Against the Social Discount Rate', in Laslett and Fishkin (1992*a*).

DALY, HERMAN (1992), *Steady-State Economics* (2nd edn.), London: Earthscan.

—— (1995), 'On Wilfred Beckerman's Critique of Sustainable Development', *Environmental Values*, 4/1: 49–55.

—— and COBB, JOHN (1989), *For the Common Good: Restructuring the Economy toward Community, the Environment and a Sustainable Future*, Boston: Beacon Press.

DASGUPTA, P., and HEAL, G. (1979), *Economic Theory and Exhaustible Resources*, Cambridge: Cambridge University Press.

DE GEORGE, R. (1981), 'The Environment, Rights and Future Generations', in Partridge (1981*a*).

DELATTRE, E. (1972), 'Rights, Responsibilities and Future Generations', *Ethics*, 82: 254–8.

DERRIDA, JACQUES (1991), ' "Eating Well", or the Calculation of the Subject: An Interview with Jacques Derrida', in Cadava et al. (1991).

—— (1992), 'Force of Law: The "Mystical Foundation of Authority" ', in Cornell et al. (1992).

DE-SHALIT, AVNER (1995), *Why Posterity Matters: Environmental Policies and Future Generations*, London: Routledge.

DOBSON, ANDREW (1995), *Green Political Thought: An Introduction* (2nd edn.), London: Routledge.

——(1996), 'Environmental Sustainabilities: An Analysis and a Typology', *Environmental Politics*, 5/3: 401–28.

——(ed.) (1999), *Fairness and Futurity: Essays on Sustainability and Justice*, Oxford: Oxford University Press, forthcoming.

——and LUCARDIE, PAUL (eds.) (1993), *The Politics of Nature: Explorations in Green Political Theory*, London: Routledge.

DOWIE, M. (1995), *Losing Ground: American Environmentalism at the Close of the Twentieth Century*, Cambridge, Mass.: MIT Press.

DWORKIN, RONALD (1993), 'Integrity', in Fisk (1993).

ECKERSLEY, ROBYN (1992), *Environmentalism and Political Theory: Toward an Ecocentric Approach*, London: UCL Press.

——(1993), 'Free Market Environmentalism: Friend or Foe?', *Environmental Politics*, 2/1: 1–19.

——(1994), 'Natural Justice: From Abstract Rights to Contextualised Needs', *Environmental Values*, 3/2: 161–72.

*Ecologist* (1993), *Whose Common Future? Reclaiming the Commons*, London: Earthscan.

EDEN, S. (1994), 'Using Sustainable Development: The Business Case', *Global Environmental Change*, 4/2: 160–7.

EDWARDS, B. (1995), 'With Liberty and Environmental Justice for All: The Emergence and Challenge of Grassroots Environmentalism in the United States', in Taylor (1995).

EKINS, PAUL (1995), 'Economics and Sustainability', in Ravaioli (1995).

ELLIOT, R. (1984), 'Rawlsian Justice and Non-human Animals', *Journal of Applied Philosophy*, 1: 95–106.

ELLIOTT, J. (1994), *An Introduction to Sustainable Development: The Developing World*, London: Routledge.

EPSTEIN, BARBARA (1994), 'Ecofeminism and Grass-Roots Environmentalism in the United States', in Hofrichter (1994).

EVANS, EDWARD (1987), *The Criminal Prosecution and Capital Punishment of Animals: The Lost History of Europe's Animal Trials*, London: Faber & Faber.

FEINBERG, JOEL (1981), 'The Rights of Animals and Unborn Generations', in Partridge (1981*a*).

FEUER, LEWIS (ed.) (1969), *Marx and Engels: Basic Writings on Politics and Philosophy*, London: Fontana.

FISCHER, F., and BLACK, M. (1995), *Greening Environmental Policy: The Politics of a Sustainable Future*, London: Paul Chapman Publishing.

FISHKIN, JAMES (1992), *The Dialogue of Justice: Toward a Self-Reflective Society*, New Haven: Yale University Press.

FISK, M. (ed.) (1993), *Justice*, Atlantic Highlands, NJ: Humanities Press.

FOSTER, JOHN, and HOLLAND, ALAN (eds.) (1997), *Valuing Nature? Economics, Ethics and the Environment*, London: Routledge.

FOX, WARWICK (1986), *Approaching Deep Ecology: A Response to Richard Sylvan's Critique of Deep Ecology*, Hobart: University of Tasmania.

GALSTON, WILLIAM (1980), *Justice and the Human Good*, Chicago: Chicago University Press.

GIBBS, LOIS (1994), 'Foreword', in Hofrichter (1994).

GILLIGAN, CAROL (1982), *In a Different Voice*, Cambridge, Mass.: Harvard University Press.

——(1996), 'Remapping the Moral Domain', in Heller et al. (1996).

GLAESER, B. (ed.) (1984), *Ecodevelopment: Concepts, Projects, Strategies*, Oxford: Pergamon Press.

——and VYASALU, V. (1984), 'The Obsolescence of Ecodevelopment?', in Glaeser (1984).

GOODIN, ROBERT (1985), *Protecting the Vulnerable: A Reanalysis of our Social Responsibilities*, Chicago: University of Chicago Press.

——(1992), *Green Political Theory*, Cambridge: Polity Press.

GOODLAND, R., and LEDEC, G. (1987), 'Neoclassical Economics and Principles of Sustainable Development', *Ecological Modelling*, 38: 19–46.

GOODWIN, BARBARA (1992), *Justice by Lottery*, New York: Harvester Wheatsheaf.

GORE, C. (1993), 'Entitlement Relations and "Unruly" Social Practices: A Comment on the Work of Amartya Sen', *Journal of Development Studies*, 29/3: 429–60.

GOTTLIEB, A. (ed.) (1989), *The Wise Use Agenda: The Citizen's Policy Guide to Environmental Resource Issues*, Bellevue: Free Enterprise Press.

GOWER, B. (1995), 'The Environment and Justice for Future Generations', in Cooper and Palmer (1995).

GREY, W. (1996), 'Possible Persons and the Problem of Posterity', *Environmental Values*, 5/2: 161–79.

GRUBB, MICHAEL, et al. (1993), *The Earth Summit Agreements: A Guide and Assessment*, London: Earthscan.

GRUMBINE, R. EDWARD (1994), 'Wildness, Wild Use and Sustainable Development', *Environmental Ethics*, 16 (Fall): 227–49.

GUNN, A. (1984), 'Preserving Rare Species', in Regan (1984).

HABERMAS, JUERGEN (1993), 'Justice and Solidarity', in Fisk (1993).

HAMMOND, MICHAEL, and HOLLAND, ALAN (1995), 'Ecosystem Health: Some Prognostications', *Environmental Values*, 4/4: 283–6.

HAND, S. (ed.) (1989), *The Levinas Reader*, Oxford: Oxford University Press.

HARCOURT, W. (ed.) (1994), *Feminist Perspectives on Sustainable Development*, London: Zed Books.

HARDIN, G. (1981), 'Who Cares for Posterity?', in Partridge (1981*a*).

HARTNEY, MICHAEL (1995), 'Some Confusions Concerning Collective Rights', in Kymlicka (1995*b*).

HAYEK, F. VON (1993), '"Social" or "Distributive" Justice', in Ryan (1993).

HAYWARD, TIM (1994), *Ecological Thought: An Introduction*, Cambridge: Polity Press.

HEILBRONER, ROBERT (1981), 'What has Posterity Ever Done for Me?', in Partridge (1981*a*).

HELD, DAVID (ed.) (1991), *Political Theory Today*, Cambridge: Polity.

HELLER, T., et al. (eds.) (1996), *Reconstructing Individualism: Autonomy, Individually and the Self in Western Thought*, Stanford, Calif.: Stanford University Press.

HOBAN, T., and BROOKS, R. (eds.) (1996), *Green Justice: The Environment and the Courts* (2nd edn.), Oxford: Westview Press.

HOFFERT, R. (1986), 'The Scarcity of Politics: Ophuls and Western Political Thought', *Environmental Ethics*, 8/1: 5–32.

HOFRICHTER, RICHARD (ed.) (1994), *Toxic Struggles: The Theory and Practice of Environmental Justice*, Philadelphia: New Society Publishers.

HOLLAND, A. (1994), 'Natural Capital', in Attfield and Belsey (1994).

——(1997), 'Substitutability: Or, Why Strong Sustainability is Weak and Absurdly Strong Sustainability is not Absurd', in Foster and Holland (1997).

HOLMBERG, J., et al. (1991), *Defending the Earth: A Guide to Sustainable Development*, London: IIED/Earthscan.

HORTON, JOHN, and MENDUS, SUSAN (eds.) (1994), *After MacIntyre: Critical Perspectives on the Work of Alasdair MacIntyre*, Cambridge: Polity Press.

IRVINE, SANDY, and PONTON, ALEC (1988), *A Green Manifesto*, London: Optima.

JACOBS, MICHAEL (1995), 'Sustainable Development, Capital Substitution and Economic Humility: A Response to Beckerman', *Environmental Values*, 4/1: 57–68.

——(1999), 'Sustainable Development: Faultlines of Contestation and the Radical Model', in Dobson (1999).

JACOBS, P., and MUNRO, D. (1987), *Conservation with Equity: Strategies for Sustainable Development*, Cambridge: International Union for Conservation of Nature and Natural Resources.

JAMIESON, DALE (1994), 'Global Environmental Justice', in Attfield and Belsey (1994).

JEFFREYS, K. (1994), 'Free-Market Environmentalism: Can it Save the Planet?', *Economic Affairs*, 14/3: 6–9.

JOHNSON, ANDREW (1995), 'Barriers to Fair Treatment of Non-human Life', in Cooper and Palmer (1995).

KAVKA, G. (1981), 'The Futurity Problem', in Partridge (1981*a*).

KLAASSEN, G., and OPSCHOOR, J. (1991), 'Economics of Sustainability or the Sustainability of Economics: Different Paradigms', *Ecological Economics*, 4: 93–115.

KLINGER, J. (1994), 'Debt-for-Nature Swaps and the Limits to International Co-operation on Behalf of the Environment', *Environmental Politics*, 3/2: 229–46.

KLOPPENBURG, J. (ed.) (1988), *Seeds and Sovereignty: The Use and Control of Plant Genetic Resources*, Durham, NC: Duke University Press.

KORTEN, D. (1991–2), 'Sustainable Development', *World Policy Journal*, 9: 157–90.

KRAUSS, CELENE (1994), 'Blue-Collar Women and Toxic-Waste Protests: The Process of Politicization', in Hofrichter (1994).

KVERNDOKK, S. (1995), 'Tradeable CO2 Emission Permits: Initial Distribution as a Justice Problem', *Environmental Values*, 4/2: 129–48.

KYMLICKA, WILL (1990), *Contemporary Political Philosophy: An Introduction*, Oxford: Oxford University Press.

——(1995*a*), *Multicultural Citizenship: A Liberal Theory of Minority Rights*, Oxford: Oxford University Press.

——(ed.) (1995*b*), *The Rights of Minority Cultures*, Oxford: Oxford University Press.

LASLETT, PETER, and FISHKIN, JAMES (eds.) (1992*a*), *Justice between Age Groups and Generations*, New Haven: Yale University Press.

————(1992*b*), 'Processional Justice', in Laslett and Fishkin (1992*a*).

LEE, K. (1993), *Compass and Gyroscope: Integrating Science and Politics for the Environment*, Washington: Island Press.

LÉLÉ, S. (1991), 'Sustainable Development: A Critical Review', *World Development*, 19/6: 607–21.

LEONARD, H. (1989), *Environment and the Poor: Development Strategies for a Common Agenda*, Oxford: Transaction Books.

LEVINAS, E. (1969), *Totality and Infinity: An Essay on Exteriority*, Pittsburgh: Duquesne University Press.

——(1989*a*), 'Time and the Other', in Hand (1989).

——(1989*b*), 'Ideology and Idealism', in Hand (1989).

——(1989*c*), 'God and Philosophy', in Hand (1989).

LOCKE, JOHN (1690/1924), *Two Treatises of Government*, London: Dent (1st pub. 1690).

LUCASH, F. (ed.) (1986), *Justice and Equality Here and Now*, Ithaca, NY: Cornell University Press.

LUKE, T. (1995), 'Sustainable Development as a Power/Knowledge System: The Problem of "Governmentality"', in Fischer and Black (1995).

LUPER-FOY, S. (1992), 'Justice and Natural Resources', *Environmental Values*, 1/1: 47–64.

——(1995), 'International Justice and the Environment', in Cooper and Palmer (1995).

MACHAN, T. (ed.) (1974), *The Libertarian Alternative*, Chicago: Nelson Hall.

MACINTYRE, A. (1985), *After Virtue: A Study in Moral Theory* (2nd edn.), London: Duckworth.

——(1988), *Whose Justice? Which Rationality?*, Notre Dame, Ind.: University of Notre Dame Press.

MCKIBBEN, BILL (1990), *The End of Nature*, Harmondsworth: Penguin.

MACKLIN, R. (1981), 'Can Future Generations Correctly be Said to Have Rights?', in Partridge (1981a).

MCMANUS, P. (1996), 'Contested Terrains: Politics, Stories and Discourses of Sustainability', *Environmental Politics*, 5/1: 48–73.

MANNING, R. (1981), 'Environmental Ethics and Rawls' Theory of Justice', *Environmental Ethics*, 3: 155–66.

MARTÍNEZ-ALIER, J. (1993), 'Distributional Obstacles to International Environmental Policy: The Failures at Rio and the Prospects after Rio', *Environmental Values*, 2/2: 97–124.

MARX, K. (1969), *Critique of the Gotha Programme*, in Feuer (1969).

MAYNARD, R. (1974), 'Who Conserves our Resources?', in Machan (1974).

MEADOWS, DONELLA, et al. (1972), *The Limits to Growth*, London: Pan.

——et al. (1992), *Beyond the Limits*, London: Earthscan.

MILL, J. S. (1863/1972), *Utilitarianism*, Dent: London (1st pub. 1863).

MILLER, D. (1976), *Social Justice*, Oxford: Clarendon Press.

——(1994), 'Virtues, Practice and Justice', in Horton and Mendus (1994).

——(1995), 'Introduction', in Miller and Walzer (1995).

——(1999), 'Social Justice and Environmental Goods', in Dobson (1999).

——and WALZER, M. (eds.) (1995), *Pluralism, Justice and Equality*, Oxford: Oxford University Press.

MITLIN, D. (1992), 'Sustainable Development: A Guide to the Literature', *Environment and Urbanization*, 4/1: 111–24.

MOFFATT, I. (1992), 'The Evolution of the Sustainable Development Concept: An Australian Perspective', *Australian Geographical Studies*, 30/1: 27–42.

——(1994), 'Measuring and Assessing Indicators of Sustainable Development: A Pilot Survey', *International Journal of Sustainable Development and World Ecology*, 1: 170–7.

——(1996), *Sustainable Development: Principles, Analysis and Policies*, Carnforth: Parthenon Publishing Group.

MULHALL, S., and SWIFT, A. (1992), *Liberals and Communitarians*, Oxford: Blackwell.

NAESS, ARNE (1989), *Ecology, Community and Lifestyle*, Cambridge: Cambridge University Press.

NIELSEN, K. (1995), 'Global Justice, Capitalism and the Third World', in Attfield and Wilkins (1995).

NORGAARD, R. (1985), 'Environmental Economics: An Evolutional Critique and a Plea for Pluralism', *Journal of Environmental Economics and Management*, 12: 382–94.

——(1987), 'Economics as Mechanics and the Demise of Biological Diversity', *Ecological Modelling*, 38: 107–21.

——(1988), 'Sustainable Development: A Coevolutionary View', *Futures*, 20/6: 606–20.

NORTON, B. (1982), 'Environmental Ethics and the Rights of Future Generations', *Environmental Ethics*, 4: 319–77.

——(1989), 'Intergenerational Equity and Environmental Decisions: A Model Using Rawls' Veil of Ignorance', *Ecological Economics*, 1: 137–59.

——(1991), *Toward Unity among Environmentalists*, Oxford: Oxford University Press.

——(1992), 'Sustainability, Human Welfare and Ecosystem Health', *Environmental Values*, 1/2: 97–112.

NOZICK, R. (1974), *Anarchy, State and Utopia*, Oxford: Blackwell.

NUSSBAUM, M. (ed.) (1995), *Women, Culture and Development: A Study of Human Capabilities*, Oxford: Clarendon Press.

OKIN, S. (1989), *Justice, Gender and the Family*, London: HarperCollins.

O'NEILL, J. (1993), *Ecology, Policy and Politics: Human Well-Being and the Natural World*, London: Routledge.

O'NEILL, ONORA (1991), 'Transnational Justice', in Held (1991).

——(1995), 'Justice, Gender and International Boundaries', in Attfield and Wilkins (1995).

——(1996), *Towards Justice and Virtue: A Constructive Account of Practical Reasoning*, Cambridge: Cambridge University Press.

OPHULS, W., with BOYAN, A. (1992), *Ecology and the Politics of Scarcity Revisited*, New York: W. H. Freeman.

O'RIORDAN, T. (1991), 'The New Environmentalism and Sustainable Development', *Science of the Total Environment*, 108: 5–15.

——(1993), 'The Politics of Sustainability', in Turner (1993).

PALMER, J. (1995), 'Just Ecological Principles?', in Cooper and Palmer (1995).

PARTRIDGE, E. (ed.) (1981a), *Responsibilities to Future Generations*, New York: Prometheus Books.

——(1981b), 'Can Future Generations be Said to Have Rights?', in Partridge (1981a).

PASEK, J. (1994), 'Economic and Environmental Justice: The Contribution of Philosophy', *Contemporary Political Studies*, 2, ed. Patrick Dunleavy and Jeffrey Stanyer.

PEARCE, D. (ed.) (1991), *Blueprint 2*, London: Earthscan.

——(1993), *Blueprint 3: Measuring Sustainable Development*, London: Earthscan.

——(1995), *Blueprint 4: Capturing Global Environmental Value*, London: Earthscan.

——et al. (1989), *Blueprint for a Green Economy*, London: Earthscan.

——et al. (1990), *Sustainable Development: Economics and Environment in the Third World*, London: Edward Elgar/Earthscan.

PEZZEY, J. (1992), 'Sustainability: An Interdisciplinary Guide', *Environmental Values*, 1/4: 321–62.

PRITCHARD, M., and ROBISON, W. (1981), 'Justice and the Treatment of Animals: A Critique of Rawls', *Environmental Ethics*, 3: 55–61.

PULIDO, LAURA (1996), *Environmentalism and Economic Justice*, Tucson: University of Arizona Press.

RAPPORT, D. (1995), 'Ecosystem Health: More than a Metaphor?', *Environmental Values*, 4/4: 287–309.

RASHDALL, H. (1915), *Property: Its Duties and Rights*, London: Macmillan.

RAVAIOLI, C. (ed.) (1995), *Economists and the Environment*, London: Zed Books.

RAWLS, J. (1973), *A Theory of Justice*, Oxford: Oxford University Press.

——(1993), *Political Liberalism*, New York: Columbia University Press.

RAZ, J. (1986), *The Morality of Freedom*, Oxford: Clarendon Press.

Real World Coalition (1996), *The Politics of the Real World*, London: Earthscan.

REDCLIFT, M. (1987), *Sustainable Development: Exploring the Contradictions*, London: Methuen.

——(1992), 'The Meaning of Sustainable Development', *Geoforum*, 23/3: 395–403.

——(1993), 'Sustainable Development: Needs, Values, Rights', *Environmental Values*, 2/1: 3–20.

Red-Green Study Group (1995), *What on Earth is to be Done?*, Manchester: Red-Green Study Group.

REGAN, T. (ed.) (1984), *Earthbound: New Environmental Essays in Environmental Ethics*, Philadelphia: Temple University Press.

ROUSSEAU, JEAN-JACQUES (1762/1968), *The Social Contract*, Harmondsworth: Penguin.

RYAN, A. (ed.) (1993), *Justice*, Oxford: Oxford University Press.

SAGOFF, M. (1988), *The Economy of the Earth*, Cambridge: Cambridge University Press.

——(1993), 'Environmental Economics: An Epitaph', *Resources*, 111 (Spring): 2–7.

SANDEL, M. (ed.) (1984a), *Liberalism and its Critics*, New York: New York University Press.

——(1984b), 'Justice and the Good', in Sandel (1984a).

SCHMIDHEINY, S. (1992), *Changing Course: A Global Business Perspective on Development and Environment*, Cambridge, Mass.: MIT Press.

SEDJO, R. (1988), 'Property Rights and the Protection of Plant Genetic Resources', in Kloppenburg (1988).

SELMAN, P. (1996), *Local Sustainability: Managing and Planning Ecologically Sound Places*, London: Paul Chapman Publishing.

SEN, A. (1984), *Resources, Values and Development*, Oxford: Blackwell.

SIMON, J. (1994), 'More People, Greater Wealth, More Resources, Healthier Environment', *Economic Affairs*, 14/3: 22–9.

SIMON, R. (1984), 'Troubled Waters: Global Justice and Ocean Resources', in Regan (1984).

SINGER, B. (1988), 'An Extension of Rawls' Theory of Justice to Environmental Ethics', *Environmental Ethics*, 10: 217–32.

SKOLIMOWSKI, H. (1995), 'In Defence of Sustainable Development', *Environmental Values*, 4/1: 69–70.

SOLOW, R. (1992), 'An Almost Practical Step toward Sustainability', Address to 'Resources for the Future', Washington.

STONE, C. (1974), *Should Trees Have Standing? Towards Legal Rights for Natural Objects*, Los Altos, Calif.: Kaufman.

STROUP, R., and SHAW, J. (1989), 'The Free Market and the Environment', *Public Interest*, 97 (Fall): 30–43.

SZASZ, A. (1994), *Ecopopulism: Toxic Waste and the Movement for Environmental Justice*, Minneapolis: University of Minnesota Press.

TALIAFERRO, C. (1988), 'The Environmental Ethics of an Ideal Observer', *Environmental Ethics*, 10/3: 233–50.

TAYLOR, B. (ed.) (1995), *Ecological Resistance Movements: The Global Emergence of Radical and Popular Environmentalism*, New York: SUNY Press.

TAYLOR, C. (1986), 'The Nature and Scope of Distributive Justice', in Lucash (1986).

——(1994), 'Justice after Virtue', in Horton and Mendus (1994).

'T SAS-ROLFES, M. (1994), 'Trade in Endangered Species: Is it an Option?', *Economic Affairs*, 14/3: 10–12.

TURNER, R. K. (ed.) (1993), *Sustainable Environmental Economics and Management*, London: Belhaven.

VANDEVEER, D. (1979), 'Of Beasts, Persons, and the Original Position', *Monist*, 62/3: 368–77.

VICTOR, P. (1991), 'Indicators of Sustainable Development: Some Lessons from Capital Theory', *Ecological Economics*, 4: 199–213.

WALZER, M. (1983), *Spheres of Justice: A Defence of Pluralism and Equality*, Oxford: Blackwell.

——(1994), *Thick and Thin: Moral Argument at Home and Abroad*, Notre Dame, Ind.: University of Notre Dame Press.

——(1995), 'Response', in Miller and Walzer (1995).

WARNKE, G. (1992), *Justice and Interpretation*, Cambridge: Polity Press.

WCED (1987), *Our Common Future*, Oxford: Oxford University Press.

WENZ, PETER (1983), 'Ethics, Energy Policy and Future Generations', *Environmental Ethics*, 5: 195–209.

——(1988), *Environmental Justice*, New York: SUNY Press.

WISSENBURG, MARCEL (1993), 'The Idea of Nature and the Nature of Distributive Justice', in Dobson and Lucardie (1993).

——(1998), 'The Rapid Reproducers Paradox: Population Control and Individual Procreative Rights', *Environmental Politics*, 7/2.

——(1999), 'An Extension of the Rawlsian Savings Principle to Liberal Theories of Justice in General', in Dobson (1999).

WOOD, A. (1993), 'The Marxian Critique of Justice', in Fisk (1993).

WOOD, D. (1988), 'Crop Germplasm: Common Heritage or Farmer's Heritage?', in Kloppenburg (1988).

World Energy Council (1994), *New Renewable Energy Resources*, London: Kogan Page.

YOUNG, I. (1993), 'Social Movements and the Politics of Difference', in Fisk (1993).

# INDEX